Discovering
the Laws of Life

JOHN MARKS TEMPLETON

DISCOVERING THE LAWS OF LIFE

Foreword by
NORMAN VINCENT PEALE

CONTINUUM | NEW YORK

1995
The Continuum Publishing Company
370 Lexington Avenue, New York, NY 10017

Copyright © 1994 by John Marks Templeton

Printed in the United States of America

Library of Congress Cataloging-in-Publication Data

Templeton, John, 1912–
Discovering the laws of life / John Marks Templeton ; Foreword by Norman Vincent Peale.
      p.   cm.
   ISBN 0-8264-0636-X (alk. paper)
   1. Conduct of life—Quotations, maxims, etc.   2. Spiritual life–
–Quotations, maxims, etc.   3. Devotional calendars.   I. Title.
         BJ1581.2.T426   1994
      170′.44—dc20   93-30371
               CIP

CONTENTS

FOREWORD

I have known John Marks Templeton for many years and have admired him greatly. From humble beginnings in a rural Tennessee farming community, he rose to lead a thirty-billion-dollar group of investment companies. His financial acumen and wisdom have helped thousands of investors, large and small, to grow their assets and develop wealth.

However, his financial skills and achievements are not what have produced my admiration, remarkable though they may be. What has impressed me most is his dedication and drive in the spiritual realm.

Long before he reached his present success, John Templeton awakened spiritually. Early in life, he began to tithe and to give his time unselfishly to philanthropic causes. He has since established several foundations to advance spiritual development. He has served tirelessly on the boards of key philanthropic and religious organizations. His most recent effort, the Humility Theology Information Center of the John Templeton Foundation, is typical, representing a commitment to discover and communicate the key factor in helping people develop humility, a spiritual quality that summarizes the character of Sir John.

Perhaps his best-known effort has been the establishment of the Templeton Prize for Progress in Religion. Given annually, the monetary value of this award now exceeds that of the Nobel Prizes. The international importance of this gift has been recognized by no less than England's Queen Elizabeth II, who knighted John Templeton in 1987 for his service to philanthropy.

Once, when I had a conversation with him about spiritual faith, he summed up his thoughts by saying: "The most important thing in human life is to seek and do the will of God. A person who does this is living by faith. He or she doesn't have to look around trying to find faith; it springs from within."

It is from this background, then, that Sir John has developed his wonderful collection of "the laws of life." When I first heard of the concept, that there are universal principles present in every society and every religion that can lead us to a common understanding, I knew he was on to something important. It has been my experience that he is correct, that these principles do exist and that we can write them down and teach them to future generations.

This aspect of teaching the laws is vitally important. In an interview with the Peale Center's *Plus Magazine,* Sir John shared what he taught his own children about happiness: "I taught them the principle of free will tied to happiness. Each of us is given a free will, and we can create our own happiness and our own heaven or hell. You can do it by choosing your thoughts. Choose negativity and you will get unhappiness and hell. Choose confident living and positive thoughts and you will produce a heaven of happiness."

This idea of teaching and learning is the key to *Discovering the Laws of Life.* Having passed my own 95th birthday, I know we never stop learning and needing to learn. Sir John has done us all a great service by distilling and passing on these principles that have guided his own life into happiness, success and incredible usefulness to others.

NORMAN VINCENT PEALE

The Hill Farm
Pawling, New York
July 1993

INTRODUCTION

Following in the footsteps of Benjamin Franklin and others who have tried to pass on their learning to others, this book has been written from a lifetime of experience and diligent observation in the hope that it may help people in all parts of the world to make their lives not only happier but also more useful. It is intended for everyone, for the young who each day are being introduced to the laws that can make their lives more productive, as well as for the older and more experienced who seek confirmation and affirmation of the laws of life.

Outlined in my earlier book, *The Templeton Plan: 21 Steps to Personal Success and Real Happiness,* are some of the laws that should prove helpful as you proceed along the road to spiritual maturity:

- TRUTHFULNESS when a lie would be so much easier;
- RELIABILITY when you could slack off;
- FAITHFULNESS during moments of doubt;
- PERSEVERANCE when you think you're too tired to go on;
- ENTHUSIASM while encountering roadblocks;
- ENERGY at the moment you feel burned out;
- HUMILITY while others heap praise on you;
- PLEASING others before thinking of your own pleasure;
- GIVING to others before thinking of receiving;
- LEARNING from others because you realize there's so little you know;
- ALTRUISM even though you may sense around you an atmosphere of selfishness;
- JOY at the very moment when your prospects seem the darkest.

Indeed, this is a short list of the laws of life. There are many more laws, and, in this book, you will find 200 major ones, culled from a list of many hundreds. They come from a vast array of sources—from the

Scriptures, from storytellers such as Aesop, from scientists such as Isaac Newton, from artists and historians.

The poet Henry Wadsworth Longfellow wrote: "Lives of great men oft remind us that we can make our lives sublime and departing leave behind us footprints in the sands of time." The truth of this statement can be demonstrated if we look to the lives of the famous as well as the unsung heroes of the past and present, for there we will find many models for useful, happy living. And, when we examine their words and deeds, we will discover the principles that inspired and sustained their benefits to future generations.

Some laws in this book are based on quotations from sources as far-reaching and varied as *Aesop's Fables,* Lao Tse's *Tao Te Ching* and Wayne Dyer's *The Sky's The Limit.* Drawn from the scriptures of different traditions, as well as from schools of philosophical thought both ancient and modern, each quotation points to a particular law that holds true for most people under most circumstances. The essays are designed to inspire and encourage you—to help you consider more deeply the laws you live by and to reap the rewards of their practical application.

The laws described here are like tools. When you apply them consistently, they have the power to transform your life into a more deeply useful and joyful experience. Even if your life is already working well, it's possible that it will work even better as you incorporate the wisdom contained in these pages. If I had found a book of 200 basic laws of life during my college years, I could have been far more productive then and in the years that have followed.

Although *Discovering the Laws of Life* can be read like any other book of inspirational material, its organization follows that of an academic study program. The laws are arranged into the forty weeks of the typical school year, with five days of "homework" for each week. At the end of that year, you will have read, studied and learned the meanings of the two hundred laws of life contained in this book. This organization should also prove useful for families who want to study these laws in daily sessions, for Sunday schools in many churches, for private religious schools and for public schools in those countries which permit or require schools to include religious education.

You may also benefit from the laws included here by applying them to various activities in your own life. For example, you might form an informal discussion group with your friends, or with a church or school group. Many people have benefited by coming together with others to explore topics of mutual interest. Such a group might share not only a variety of points of view on the importance and meaning of the laws of life, but can also provide support and encouragement for individual members as they begin to make changes in their lives. If you choose such an approach, you might select a single essay, read it as a group and spend an hour or so discussing the ideas. Group trust should develop, allowing you to deepen your relationship to the concepts and to each other by sharing your personal successes and failures as you apply the laws to your life.

Once your group is working together effectively, you might select all the essays relating to a particular law—"Giving," for instance—and concentrate intensively on that law. Your group might then find a way to actively help other spiritual pilgrims. You might create a "Circulation Day" in your hometown. Those of you with things to give away could take those items to a central location where homeless people and others are invited to take what they need. The group would experience the great satisfaction of seeing their unwanted things put to good use by those who need them; they would also create a place in their lives into which more good could flow. From direct experience of this kind they could learn the truth of the statement, "It is more blessed to give than to receive."

Another approach is to use the ideas in this book privately. Try to set aside a block of time when you aren't likely to be disturbed. When you feel your mind settling down, let yourself formulate a question about something that may be troubling you. With the question in mind, open *Discovering the Laws of Life* to the table of contents. Many times you may find the solution to a stubborn problem.

There are other ways to approach the ideas in this book so that they will be more real for you. If you don't have access to a group, you may enjoy keeping a journal in which you can record your responses to what you've read. You may find that you can keep track of your goals and progress more easily if you keep to a regular daily or weekly writing schedule.

If you have a family, these essays could be a way to improve communication, especially with your children. In the early years, values are formed that affect the rest of your child's life. As you discuss the laws contained in this book, you can play a constructive role in the creation of your child's value system. For example, your child might like to read aloud one law at dinner for family discussion. If your child is an adolescent, the key to success may be to allow him or her to fully express opinions and experiences. Once your teenager has stated a position, you can present a particular law of life and discuss its many ramifications as simply another point of view without trying to pressure the child into agreement. In fact, in all likelihood you will not get instant agreement, but you will have planted a seed that may bear fruit as he or she matures.

I'm confident that you will probably find other ways to use this wisdom of the ages, and, indeed, I would welcome the submission of additional laws as you think of them. Those that have stood the test of time may be incorporated in a future edition of *Discovering the Laws of Life*. It would also be helpful to know how you have used the book and what results you have had. Your ideas and reflections would be most appreciated.

Maybe one of the laws in this book will encourage you to try something that until now you've only dreamed of attempting. Maybe you will be inspired to create a laws of life contest in your own hometown. It would indeed be progress if the youth of this nation were to concentate their efforts on the subjects of love, justice, kindness, friendliness, helpfulness, forgiveness, self-respect, charity and loyalty. If *Discovering the Laws of Life* can push that goal a few inches forward, it will have proven worthwhile.

A few years ago, I began offering support for a laws of life essay contest in my boyhood home, Franklin County, Tennessee. Mr. and Mrs. Handly Templeton help in running the program. Prizes for the essays—they run from one hundred to two thousand words in length—are awarded semi-annually, with a first prize of $2,000, a second prize of $800 and a number of runner-up prizes. The response has been gratifying. The number of entrants for each six-month period has risen to its present size of six hundred students. It would give me great pleasure to learn that your hometown wants to embark on its own version of the Franklin County program.

In my teenage years, I was inspired by the courage and vision of Rudyard Kipling's poem "If." This poem taught me to dream—but also to be master of my dreams. I learned from the great English poet that the earth belongs to us all and that, with courage and enthusiasm, progress is likely to follow. The final stanza of "If" still rings in my ears:

> *If you can fill the unforgiving minutes*
> *With sixty seconds' worth of distance run,*
> *Yours is the Earth and everything that's in it,*
> *And—which is more—you'll be a Man, my son!*

Behind this book is my belief that the basic principles for leading a "sublime life," to paraphrase Longfellow, can be examined and tested just as science examines and tests natural laws of the universe. I have a vision that by learning the laws of life and applying them to everyday situations, more and more people will find themselves leading joyous and useful lives.

It has been well said that "Life is a tough school because the exams come first and the learning afterwards." This book is a small attempt to provide some learning before the exams arrive.

Without the help of many individuals who shared their ideas and wisdom with me, this book would not have been possible. Over the years I have employed most of these people for their help in providing ideas, writings, explanations, examples and editing for this collection of laws. Some of these contributors were ministers and lay people associated with religious groups; others were simply private individuals who share a similar hopeful outlook on life and a fundamental belief in the principle that "Life works better when you play by the rules."

For their contributions to *Discovering the Laws of Life* in the form of ideas, writings and editing, I would like to express my gratitude to the following: Clare Austen, Robert Brumet, Douglas Bottorff, Amy Butler, Janet Carney, Edward Conrad, Judy Covell, Matt Dioguardi, James Ellison, Sharon Frisby, Mari Gabrielson, Pauline Garcia, Jean Grissom, Ellie Harold, David Hayward, Marie Juneau, William Juneau, Mary Ann Keen, Mary Louise Kitsen, Kathy Long, Matthew Long, Tricia McCannon, Doris Maxwell, Kim Neafoy, Marty Newman, Marshall Norman, Cheryl Ramos, Nancy Reed, Paul Roach, Frances Schapperle, Joanne Starzec, Sylvia Taylor, Becky Templeton, Tom Thorpe, Patricia Trentacoste, Duke Tufty, Lois Webb, Crystal Yarlott, my colleagues in business and charities, and my wife and family.

You may join this group by sending me a law of life you have discovered with an essay of five hundred to six hundred words about it. Your law may be derived from any religious tradition—Jewish, Muslim, Hindu, Buddhist and others, as well as Christian. If I decide to include it in a later edition of *Discovering the Laws of Life,* I will pay you $200. You may send your law to me in care of the John Templeton Foundation, P. O. Box 1040, Bryn Mawr PA 19010-0918, U.S.A.

JOHN MARKS TEMPLETON

The golden rule.

Jesus gave his own wording to the Golden Rule and it is expressed in various forms in every major religion. Similar ideas of conduct are found in the literature of Hinduism, Buddhism, Islam and in the writings of Aristotle, Plato and Seneca. Confucius taught the negative form. In Jewish literature the negative form of the Rule appears in various places as "What you hate do not do to anyone." The words used by Jesus for the Golden Rule are found in Matthew 7:12 and also Luke 6:31. In five different translations of the New Testament the Golden Rule is stated in the following words:

1. *King James Version:*

   And as ye would that men should do to you, do ye also to them likewise.

   Therefore all things whatsoever ye would that men should do to you, do ye even so to them: for this is the law and the prophets.

2. *Revised Standard Version:*

   And as you wish that men would do to you, do so to them.

   So whatever you wish that men would do to you, do so to them; for this is the law and the prophets.

3. *New English Bible:*

   Treat others as you would like them to treat you.

   Always treat others as you would like them to treat you: that is the Law and the Prophets.

4. *Phillips Modern English:*

Treat men exactly as you would like them to treat you.

Treat other people exactly as you would like to be treated by them—this is the meaning of the Law and the Prophets.

5. *Jerusalem Bible:*

Treat others as you would like them to treat you.

So always treat others as you would like them to treat you: that is the meaning of the Law and the Prophets.

WEEK ONE : LAW B

Listen to learn.

There's an old saying that God gave us two ears and one mouth so we may hear more and talk less. How well we use our ears will play an important part in determining what we learn as we go through life.

A major reason why relationships break down is that one or more of the parties involved hasn't learned to listen. Listening is a learned skill and when we develop it to the fullest, we not only increase our capacity to learn but increase our ability to maintain healthy relationships.

Ironically, deaf people are often better listeners than those of us who can hear. As those deaf people who sign communicate, they must remain focused on the movement of each other's hands. Those of you who can hear must develop that high level of concentration in order to be good listeners.

There are two kinds of listening—active and passive. Most of us are good at passive listening. We appear to be listening when, in fact, our minds have wandered off to the movie we saw last night or what we're going to wear tomorrow. We do it during lectures, we do it during sermons, we do it during television shows, and even with close friends and family members.

Active listening is difficult because it requires staying focused on what the speaker is saying. It depends on using our ears the way a photographer uses a camera. To get the best pictures, the photographer must adjust the lens until the settings are right. As active listeners, we must constantly adjust our attention to remain aware of what the speaker is telling us.

A presentation by the Sperry Corporation on effective listening quotes studies showing that students spend 60 percent to 70 percent of classroom time listening. In business, listening is cited as one of the most important skills a manager can possess. Sadly, most of us are ineffective listeners.

Have you ever played the childhood game "Gossip," in which people sit in a circle and someone whispers a story into the ear of the person next to him? That person turns and whispers the story to the next person and so on until everyone in the circle has heard and retold the story. When the last person tells the story, it's usually so far removed from the original that it bears no resemblance to it. This is the result of poor listening.

When we misunderstand or don't understand what we hear, our tendency is to blame the speaker. In fact, it could be our poor listening habits. It takes practice and concentration, but we can all become better listeners and better listeners are better learners. God not only gave us two ears and one mouth, God also gave each of us the potential to learn. The more we listen and learn, the better able we are to realize the God-given potential that each of us possesses.

One of the great laws of life tells us that we must practice being truly interested in other people if we want to know them and form a close connection with them. A wonderful way to begin is quite simply to focus our attention on who they are and what they say to us. We must practice asking them questions about themselves instead of talking solely about ourselves. It's amazing how receptive people are to our questions about them. When we truly show an interest in another person and really listen to that person without constantly referring to ourselves, we have begun a relationship that will only grow stronger over time.

It is better to love than be loved.

St. Francis

Consider the sun—a self-sustaining unit that receives energy from thermonuclear reactions near its center. The energy released in these reactions is so great that the sun could shine for billions of years with little change in its size or brightness.

Love is like the sun. It sustains itself. It needs neither thanks nor reward for it to give out its powerful and healing energy. Love is always there, even when the clouds of human emotions hide it, just as the sun is there when clouds hide it from the earth. Our lives thrive on the energy of love. But because love sustains itself and creates its own energy, we need not look for it outside ourselves. It lies deep at the center of our being.

As we release the energy of our love, a chain reaction takes place similar to the thermonuclear reactions within the sun that change hydrogen into hellium. The energy of love flows within us, changing and enlarging us. Love opens hearts once closed tightly by bitterness and, in the place of bitterness, we become flooded with acceptance and joy. Hate no longer erodes our soul; care and concern replace apathy. The changes are evidenced in our lives as we begin to love ourselves and see ourselves as love. Because we *are* love, we don't need to search for love outside ourselves.

The energy of love is a healing balm. Just like the sun, it has no perception of good or evil. It just is. It doesn't say, "I'll love this person because it's the right thing to do," or "I'll love this person because I will gain position and wealth in return." When we allow love to live within us, it automatically radiates out to every aspect of our environment. Just as photosynthesis is the process by which the sun and plants together make food, a similar process takes place within us as we allow the energy of love to transform us. Love becomes food for ourselves and others. But, unlike plants that receive the sun's energy as a continuing process of nature, we must allow the process to happen within us. As we allow the energy of love to fill us, we must allow that energy to flow out of us. Love is what we are all searching for because love is what our basic nature is.

Once the spark is kindled within and begins to burn brightly, we can't stop it from flowing from us to others. Some may not come close enough to feel the warmth of our love. Others may bask in the glow of our energy. Because we are love, because we sustain ourselves and bless others, it doesn't matter if we receive thanks or recognition. Like the durability of the sun, love gives and gives with no diminution of its supply. Our lives become brighter the more we express love. We can shine like the sun and, when we are in our rightful place, we can radiate love for all persons without any exceptions.

WEEK ONE : LAW D

Thanksgiving leads to having more to give thanks for.

Thanksgiving is a creative force that, if lived on a continuous basis and not just for one day each year, will create more good in your life and more to be thankful for. Perhaps we could call this the life of thanks-*living*. Thanksliving is an attitude of perpetual gratitude that will draw good to you. It is based on the premise that "thanksgiving leads to having more to give thanks for." We have the power to create whatever we need in our life and this power, available to each of us because it lies within us, is the power of the mind.

Let's look at three ways to practice thanksliving. The first way is to search for the good and praise it. We tend to attract that which we give our attention to. Where your attention goes, your energy flows. A good idea can get even better as its possibilities for greater good are explored. The more good you can see and praise, the more you direct creative energy to positive results. Even in situations that at first appear difficult or unpleasant, see all the good you can. And bless the good you can see. Praise the good and watch it multiply.

A second way to experience thanksliving is to give thanks ahead of time for whatever good you desire in your life. Feel as if you have *already* received this good. There is a law of life that can be stated in these words: "Thoughts held in mind will reproduce in the outer world after their own kind." In other words, we create our outer life according to the way we have created our *inner* life—with thoughts, beliefs and attitudes. Thanksliving will help us to create what we want. Thanksgiving is then seen not as an effect of something we have received, but rather the cause of some future good that will inevitably be drawn to us. Instead of postponing your good, satisfied feelings until after the fact, practice having the good feelings now. If what you desire is a more prosperous lifestyle, start feeling like a grateful, prosperous person today. Your attitude tends to draw prosperity to you like a magnet.

A third way to experience thanksliving—perhaps the most difficult, yet the most powerful of all—is to give thanks for your problems and challenges. By facing our challenges and overcoming them, we grow stronger, wiser and more compassionate. One of the best ways to learn mathematics is to be given problems to solve. One of the best ways to prepare for an athletic event is to practice with a strong, competitive opponent. Adversity, when overcome, strengthens us. So we are giving thanks not for the problem itself but for the strength and the knowledge that will come from it. Giving thanks for this growth ahead of time will help you to grow through—not just go through—your challenges.

The mind has power to cause. Thoughts and feelings have creative power. An "attitude of gratitude" (*i.e.,* thanksliving) is attractive; it is a power that will draw more good to you.

WEEK ONE : LAW E

You cannot be lonely if you help the lonely.

Few remember the days when special services were paid for by sharing what you had with the one who provided the service. A farmer could offer sacks of grain to the town doctor for setting a broken arm. Chickens might be given to the blacksmith and his family or potatoes to the village midwife for assistance in the delivery of a child.

An old friend often reminisced of his childhood days when his mother, Sarah, became very skillful at making tantalizingly delicious dishes from frequent gifts of cabbages, rutabagas, and yams. His father was a minister and the family of the town parson was held in high regard in southern Mississippi. A visit to the Reverend and his wife in their modest, frame cottage was a rare treat indeed. The moment a knock was heard at the door, Sarah bustled with a flourish to greet her guests with hugs, kisses, and warm words of welcome. Always dressed in the traditional black clerical suit with starched white collar, the round Reverend followed her to extend a warm hand and twinkling smile, saying, "The Lord blesses you, come in." Their gentle manner was the same, whether their visitor was a cherished relative, a pauper needing a meal, or the town's mayor.

As time laid to rest Sarah's best friend, she elected to move to a port city on the Texas coast to be closer to her son and daughter. As was her custom for over fifty years, she arose daily before dawn, dressed meticulously with cloak and a tiny veil, and walked to the church. She polished and prepared all the vessels and linens necessary for the priest to offer the sacrament. She tended to every menial task needed by the church personnel. Upon finishing, she went out, walking to the hospital to visit and cheer those who were ill. Afterwards, one by one, she visited the homes of the shut-ins, sharing her joy and kindness and what might be needed of her slender pension.

When news came that Sarah had left this life, a touching story was told. That day she had made her service offering at the church, as always. Returning home, she gathered a few items of hand-washed laundry from the clothes line and laid her wrap over the back of the sofa. When she was found, she was resting, eyes closed, in her favorite lounge chair, a gentle, sweet smile on her lips and the tiny net veil still in place.

No sermon or lecture could convey the essence of gratitude and joy as would spending a few hours in the presence of this special lady. To Sarah, loneliness was an ill to be tended to and abolished. She used every waking moment to instill or perpetuate a bit of happiness in someone's life.

Mother Teresa has reported in some of her television interviews that she finds the greatest poverty and desolation among the wealthy of the world today. She noted that there is a stark need for missions to offer love and nurturing to the barren of heart.

When one seeks to fill a need in humanity, the opportunities are limitless. Within three blocks of one's own home or less, anyone can find desperation and helplessness. Often those most pained cannot discern for themselves the source of their anguish. Hunger, shelter, and the need for gainful productivity are easily recognized. Emotional pain and inner desolation may require more effort and sensitivity.

Anyone looking within themselves can find valuable assets, special resources, and talents that can be shared. When thoughts are turned outward in search of usefulness, loneliness melts and disappears.

Beginning with one effort, such as spending an unselfish hour with someone less fortunate, produces a miracle for the giver and the receiver. If these two should remember another friend in need and go together to them, three or more agents of caring are now in action. This positive force multiplies in energy, which moves joy and love and sustenance into the world to dispel sorrow and lack. Sharing these priceless gifts of caring, encouragement, appreciation, and praise can fill our day with rich purpose.

"There are those who have little and give it all. These are the believers in life and the bounty of life and their coffers are never empty" (Kahlil Gibran, *The Prophet*).

WEEK TWO : LAW A

You are sought after if you reflect love, joy, peace, patience, kindness, goodness, faithfulness, gentleness and self-control.

Living is a process of learning and growing from the lessons we learn. One lesson worth learning early is that life gives back to us what we give to it. St. Paul's formula will help us give our best to the world and in the process gain friends and influence the world around us.

Each quality St. Paul mentions carries with it its own reward and, as we take the time to develop them, our lives take on a fuller dimension. When we learn to reflect love, joy, peace and patience, we benefit as well as those we come in contact with. We can't reflect something unless it's within us to reflect. When we are truly reflecting, joy, peace and patience, others are glad to be associated with us. When we reflect those qualities in our lives, others benefit because those qualities have the effect of rubbing off on them.

As we go on to develop kindness, goodness, faithfulness and gentleness, others know they can trust us. They know they will be treated the way they deserve to be treated. When we deal with people honestly, and with kindness, faithfulness and gentleness, we send them the message that we care. In return, we are treated the same way, because what we give to others comes back to us.

When we develop self-control, we gain a balance in our lives that enables us to live the other qualities more fully and completely. Without self-control we lack the ability to be patient with ourselves and with others. Without self-control we lack the ability to love unconditionally. Self-control gives us the ability to put the ego in the correct perspective so that we don't harm ourselves or others. When we are able to do this, we realize the true value of the ego as being the vehicle for our expression and not a domineering tyrant that has to have its way. The ego that insists on having its own way is a destructive ego, both to the self and to others. It can lead to destructive habits; it can seek its good without being concerned about the welfare or good of others. Mastering self-control is a key to gaining mastery over our lives.

If we really want to be sought after, to "gain friends and influence people," we must develop the characteristics championed by St. Paul. As we develop them, we will reflect them in our lives, and others will be drawn to us like magnets. They will seek our company because of the comfort, companionship, friendship and love they experience with us. And we will find we are our own best friend because those same qualities help us to love ourselves. They help us to be at peace with ourselves, to have more patience and joy in our hearts. We will learn how to treat ourselves with kindness, goodness, faithfulness and gentleness. We will give to life what we seek from life and we will be rewarded with the greatest treasure—wholeness of life.

WEEK TWO : LAW B

A smile breeds a smile.
Ted Engstrom

"Smile and the world smiles with you, cry and you cry alone." Everyone likes to be around someone who smiles easily. Perfect strangers can pass in the street and if one of them smiles, the other is likely to smile in return. Most everyone appreciates the person who can generate a smile from us. A smile, no matter how brief, can lift us up from the mundane task in front of us. A smile reaches down inside of us and pulls up to the surface reasons for rejoicing in our lives. This is the gift we can pass on to everyone we meet—a gift we can give to ourselves, a gift that costs us nothing. Living life with a smile is like throwing yeast into a bowl of flour, adding warm water and waiting for the flour to rise. It multiplies many times over.

A smile can be triggered by a thought, an idea, or remembrances of times past. If we linger with it for a moment, we can capture it and let it enhance life. We can allow the effect of that smile to permeate our being, warming us and reminding us to be happy and relaxed. A smile from another can shake us loose from our perception of life's severity, can connect us to that person. In that brief passage of time, we have gained a friend. If we choose to ignore the smile, we miss out on a gift of friendship.

Most of us tend to be drawn to those who have a positive outlook on life. An optimist has a reason to smile, and his smile reveals his faith in life. The pessimist, on the other hand, thinks he has no reason to smile and lives his life without smiles, without faith, and alone. The ability to smile in the face of life's adversities has escaped the pessimist. He has unconsciously chosen to ignore the many blessings life has given him.

When we learn to smile in the face of life's adversities, we can overcome our problems more effortlessly. We don't become chained to them. Living life with a smile enables us to see the joy of life no matter what is going on around us. We can spread that joy with a simple smile to others. Even if we can generate only half a smile from them, for a brief moment they may have let the light of joy enter their lives.

A smile *is* contagious! There might not be any visible sign that we've acknowledged the smile, but that "something" within us will tell us we've been given a gift. In choosing to return the smile, we say "yes!" to life. We say to ourselves that even in the face of adversity we have faith in the process of life. We allow our smile to spread that faith and joy to all we meet.

Although it is true that there may be times when it is inappropriate to giggle or laugh aloud, your genuine smile is never out of place. Can you think of a time or place when the world could not use a little more light and love? Every person has the capacity to bring these vital qualities to life with their smile. While not all of us will smile in the same situations or in the same way, you will bring a little more warmth into a sometimes cold world with a smile that brings forth the best part of you. The smile you bring to a difficult life challenge infuses it with the light of understanding and with love, which attracts harmonious solutions. It also inspires those around you to respond in a similar manner. Your smile makes a difference wherever you are!

When you choose to smile, even when the situation does not seem to warrant it, you will find yourself reliving in an unconscious way all the times your smile did come easily and feel good—and soon you will rediscover ease and good feeling in this present circumstance. As you touch once again the light and love within you and begin to share this with the world, you set off an irresistible chain of cause and effect that restores understanding and harmony to the situation. Your smile will breed many more smiles because of the good feeling that is generated just in being around you. When the bullet that began the American Revolution was fired at Concord, it was called "the shot heard 'round the world." Your smile, aimed in the direction of any hostile emotions, could be the smile *felt* around the world today by all people everywhere. "Brighten the corner where you are"—the world needs your smile.

WEEK TWO : LAW C

None knows the weight of another's burden.

George Herbert

A middle-aged man attended a male therapy support group one evening when he felt he was at his lowest ebb. His wife was leaving him. His business was teetering near bankruptcy. He had gained weight over the last few years and his self-esteem wasn't very high. Even his hair was thinning.

The moderator explained that they would go around in a circle and each man would take a few minutes to explain what wasn't working in his life. On the second round, they would discuss what they were going to do to change it.

The middle-aged man listened patiently as each of the other members spoke. When it came time for him to unburden himself, he knew that his was one of the saddest stories there. A secret part of him felt almost proud to be so pathetic.

As they continued around the circle, he found himself trying to second guess why each man had come and then he noticed that the last person in the circle was a handsome young man about twenty years old.

Why, he thought, would such a young man be here? The youngster's face looked sympathetic as he nodded at each person's story. When the time came for him to speak, he was smiling.

"My friends," he said almost wistfully, "I have been diagnosed with terminal cancer." The gasp was audible in the room. "My doctors have given me three to six months to live. I have struggled with this for a month now and have finally made a decision." His voice gained self-confidence as it grew. "I am going to take up flying lessons."

The words hung in the air. Flying lessons?

"I have chosen to live."

Flying lessons! The middle-aged man drew in his breath. His mind flew over all of the imaginary reasons he had created for this young man to have spoken, realizing each of them had been trite and pretentious next to the reality of his plight. Then his thoughts rested, for the first time without self-pity, on his own small problems. He felt almost ashamed.

The boy was dying. He would not even get a chance to live his life. And he—he had lived so many years, over twice the boy's age. And what had he really done with it? And yet here was the boy with almost a look of triumph, a look of . . . could he say it . . . joy!

What had the boy said? He chose to live!

When the man left that night, he and all the other members of the circle had once again taken up the torch of believing in their own lives. They had seen light in another and it reminded them that they had a choice about how they might carry their own burdens.

We all carry our past with us. Sometimes it is very visible, as visible as the faces we pass in the streets. But usually it is hidden from all but the most discerning eyes. We cannot know what has happened in another's life, unless we have truly walked in that person's shoes.

So often it is easier to judge others quickly and be done with it. "I would never have made that decision!" "How can she live like that?" "He'll never amount to anything!" "She's hopeless." We have all found ourselves espousing that kind of doubtful wisdom.

Unfortunately, that kind of "justice" is often self-fulfilling; it closes the door of understanding between one individual and another. It is only through seeking to understand one another from the heart that we can learn compassion. And the compassion that we show others allows us to forgive our own shortcomings. The next time you find yourself wanting to prejudge another, stop and ask how often we too have been judged by those who have not walked in our shoes.

Getting a glimpse into others' misfortunes, our attitude towards them and ourselves can change. "Walk a mile in my shoes," that old song says, "before you criticize and choose. Walk a mile in my shoes."

Agape given grows, *agape* hoarded dwindles.

Probably no other word in our language has been given so many definitions or been written about in such depth in poems, plays, novels and philosophical and theological texts as love. Regardless of how it is defined or what is written about it, surely the most important thing about love is what we do with it.

The Greeks developed several definitions of love. *Eros* is romantic love, the kind that puts butterflies in your stomach. *Storge* is the type of love that we feel for members of our family; it is the love of security. *Phileo,* or comradeship, is the type of love we feel for our friends. The most important love, however, is *agape*.

Agape is the unselfish love which gives of itself and expects nothing in return. It is the love that grows as you give it to others. Miraculously, the more *agape* you give, the more you have to give. It is the love that Jesus taught us to practice.

The writer C.S. Lewis likened *agape* to the tools it takes to grow an abundant garden. We have a choice. We can let the garden of our life grow wild and unattended until it fills with weeds, or we can take up the proper tools and tend to our garden until we create a place of unimaginable loveliness—full of flowers and all the vegetables we need. The most important tool is our willingness to extend our love to others. *Agape* is the unconditional love God gives us regardless of what we look like, how much money we have, how smart we are, and even regardless of how unloving our actions may sometimes be. God loves unconditionally and that is what He wants us to do. When we practice *agape* it becomes easier to love our enemies, to tolerate those who annoy us, and to find something to like in every person we meet.

It is not only musicians and athletes who must train constantly to develop their skills. To develop *agape* we must practice until it becomes second nature—as natural to us as breathing. When it does, love will flow out of us and into us as easily as air flows in and out of our lungs when we inhale and exhale.

Agape is a deliberate choice, one you can make right now. It does not depend on how you feel, but on loving *regardless* of how you feel.

It resembles an exercise program. When you start a program like walking, or running, or lifting weights, you don't immediately sign up for a marathon or reach for the heaviest weight. You exercise every day and, as you do, you are able to walk farther, run faster or lift heavier weights.

The rewards of consistent exercise include feeling good about your accomplishments and improving your ability. The rewards of practicing *agape* include feeling good about others and yourself—two important components to living a happy life.

WEEK TWO : LAW E

A measure of mental health is the disposition to find good everywhere.

Have you ever noticed how some people seem to be happy no matter what is happening in their lives? There is a buoyancy to their personalities. A kind of glowing field of energy seems to come from their faces, their words, even the way they walk.

Other people seem to be predisposed to gloomy negative thoughts, no matter what the situation. You could walk in on a beautiful summer's day and say: "Isn't it a great day? I just love this kind of weather."

They would immediately tell you how much they hate the heat: "Miserable, sweaty, can't get any work done, hard to concentrate. It's fine if you're a tropical plant."

The next day it's raining. Miss Positive lunches with a negative friend. "I just love it when it rains," she says. "It's a nice break from the heat, don't you think?"

Mr. Negative grumbles: "Are you kidding? This is even worse than yesterday. I mean, if you're a duck, it's great!"

Sisters and brothers can grow up in the same family, have the same basic environment, yet turn out completely different from one another. Somewhere along the way, one chooses to look at life as if anything is possible. The other decides life is a drag, other people are hateful and he doesn't much like the world.

These two personality types are generally referred to as the optimist and the pessimist. One is bound to see the good in all things, the other the bad. We all have the capacity to see both, but how much attention we give to either side over a period of a lifetime will often define the entire experience of our lives.

The dictionary defines pessimism as the doctrine or belief that the existing world is the worst possible one, the belief that the evil in life outweighs the good, and the practice of looking on the dark side of things.

Optimism, its opposite, is defined as the doctrine that the existing world is the best possible, the belief that good ultimately prevails over evil, and the tendency to take the most hopeful or cheerful view of matters or to expect the best outcome.

You notice that both of these are subjective realities. They are attitudes, not events. They are a way of believing in ourselves or our world that either limits us or frees us to experience life positively. It is important to remember we have a choice about our attitudes, since we know that our own reactions can color how we perceive life.

Few would argue that choosing to take the optimist's point of view makes our lives happier. However, the pessimist would say that: "If you don't believe or expect the best, you'll never be disappointed. By expecting the worst, you have nothing to lose." One of the problems with this is that it also means you are either *not* directing your life toward any achievable goals or else you're subconsciously directing yourself toward failure. Fear of failing becomes a self-fulfilling prophecy.

The force of the human mind cannot be underrated. The human will has overcome seemingly insurmountable obstacles throughout history. From physical discoveries like climbing Mt. Everest, to documented cases of heroic rescues by people normally too frail to manage them, a positive human desire has proven over and over again that almost anything is possible.

Every great endeavor has had an optimist at its helm. Without optimism, Magellan would never have circumnavigated the globe. Without optimism, Charles Lindbergh would never have made his way across the Atlantic Ocean on the first solo flight, thus opening the way for intercontinental travel. And, without a belief that things could change for the better, there would never have been social or political reforms in any countries.

The optimist is also the dreamer. Without him, we would never have had electricity. Inventors, by definition, are people who believe in the reality of something they cannot see. They seek to make it real in the face of existing facts. A pessimist cannot be an inventor because he has lost the ability to dream.

Every day each of us has a choice about how we will respond to the events in our lives. Choosing the good creates a positive mental attitude. It allows for balance in our lives. It keeps us focused on what *does* work in our lives, it permits the opening through which anything—even miracles—can happen.

Giving friendship is more rewarding than giving luxuries.

No doubt you have heard this many times growing up. Perhaps you came to believe that the reward one receives for giving is good feelings inside or a happier afterlife. You can be assured you will have good feelings if you are a giving person. What is also true is that giving freely and lovingly, with no exceptions, will also produce tangible rewards.

Most of us think we would be much happier as a result of *receiving* more love and more money, rather than *giving* it away. We have heard all our lives phrases like "to have a friend be a friend" and "it is more blessed to give than to receive." But all too often we fail to see the correlation between the truth of these statements and the deficit we sense in these areas of our lives. We think winning the lottery would make us happy. We don't usually think that contributing to a needy person or worthy cause, or giving simply because we are asked, would do so. We dream of someone out there who will show up in our lives and adore us and love us so much we will be content. Not all of us think of who we could love, or show love to, such as our lonely neighbor, or parents, or friends, so that we could be happy. And yet, that is exactly how it works.

As we give lovingly and willingly, we get back the very feelings which feed our spirits so that we can create in our lives the things we want most, and can keep: self-esteem and confidence in our ability to succeed in relationships as well as in business. In this state of mind we can create in our lives blessings we desire.

In relationships, we often confuse our own happiness in being loving with the love we are receiving from another. What is the object of our affection? It really can be an object. Remember falling in love with an object, perhaps a car? The car did not give us love back, but in our state of bliss we felt expansive, warm, generous, successful and attractive. These are all feelings we possess in our being; the object doesn't bestow them on us. We think we have them because of the car, but it is only in choosing the car we allow ourselves to *experience* the feelings that are available to us anyway.

I have a friend who remembers the happiest time of his life as the first thirty days he owned a speedboat. He and his family had dreamed of owning a boat and he thought his purchase would keep his unfaithful wife from wandering and cause his children to love and respect him more. During the early days of boat ownership, he felt like a successful father and husband. He felt youthful, handsome, and more confident. These feelings were reflected in his work's success. His clients were easier to get along with, and he made more money, even though he was working fewer hours than he normally did because he spent a lot of time at the lake.

At the end of the thirty days, the premium book from the loan company arrived and suddenly he faced a big payment for the big boat. His wonderful feelings drained away. His boat still looked pretty, still went as fast, still impressed his friends, still thrilled his kids. My friend, however, didn't really enjoy the boat any more except for short periods of time when his kids were water skiing and having fun. Every time he thought about the boat he remembered the heavy monthly payment and the expensive maintenance. He worried about having to work harder to afford the boat. His wife soon started another affair and his kids seemed to want him only as a chauffeur for their water skiing.

The boat did not change. The boat was an inanimate object that did not give anything and did not take anything away. My friend changed from experiencing and giving loving feelings to withholding them because his family had not changed the way he expected. His worry and discomfort were communicated to his family and friends. His work fell off and he began having financial problems; eventually he had to sell the boat.

We must be very careful. Giving because we think we will get something back will not work. We must be 100 percent willing to give and never experience any return, or it will not work. Truly free giving will produce the wonderful feelings we all possess in our being, and we can choose to express that way, and consequently feel that way all the time.

As long as we choose to experience love and happiness, and give freely from those feelings, the rewards will be greater than we ever imagined.

WEEK THREE : LAW B

Love given is love received.

There's a strange thing you can observe about love. People search, run after, try to earn, to get, to grasp and hold onto something that is as naturally theirs as the air they breathe! And what mental and emotional rigors we put ourselves through in order to get it. Many of us think it all depends on having the right person see us in just the right way, so that person will feel the right way and love us. That raises the pressure of trying to be just what the person wants, trying to please, trying to be good enough to deserve their love. Having to look just right, say the right things, do the right things. Otherwise, we will not "get" the love we want or, if we have it, we might lose it. Nothing makes people more emotionally crippled, dependent, self-pitying, bitter and cynical than thinking they don't have love unless someone gives it to them.

Of course, whether we admit it or not, we all instinctively want to experience love. The reason it's considered the treasure of life is that love is the very nature of every soul. It's the nature of your soul to give and create experiences of love, because love originates in the essence of your being. The power, force and energy of love reside self-existent within us as our very lifeblood.

An ancient story tells how the greatest gift of life was hidden. When the gods were creating mankind, they wondered where to hide this most precious and powerful treasure so that it would not be misused or mistreated by the unwise. "Shall we hide it atop the highest mountain? Shall we bury it deep in the earth or at the very bottom of the deepest ocean? Or shall we conceal it in the heart of the thickest, darkest forest?" After pondering, they finally hit on the answer. They would implant the gift within the human beings themselves, for surely they would not think to look there. And just to make sure, they designed human eyes to look only outward, not inward.

And now the secret is yours. You can look within to find the treasure, and experience it all you want—by giving it. The sure way to experience love is to give it. Giving love demonstrates to yourself that you have it, because you can't give something you don't have, can you? There is no one without love to give. You need not search out the right people who will recognize and understand it just the way you do, nor expect it to be given back to you by those to whom you gave it, nor, if they do give it back, give it back in just the same way. But be assured that not even the smallest thought of love that you give will fail to return to you.

Start with whoever is around you: men, women, girls, boys, old people, young people, yourself. Giving love doesn't mean contrived sentimentality or flattery. It's simply a natural attitude and demeanor of goodwill, kindliness, support, caring and benevolence. It's a willingness to do what you can to be helpful, to make things a little better for someone. Giving love consciously through thoughts, words and deeds will help you become your own force field of love. It will be impossible for it not to attract that which is like itself.

Because you will feel the power and beauty of love within you so strongly, you will cease to differentiate between love given and love received. You will eventually take little notice of whether it's attracted back to you. The gift, the giving and the receiving, will be one harmonious flow of the most powerful force in the universe.

WEEK THREE : LAW C

Laws of life guide your actions and reactions.

According to *The American Heritage Dictionary,* a law is a "rule established by authority, society or custom." A rule is defined as: "an authoritative direction for conduct or procedure" or "a standard method or procedure." A law then is an agreed-upon governing tactic that guides or directs the activities or actions of a people. And, as people and cultures change, the needs of the people change as do the laws by which they live.

What is spiritual law then? We may answer that it's an invisible law and, being of spirit, is not dictated by the laws of our physical world. It is not shaped by current opinion or whim. It is not determined by people. For those who understand that life and living involve more than the merely physical, it becomes obvious that there is a creative principle that supports and creates all life.

The followers of the ancient Chinese sage Lao Tzu, understand spiritual law as the *Tao*. The simplest interpretation of Tao or spiritual law is: "This is how things work." One way to comprehend this law is to realize the relationship between the mind and its thoughts, feelings and ideas and the physical activities that give those thoughts, feelings and ideas expression. There is a definite relationship between the invisible thoughts and feelings of our minds and the visible actions we take as a result of them. To understand spiritual law is to realize that one cannot think and feel one way and act in an opposite way.

If you're feeling angry and your thoughts are negative, it's not possible to be happy, healthy and loving in your interactions with yourself and others. Sometimes you may pretend to be happy when you're really angry, but chances are your anger will manifest itself as a stomach ache, a headache, or perhaps in harsh treatment of a pet or another person. It is impossible to be one way inside ourselves and be completely different on the outside. This is the law of how all things work: as within, so without.

WEEK THREE : LAW D

Pray without ceasing.
I Thessalonians, 5:17

Since the beginning of time, prayer has been observed in almost every culture recorded and studied by man. Today, we witness many of those around us in church, at business meetings, at sports functions, or in times of crisis invoking God to help them complete the task at hand in accordance with His will.

For those brought up in church-going, it would seem unnecessary to repeat the promises made to those who pray. "Ask and it will be given unto you" *(Luke 11:9)* or "And all things, whatever you ask in prayer, believing, you will receive" *(Matthew 21:22)* are often memorized by many in early childhood, possibly at Sunday School.

And yet, as we grow from childhood to adulthood, and our lives become more complex and our concerns more encompassing, prayer is often the last resort for many. We forget to "pray without ceasing." We need to be reminded not only how and when to pray, but also why we should pray.

I attribute a large part of my own formula for success to the power of prayer in my daily life. In fact, I start all my shareholders and directors meetings with prayer. Whatever you do in life, whether you get married, bring a case to a law court, operate on a child, or buy a stock, it is wise to open with prayer. And that prayer should be that God will use you as a clear channel for His wisdom and His love.

The four words, "Thy will be done," are probably the most difficult and yet the most important part of any prayer. Perhaps some of us stopped praying either because we didn't feel our prayers were being answered, or we didn't like the answers we received from God. Sometimes we have a tendency to ask God to do things for us, hoping He will agree that our requests make sense and will grant them. This relationship with God playing the part of a divine fairy godfather may not always work out to our liking, but it doesn't mean God isn't listening. It may mean either that God has a better plan or we're not fully understanding the meaning of the words, "Thy will be done."

In C. S. Lewis's book, *Letter to Malcolm: Chiefly on Prayer,* he notes that "Thy will be done" doesn't necessarily mean we must submit to disagreeable things that God has in store for us, but rather that there is a great deal of God's will to be done by his creatures. The petition, then, is not merely that we may patiently suffer God's will, but also that we may vigorously do it. Lewis also notes the tendency to overlook the good that God offers us because, at that moment, we expected something else. But that doesn't mean our prayers aren't answered, only that we don't recognize God's message.

By communicating with God on a regular basis, we receive his guidance and the power to understand and do His will. The more we talk with God, the more He reveals Himself to us. Chester Tolson and Clarence Lieb, in their book *Peace and Power through Prayer,* suggest that by understanding the implication of God's will being done, "man receives a new wave of spiritual energy."

"Pray without ceasing" and allow it to work in our lives daily in tune with God's will, and we will fully benefit from what some have described as one of the most powerful weapons on earth.

The impossible is the untried.
Jim Goodwin

"It's simply impossible! It can't be done!" Many of us find it convenient to fall back on one of the most popular words in the English language—"impossible"—when faced with a challenging project or problem.

Clearly not everything is possible in this life, but frequently we throw in the towel because it's expedient to do so. Isn't it easier to assume that a stubborn problem cannot be solved than to put time and energy into finding a solution? Isn't it easier to give up on a quarrelsome colleague than to try to find a common meeting ground with him? Yes, impossible is indeed a convenient word.

But, in fact, the impossible is merely the untried. Earlier in this century, most would have agreed it was impossible to jump from an airplane in flight and live to tell about it. If everyone had decided to file that dream away as an impossibility, then today there would be neither parachutes nor parachutists. Yet at least one person believed in the possible and worked to find a solution to the problem of gravity and the rapid acceleration of falling objects.

In the early phases of development, parachutes sometimes failed, but the inventors refused to cry "Impossible." They tried and tried again, until they found workable answers. It is the same with us and our own individual problems. We must search for answers to our money needs, our friendship and spiritual needs, our needs at school and at work. We must make efficient use of our time instead of complaining that there aren't enough hours in the day. We'll never know if there is a solution to our time crunch, unless we say to ourselves, "Yes, it's possible. It can be done!"

Rebecca was born without a left arm from above the elbow. Luckily her parents were supportive as well as loving: they believed that the impossible is the untried. As a result, Rebecca learned to swim, to ride a bike, to shuffle a pack of playing cards and to tie her shoes. She grew up with a sense of pride, with a belief in her abilities and with a desire to be useful to others.

"The impossible is the untried" is a law of life that will help us attain the apparently unattainable, and to believe that the inconceivable can, in fact, be conceived and then carried out.

I shall allow no man to belittle my soul by making me hate him.

Booker T. Washington

Whom does hate change? What conditions does it improve? The answer may be surprising. Hate, like prayer, changes the person involved in the activity, not the person the activity is aimed at. If you kick a brick wall that's in your way, you're the one who gets hurt, not the wall. Hate doesn't change the person being hated; it diminishes the person doing the hating.

We are all responsible for controlling our outlook and attitudes. The only person we can truly change or control is ourself. African-American educator Booker T. Washington was keenly aware of this truth when he vowed: "I shall allow no man to belittle my soul by making me hate him."

An emancipated slave, Washington lived in poverty so severe that he went to work at the age of nine. He could easily have blamed his situation on circumstances and used these as an excuse to hate. Instead of permitting this emotion to fester within his soul, he managed to harness his energies and channel them into improving his own condition and that of others.

Washington worked as a janitor to obtain an education—the method he believed would lead to self-improvement and eventual improvement of conditions for all humankind. He took command of his life rather than viewing himself as a victim of his circumstances. After graduation and some teaching experience, he was eventually asked to head a new school for blacks at Tuskegee, Alabama. He accepted.

The challenges of little money, no equipment, and only two converted buildings did not make the new administrator envy wealthy schools or hate those who were more fortunate. Instead, Washington began working toward his goal. He permitted no negative interferences. During his administration, Tuskegee Institute grew to have nearly two hundred faculty members and one hundred well-equipped buildings.

When Washington's emphasis on education drew criticism from members of the black community who believed that political activism was the path to genuine progress, Washington calmly followed the direction he believed to be true. Rather than seeing the differences as an excuse to hate and fight, the educational leader continued his positive work on the academic front.

A person is in control of what he will allow into his conscious awareness. By concentrating on retaining mastery over the inner self, a wise person averts negative emotions and destructive activities. Negativity cannot have positive results. Washington realized this truth. Rather than wasting valuable energies in unproductive arguments, he followed inspiration to fulfill his vision of education. He allowed no man to belittle his soul because he remained responsible for his inward self. Like other great men and women, Washington was aware that only he could control his inner being.

WEEK FOUR : LAW B

Success is a journey, not a destination.
Wayne W. Dyer

The dictionary defines success both as a favorable or satisfactory outcome and as the gaining of wealth, fame and rank. Success can come in many ways—for example, graduating from college, winning a football game, getting high scores on a test or going out with someone you like. These are easily measurable ways of charting what the outer world terms as "success."

There are far more subtle ways as well, that are nonetheless just as spectacular even if they aren't accompanied by social fanfare: Helping a friend who really needs you; keeping a secret you promised to honor; staying on a diet or exercise program; and not giving in to peer pressure because someone whose high opinion you desire wants you to. In fact, honoring the personal commitments you've made with yourself may be a higher form of success than all the fanfare—exactly because it *is* deeply personal.

It has been said that "Success is a journey, not a destination—half the fun is getting there." So how do we get there and what makes the difference between a life full of struggle and one that is full of earned pleasure? Two of the most fundamental laws of the universe—the law of attraction and the law of inertia—may help place that question in a clear context.

The law of inertia states: "It is easier for something in motion to stay in motion. Conversely, once an object (or person) is at rest, it is easier to stay at rest." This is tantamount to saying that fifty percent of the doing of a task is to begin it. Once it is begun, the law of inertia will tend to propel you to finish it. It is, in fact, harder *not* to finish it—to stop in the middle—than to keep going. On the other hand, when you are at rest—unmotivated or quiet or withdrawn—it is easier to stay there than to make the effort to move ahead.

Once you overcome your initial inertia to stay at rest, you can use the energy of the inertia of motion to succeed at anything you commit to beginning. Thus the law, "success breeds success," is reflected in your continuing to create what you have created in the past, or what you are creating in the present.

The law of attraction, which also breeds success, states that "like attracts like." It is a law that functions like a boomerang, bringing back to you that which you project onto others, either for good or ill.

You have three options, then, of things that will be attracted to you in your universe. Two of these are easy: that which you like and that which is like yourself. By becoming the person you most admire—a person of honesty, integrity and compassion—you will in fact attract to you others of similar virtue. Your "inner success" will create your "outer success." That is why it is important to keep our personal commitments, because the loyalty and honesty reflected in such behavior will return to us from the outside.

However, from time to time you will also attract that which you dislike. That is the portion of the law of attraction that gets tricky and can create stress. No one wants to attract those qualities they hate. Yet, by assuming a non-judgmental attitude, you can neutralize those negative experiences. Whenever we resist something, it persists. By refraining from judgment, it is possible to dissipate the energy that attracts it to you.

By focusing on the good in yourself and in others, people will love to be in your presence. They will treat you as a successful person because you make them feel good about themselves.

Success is indeed a journey. It is not a destination, for a destination means the journey is over.

An attitude of gratitude creates blessings.

Do you wake up every morning with a song of praise on your lips? Do you feel full of appreciation for life as you live it each and every day? Or do you have to think long and hard before finding something to be grateful for?

Consider your response to the above questions carefully. These questions are crucial to a life of usefulness and joy. It is a law of life, and an inexorable principle, that if we develop an attitude of gratitude our happiness will increase. The very reasons for being thankful will begin to multiply. Whether you know it or not, you have multitudes of reasons to break out in a wonderful song of praise at this very moment.

But how does this positive approach really work, you may ask. You may wonder how I can be so certain that this law works. The only way to prove it to yourself is to give it a good try and see what happens. It is written, "As a man thinketh in his heart, so is he." Whatever you give your attention to and belief to becomes your experience.

Focus your attention on the way you would like to see yourself. Now, give thanks for the realization that you are becoming that person. Give thanks for all of the abundance you're now enjoying and give thanks for the abundance of every good thing that's coming to you. As you count your blessings and become more and more aware of how truly blessed you are, you will begin to build an attitude of gratitude. Your life will be blessed in ways you never thought were possible. Practice waking up each day with an expectation of good, with a wonderful feeling of thanksgiving for life itself. Your days will grow better and better.

True, you can choose to focus solely on what is lacking in your life. You can bemoan the fact that you don't have your share of earthly possessions. You can go around complaining about fate and your parents and your pocketbook, and the faults and frailties of others. These are choices that many people have made before you and continue to make.

Or you can change yourself—you can become wise to wonderful ways of playing the game of life. It's likely you already realize the wisdom of an attitude of gratitude. It's only a small step for you to begin to open to greater and greater good. As you become a good steward of the abundance that is yours right now, an increasing attitude of gratitude will bring great blessings to you and, then, through you, to our world. The attitude of gratitude—it will work for you!

Enthusiasm is contagious.

A small church in a low-income area of Brooklyn asked a businessman if the neighborhood children could play in a vacant lot he owned until another use was made for the property. The man agreed to allow the space to be used as a playground, with two specifications. The church had to pay for insurance and take responsibility for cleaning up the lot. The church decided they would manage insurance payments somehow and the entire membership agreed to meet on a certain Saturday to clean the lot.

It was not an inviting prospect. The people were certainly willing but they could not bring themselves to look at the task ahead of them with any enthusiasm. And who could blame them? The litter was terrible—there were bottles, cans, paper, even discarded needles used by drug addicts. It was decided the adults would pick up the trash and litter, and the children would hold the trash bags open for easy access. With giant-sized sighs and long faces, they began the work.

A few of the families were slightly late, including a couple with a crippled ten-year-old daughter. Many of the volunteers wondered why they had brought the girl. After all, she could hardly walk.

But she propped herself up by leaning on her crutches, leaving her hands free and, with a huge smile and happy expression, she held the plastic bag while her father filled it. They laughed and talked about the many sports and activities that would take place on the lot. And their enthusiasm was contagious! A little crippled girl had inspired the other volunteers with her attitude. Yet a few found themselves wondering why the girl was so excited. It seemed to them unlikely that she would use the lot herself. How could she? When asked, the crippled girl was again totally enthusiastic. "I'll keep score and be a referee and stuff like that," she said.

The individual who takes up any activity as a positive adventure can inspire the same attitude in others. The worker who looks for ways to enjoy his work, to be enthusiastic about it, sets the stage for others to follow his example. Always remember that what a person does, for good or for ill, can be contagious. A smile is contagious but so is a frown. Although no one can be sunny all the time, if we take up our tasks with enthusiasm, it's likely those around us will also catch our spirit. Enthusiasm really *is* contagious!

WEEK FOUR : LAW E

You fear what you do not understand.

There was recently a replay of what had been a live simultaneous broadcast between San Francisco and Leningrad. The audiences in both cities were able to see the programs presented as well as the audience in the other city. One of the most dramatic moments came near the end of the broadcast when the reality of the situation dawned on both audiences and they began to wave to each other. Tears of joy were shed in both cities. Two peoples that had been on opposite sides of a Cold War for more than a generation suddenly became aware that the people on the other side were just like them. This new level of understanding increases the potential for peace in the world.

During World War II, Allied soldiers referred to the Germans as "Jerrys." During the Korean and Vietnam conflicts, the Red Chinese, North Koreans and Vietnamese were called "Gooks." These names served to dehumanize the enemy and to create a sense of superiority and loathing (which is a form of fear) in the troops that had to fight them. If the name callers had understood that the troops on the other side were fighting for what they believed in just as they were, killing them would have become an infinitely more difficult task.

With understanding, fear and hatred are much less likely to take root. When the audience in San Francisco understood that the people in Leningrad had hopes and aspirations, just as they did, fear and misunderstanding began to evaporate. When the audience in Leningrad understood that the people in San Francisco looked like them, laughed like them, and had a similar vision of the future, the world took a giant step closer to realizing peace and brotherhood.

We tend to fear the unknown. When the hunter sought out the maneating animals for food, there would always be the sense of fear and anxiety inherent in the hunt. Not because the hunter didn't know what he would find, but because he didn't know when.

Today it is rare to encounter a maneating animal in our normal pursuits, so there is little reason for us to fear for our lives. Yet we continue to experience fear and anxiety for the future. We believe there is the potential for terrible things to happen to us and we don't know when. However, the truth is that, by approaching life without fear, things tend to work out for the best.

Take the example of recovering alcoholics. During the course of that disease, they increasingly come to deny they have a problem with alcohol. Most of them have to hit bottom, some literally have to wake up in the gutter, before they can look up and see that the solution lies in recovery. The fears and anxieties that were the cause of their drinking had to come to light so they could face and defeat them.

But you don't have to hit bottom to look up. You can begin now to understand that life without fear works out for the best. You can begin to understand that people on "the other side" are just like you and me—they only want to be free to enjoy life. You don't have to be afraid to reach out for new experience, to take new risks for an increased expectation of good. You can go forth without fear in the direction of success, harmony, health and prosperity.

WEEK FIVE : LAW A

Love has the patience to endure the fault we cannot cure.

Because the word *love* is used to describe a variety of feelings and relationships, it's easy to be confused about what love really is. Society today tends to define love as romantic love for someone of the opposite sex. But it's possible to think of love in much broader terms: the basic feeling of goodwill for another, care for their health and well-being, and the desire to have only good come to them. This includes our parents, siblings, friends, and anyone.

Sometimes when we think we love someone, we're actually loving what the other person gives us. Love at its highest level demands nothing in return. If love, in the deepest sense, is wishing only good to come to those you love, then you want them to have what they want and what will make them happy. It does not assume we know what is best for them, or that we know what will make them happy. It means we give them the right to refuse what we want to give. It means they don't have to give us anything, even if we ask.

In human relationships we sometimes forget that true love is given freely, no strings attached. We may feel hurt, but that is usually futile. If the person doesn't care for us in the same way we care for them, how can they even understand our hurt feelings? However, we may save and improve the relationship if we're honest with our friend and explain what we're expecting or wanting. A true friend will want to understand the problem, and will be willing to work toward preventing a similar misunderstanding in the future.

This is not always easy and, sometimes, even when we truly love someone without conditions or expectations, they act in unpredictable ways and we experience pain. Perhaps the person starts behaving in a way we know to be destructive and dangerous. The problem may be related to alcohol or drugs or some criminal activity or sexual promiscuity. Such situations can be difficult. We want the person to stop hurting himself or herself. We can see great danger ahead.

We must be careful not to get caught up in this behavior too, while at the same time we want to do all we can to interrupt our friend's self-destructive behavior. We can let our friend know that we cannot approve of such behavior. Sometimes letting someone know you love them, regardless of what they do, is the very thing that will cause them to turn around, although there are no guarantees. Sometimes there is nothing we can do to stop a loved one from expressing hurt and pain, and it's important to remember that ultimately we are not responsible if our friend chooses to continue along a dangerous path. We are not in a position to rescue anyone; we can only try to help the person rescue himself, and sometimes loving without condition means letting the person suffer the consequences of his or her behavior.

WEEK FIVE : LAW B

Nothing can bring you peace but yourself.
Ralph Waldo Emerson

A man who was weary of the frantic pace of city life gave up his job, sold his apartment and moved to a small cabin in the woods. He wanted to find the peace of mind that had eluded him in the city. For a few weeks, he thought he had found contentment, but soon he missed his friends and the conveniences of the city. When his restlessness grew acute, he felt the urge to move again.

This time he decided to try a small town. There would be people to talk to and he could enjoy the conveniences of the city without the pressure of bigness, noise and the constant "hurry, hurry" atmosphere. Surely, in this best of both worlds, he would find peace. But life in the small town had problems he hadn't bargained for. People were slow to accept an outsider, yet they were quick and aggressive when it came to prying into his personal affairs. Soon he discovered to his annoyance that strange rumors were circulating about him. It was clear there would be no peace for him, even in a small town. Again he grew restless and discontented; he concluded that it was not possible to find peace anywhere. He moved back to the city, resigned to a life of inner turmoil.

This unfortunate man could have profited from an important truth realized by Ralph Waldo Emerson, who wrote: "Nothing can bring you peace but yourself." Emerson understood that inner peace does not depend on where you live or even whom you're with. True peace is a quality you carry within yourself regardless of external circumstances.

To get in touch with your own inner peace, reserve some time each day—even a few minutes, if that's all you can spare—in which you can be alone and undisturbed. Sit in a comfortable chair, close your eyes, breathe deeply and slowly and let your mind and body relax. Repeat these words slowly to yourself: "I am now letting go. I am now letting go." Mentally release the events of the day, one by one, until you feel yourself moving into a realm of stillness and peace.

This simple exercise will teach you that it's not events themselves that rob you of a sense of peace; it's a negative interpretation of events that disturbs you, causing restlessness and stress.

Jesus acknowledged this truth and taught about the existence of an inner peace that "passes all understanding," a peace that is not dependent on circumstances. When you discover this inner realm for yourself, you will realize it is the only real peace you can ever have. You don't have to travel far to find it; you need only look deep within yourself. External events can change at a moment's notice and what you thought was peace can suddenly evaporate. But once it's yours, true peace will remain with you, even in the midst of a rapidly changing world.

Try not to make the same futile mistake as the man who sought external peace by moving from place to place. That route leads to disappointment. Instead, spend time each day in your quiet place. Release your cares until you make contact with your inner realm of peace. Cultivate an attitude of gratitude, of giving and forgiving. You may be amazed at how joyful you will feel, how in touch with yourself and the world.

The unexamined life is not worth living.

Socrates

The study of human behavior is not new to our time. The ancient Greeks were probably the first to ask questions about what motivates people. The origins of psychology are often linked to the Greek philosopher Aristotle who lived in the 5th Century B.C. Aristotle built upon the groundwork of Plato and Socrates. The phrase, "Man, know thyself," is attributed to Socrates, the Greek philosopher who urged his fellow Athenians to live noble lives, to think critically and logically, to have probing minds. He believed, along with Plato and Aristotle, that evil arises from ignorance and the failure to investigate the reasons why people behave as they do. He is also credited with saying, "The unexamined life is not worth living."

We all want to live noble, moral lives. One way to accomplish this is to understand the behavior of friends and associates as well as our own. Once we understand why others behave as they do, we can have compassion and empathy for them. When we recognize our roots in the same human family, we no longer feel a need to stand in judgment of them. Judgment only condemns and separates people. It places one person or group against another, whereas compassion and empathy bring people together and promote communication. "I care about you, I want to support you" is the message.

Socrates emphasized the Greek ideal of self-control. And he believed in a divine principle, expressed through an unfailing inner voice, that directs our actions along the path of morality. He taught us to explore our thinking and behavior, to reach within and to expunge those behaviors that are unworthy of us. Honest self-analysis can help us to see if we react to people and events because we've been socially conditioned in a certain way, or if our behavior is guided by the divine principle and inner voice within us. As important as it is to understand the behavior of others, our behavior is the only behavior we can change. Learning the reasons behind our own behavior helps us to be honest with ourselves; it builds integrity into our lives. We learn what is *real* to us, what *matters* to us. And we learn to act rather than simply react. We learn to be true to ourselves and to live our lives with dignity.

Introspection with an emphasis on growth and change will help us to achieve a full and fulfilled life. So will taking the time to understand the motives behind the actions of others. Learning to have compassion and empathy for others and for ourselves, leads to a peaceful, successful existence that is truly worth living.

WEEK FIVE : LAW D

Build thee more stately mansions, O my soul.
Oliver Wendell Holmes

Have you ever watched a child in a swing, lost in her own world as she swings higher and higher trying to reach up to the sky? In her childhood innocence, she has no sense of limitation. She hasn't yet learned the meaning of the word "can't." You might be thinking: "But she's just a child. Of *course* she can never touch the sky. She'll grow up and learn better."

That child's highest aspiration while sitting in the swing is to feel a part of the sky and the most fortunate among us—the poet and philosopher Henry David Thoreau is a famous example—never lose that wonderful sense that "the sky's the limit!" Thoreau decided to make his dreams come true. He was able to take the magic of childhood belief and transform it into wisdom that helped him function fully as an adult, never losing the child's keen imaginative power and sense of wonder. He believed that in following the dictates of your own heart, you create the magic that makes deepest desires come true. Listen to his words: "If one advances confidently in the direction of his dreams, and endeavors to live the life which he has imagined, he will meet with a success unexpected in common hours. He will put some things behind, will pass an invisible boundary; new, universal, and more liberal laws will begin to establish themselves around and within him; or the old laws be expanded, and interpreted in his favor in a more liberal sense, and he will live with the license of a higher order of beings. In proportion as he simplifies his life, the laws of the universe will appear less complex, and solitude will not be solitude, nor poverty poverty, or weakness weakness. If you have built castles in the air, your work need not be lost; that is where they should be. Now put the foundations under them."

Undoubtedly most of us have been told many times we can be anything we want to be. Yet so many of us grow to adulthood living mediocre lives, feeling unfulfilled and compromised. What makes the difference between the one who accomplishes his dreams and the one who falls short? The one who succeeds is more than merely a dreamer—he is also a realist. Thoreau said to not only build your castles in the air but to put the foundations under them. Put "feet on your dreams."

Ask yourself what steps you should take to make your desires into realities. For instance, you might dream of a date with someone you admire, but until you ask that person, the dream cannot become a real part of your life. Or, if you dream of making a big sale to a difficult customer, you must take the steps needed to get an appointment with him, or it will never happen.

What do you think Thoreau meant when he spoke of new, universal, more liberal laws establishing themselves around us? Could it be that when we live true to our dreams, life will cooperate in giving us those things we cannot give ourselves? By not giving up, by remaining faithful to our aspirations, is there a better chance that circumstances will work in our favor?

What are your "castles in the air"? Ask yourself how you can put feet in your dreams. Then get your feet off the ground and swing higher and higher until you reach that part of the sky that's there waiting for you.

WEEK FIVE : LAW E

You are only as good as your word.

Sally became so absorbed in the book she was reading, she decided to skip calling Millie, a school friend, even though she had promised to do so. A few days later Sally had a chance to go into a nearby city with her girlfriend who lived next door and she decided to do so. She made a last minute call to Becky, another school friend, to explain what had come up. "We can go to the Burger Heaven anytime. I know you understand," Sally said.

Two weeks later, Becky and Millie and three other girls made plans for a trip to the local zoo. "Aren't we going to invite Sally?" one of the girls asked. "Let's not," Millie replied. "She isn't good about keeping her word."

Sally was heartbroken when she discovered her friends had planned a special day without her. It never occurred to her that good friends keep their word. The saying "you are only as good as your word" is very true. And not being as good as your word can lead to great unhappiness and a lonely existence.

When it comes to keeping your word, there is no such thing as a small situation. Saying you will call someone and then neglecting to do so may seem small to you, but it can loom large in the mind of the person to whom you made the promise. Maybe that person really needs someone to talk to at the moment. Perhaps they are not very active socially and a telephone call means a great deal to them. Perhaps they simply like you very much and look forward to the promised chat. By failing to make that call not only are you risking making someone unhappy but you may also be hurting yourself. Things might go badly for you in the near future and you may need friends more than ever before. But if you were not good at keeping your word, they may have decided to give up on you.

This is the negative view of "being as good as your word." There is also a strong positive side, as Jim's case shows. Every time Jim made a promise, no matter how small or seemingly insignificant, he kept his word. If he made plans with someone and then was offered the opportunity to do something more exciting or interesting, he never hesitated.

He would say "Thank you, I'd love to do it, but I already have a commitment."

Jim's behavior invariably brought two reactions, both positive. The first friend would be pleased because he and Jim stuck to their plan, and the second friend would be impressed. While sorry that Jim couldn't join him, he appreciated the fact that Jim could be counted on. Jim was not only well-liked during his school years but he was successful as an adult. His word was his bond, and both friends and business associates liked and trusted him. "Jim's as good as his word," a professional friend said of him. There can be no higher praise than that.

WEEK SIX : LAW A

Where there's a will there's a way.
Aesop

Paul's large family had owned and operated a successful cattle ranch in Montana for three generations. Along with his friends and neighbors, he shared a love of the land and the livestock. Paul respected the ranching life and assumed, as did others, that he would continue doing it as an adult. He studied agri-business at the nearby college and worked on the ranch during summers and school breaks.

After he took a scuba diving class at the college, he started being pulled in another direction. His underwater time was in a swimming pool and a large, silty river, plus one big field trip to the ocean two states away. For Paul, who had never learned to swim, a major challenge was the course requirement to swim one mile. He had to take a swimming class on the side and run daily (not his favorite activity) to develop the necessary physical endurance to pass the test.

He recalled that some of his happiest moments as a child had been watching Jacques Cousteau's TV program about the undersea world. He started thinking more and more about this fascinating realm. He read everything on it he could find and sent for more literature to feed his growing interest. He daydreamed about exploring coral reefs and identifying exotic fish. He talked of the sea with wonder, awe, and increasing knowledge. Eager to experience tropical waters, he took his savings and flew to the Cayman Islands to dive during a spring break, an adventure that opened up a beautiful new world.

Paul's family thought it was just a passing interest like others he'd had over the years. When he began investigating dive schools around the country, however, they were concerned. This had no relation to the world they knew and they doubted its practicality. They loved Paul very much, but saw this move of his as a flight of fancy and a waste of money. Paul had deep love, respect and loyalty for his family and, like most young people, he cared about their approval. He suffered from the conflict between his own desires and theirs for him. Plus, all the schools were far from home and he knew he would miss his family.

Ultimately, he decided to do it, chose the school he thought best, and applied. It was expensive; he had to work long and hard at unpleasant jobs and live very simply to save up enough money to go. Because few people understood or supported his goal, he knew he was regarded as "different." Time passed, full of delays and setbacks. At times his dream seemed so far away, and he wondered if circumstances were telling him to give it up and settle for something more realistic. But his will held steady. He knew what he wanted and persevered in his efforts.

It took three years before Paul finally entered school. He applied himself and graduated at the top of his class, earning the school's first recommendation for a job at a dive resort in the Bahamas. After valuable experience there, he was invited back to join the school's teaching staff. He took more schooling and became qualified to instruct instructors. From the additional education, he discovered his love of the scientific aspects of his work, which opened up further avenues of potential.

His success has fed on itself and created more success. At 27, Paul is respected as one of the top people in his field. Not only is he in demand as a teacher but he also writes articles for publication, co-owns a dive shop, travels around to trade shows, has his diving equipment provided for him, and has become an accomplished underwater photographer. He meets people from all over the world. He knows he can go anywhere he likes and have work and friends. Paul's family has become very proud of his accomplishments and he enjoys his trips home to see them. He may be different, but he's the most interesting person they know—and one of the happiest!

WEEK SIX : LAW B

The borrower is servant to the lender.

Proverbs 22, 5:7

The person who borrows money often finds himself nervous or uneasy in the presence of the lender. There is comfort and confidence in managing your finances so well that you are free to choose how you spend your money. How can you enjoy spending the money when it really belongs to someone else?

A borrower may find his joy diminished because he is worrying about how to repay the loan even before he's used it. Picture a person at a party when in walks his lender. Somehow, without a word being spoken between the two on the subject of the loan, he begins to feel guilty for enjoying himself.

It could be something as small as the new tie the borrower bought to wear for the occasion. The mere sight of the lender reminds him that he should be spending the money on other things that may be more important. Buying a new tie to wear to a party is not normally a cause for shame, but if your lender thought the money was needed to pay medical bills or finance the expansion of your business, he may have doubts about trusting your judgment.

Another facet of the relationship between borrower and lender has affected people who have fallen behind with loans. In recent years it has become easy to obtain credit cards, but this convenient access to money can become a burden. It's inviting to walk past stores and decide on the spur of the moment to buy things you want but don't need. It's a pleasant experience to be able to eat in any restaurant you want and just sign a piece of paper. The use of words such as "revolving charge account" sound so harmless, but they aren't. When the cardholder loses his job or faces a real emergency, such as an accident or surgery, he suddenly finds himself unable to repay his creditors.

Phone calls start coming from the bank with greater and greater frequency. Often these calls assume a condescending tone that makes the debtor feel sorry he ever accepted the loan. Gone is the friendly spirit that was contained in the letters inviting him to "buy now and pay later." After a few months of being behind in his payments, the attitude will become "pay now or face dire consequences."

Initially, when the cardholder finds himself in the position of trying to pay the hospital or auto repair bill, plus the credit card issuer for all those nice clothes and meals in restaurants, he finds himself facing choices he never thought he would have to make. Of course, there is a sense of urgency and responsibility to repay all of those lenders. But without enough money to satisfy all of them, some will have to come first, and some will have to come last.

You can pay each of them a little, but someone will be very unhappy about the amount you're paying and then the calls from that creditor will increase in frequency and become more sinister in tone. At that point, the debtor may be able to repay the loans by borrowing from yet another source, which just delays the cycle. Or they could work out a long-term payment plan, which results in living with absolutely no luxuries until all the debts are repaid. But how many people would relish the thought of living with no margin for error, and no allowance for fun?

Unfortunately, many people have arrived at a step ever further down the ladder. When they don't want or can't get another loan and they can't see how to repay their creditors, bankruptcy is the only solution left. For most people, it is embarrassing to admit that they cannot handle their finances, and it's also inconvenient. Try and get a loan once you have filed for bankruptcy. Even begging won't help.

People don't like to be servants, but it's easy to forget that's just what you become when you cast your lot with such modern conveniences as credit cards, home equity loans, revolving charge accounts, and time payments. No matter what they're called, loans will always make the person receiving them subservient to the person giving them.

This applies to corporations and to nations as well as to people.

WEEK SIX : LAW C

There is no limit in the universe.

There is no place in the world that is truly empty, without substance or energy. Wherever we look, we see some form of life, of growth, or vitality. All around us is the matter from which we build and create.

If we turn from the physical world and look within our minds for an empty space, we will quickly realize that the mind is constantly active, filled with ideas and thoughts. Even the great mystics of the ages have taught that to still the mind is to simply realize an unseen power and activity far greater than ourselves.

This speaks of a great truth, another law of life: There is no limit in the universe. Look around at the many objects that have been made by humans. Now look beyond those things and see before you the vastness of the resources from which objects are created—and the greatest of these resources is the mind. Our minds are filled with ideas and thoughts that show us how to build or create whatever our imagination can conceive of.

As we approach the 21st Century, we are becoming increasingly aware of the great needs of our global community. Some countries are mired in poverty, without the resources to feed the hungry and without the skills to create more economical and effective ways of living. Other countries are overrun with violence and apathy, seemingly lacking in the ideas and enthusiasm to meet the needs of the people. It is easy to believe that we don't have the resources to feed all the world's people, or the medical answers to the world's diseases. War may tempt us to believe we've run out of ideas that will promote a harmonious and peaceful world.

Each day as we are challenged to meet our own needs, and each time we feel helpless to assist in meeting the world's needs, we need only remember this essential law of life: everything has been provided to meet our needs and *there is no limit in the universe*. Limits are imposed on us only when we close our minds to possibilities and our eyes to the abundance that is all around us.

WEEK SIX : LAW D

A loving person lives in a loving world.

Ken Keyes

Bill and Mike both moved to new towns with their parents. Bill disliked his new community from the first day. He felt the school was inferior to the one he'd attended in his former hometown. His new classmates seemed boring and unfriendly. "I wish we hadn't moved here," Bill told his parents. "This is a cold, dull place and I'll never fit in." Mike was far more fortunate. He discovered his new school was not only excellent academically but had many activities and challenges. "I can't believe how many new friends I made today," he stated at the dinner table after his first day at Miller High. "I feel as though some of the students have been my friends forever." Before you pity Bill for not moving to a town as warm and friendly as the one Mike moved to, you should know that they moved to the same town, the same neighborhood, and that they attend the same school.

So why did they respond to a similar situation so differently? Bill tends to expect the worst in life, whereas Mike is outgoing and friendly. He went to the new school with a smile on his face and a positive outlook. Mike is a loving person who lives in a loving world.

The loving person creates a positive atmosphere. Jill, for example, was a loving person. She was the friend you could count on. Ready to listen, to help, to comfort. When Jill's mother died of cancer while Jill was still in high school, she was surrounded by love, not only from her family but from her many friends. Jill's giving of herself was being returned tenfold. Even in great sorrow, she lived in a loving world.

The loving person can feel hurt, can experience anger, can be put out at someone for some reason. These are human emotions. Life, after all, has its share of disappointments, troubles, worries and sorrows for all of us. We cannot expect continuously happy days. But the loving person refuses to allow negative emotions to take over. The loving person forgives the person who hurt him. The loving person goes for a long walk or does a chore that takes his mind off the anger being experienced. The loving person clears the air by talking with the person he's angry at, and then gives him a hug or a handshake. No matter what degree of stress or confusion he must undergo, that person's world continues to be a loving world.

So try a smile instead of a scowl. Expect the best and not the worst. Do your utmost to be understanding and to care for the people in your life. The Bills of this world find things to complain about throughout their lives. The Mikes, on the other hand, not only look for the best but help create that best by their own attitudes. The loving person, from youth to old age, lives in a loving world and leads a full and happy life, with the strength to face problems and tragedies because of the loving world they inhabit.

WEEK SIX : LAW E

Count your blessings and you will have an attitude of gratitude.

It was only a few days until Christmas and Jennifer Noble, a Britisher, was feeling low. This was the first holiday season since her divorce and she was living in the United States, thousands of miles away from her home and her family. She had married an American eight years earlier and for the past two years they had lived in the midwest while he studied for a new career. Following the divorce, she had made a decision to remain. But most of her friends had moved on and, although she had been making new ones and was successfully rebuilding her life, on this day she was feeling very sorry for herself.

Not one to wallow in self-pity for too long, she knew the way to feel better was to make a "gratitude list." She wrote down all the things in her life she was grateful for and, as she did so, her spirits lifted. But she also knew that gratitude is not simply a feeling. It is something to be put into action and she was determined to not slide back into her "poor me" state of mind again.

In order to shake off the blues and increase her feeling of well being, Jennifer decided to help others less fortunate than herself. She went to the local Salvation Army shelter and helped them with their Christmas dinner preparations and bought a few inexpensive toys for the children there. That was her choice, and might not necessarily be yours or mine; there are choices to fit a variety of temperaments and needs. Sometimes we can give thanks for our blessings simply by picking up the telephone and calling someone we haven't spoken to for a while, or writing a note of thanks for a gift, or telling our children how much we appreciate their presence in our lives.

Actively acknowledging our good creates more good. Those who are grateful experience the wonderful balance of being both receivers and givers. Gratitude nurtures within us a positive, joy-filled consciousness and unifies us with life's flow and it is this that gives birth to inner fulfillment.

Many of the world's great figures have been faced with problems so great that at first they seemed insurmountable. What would have happened if Beethoven had wallowed in self-pity because of his deafness? The world would not have benefited from the legacy of his profoundly beautiful music. What would our transportation system be like today if the Wright brothers had given up after their first test flight? What if Herman Melville had stopped writing because, at the time of publication, *Moby-Dick* was ignored by both critics and readers?

Counting our blessings can transform melancholy into cheerfulness; laughter and joy are expressions of praise and thanksgiving for life's glories. When looking at the glass that symbolizes our life, we can view it as half full or half empty. The choice is ours. He who sees the glass as half empty, bemoans his lot; he has the attitude that the world is out to get him. But the person who cultivates an attitude of gratitude will more readily see the glass as half full, and this positive outlook is self-perpetuating. The more joyful we are, the more attractive we become. When we feel gratitude for our experiences, it becomes easier to see the good that always exists. When we give a smile to someone else, we are likely to receive one in return, and that smile reflects a happy heart that is open and receptive to what the good life has in store.

WEEK SEVEN : LAW A

We learn more by welcoming criticism than by rendering judgment.

J. Jelinek

Like everything else in life, arguments can be managed. When someone is expressing his anger at us, or seems to be overly critical, we have two basic choices. We can defend ourselves, or we can learn from the conflict. In a defensive conflict there is lots of anger, blame and criticism and a minimum of listening to what the other person is saying. Nothing is learned if no one is listening.

When we opt for that method of argument, we do whatever is necessary to protect our position, our feeling that we are right and the other person is wrong. Strategies defensive arguers use include hurling accusations back at the other person, shouting to prove a point, and walking away in a silent rage.

Using the learning method to solve conflicts, on the other hand, encourages calmness and patience under pressure. We force ourselves to remain silent long enough to hear the other person's thoughts and feelings. If we ask questions to clarify a misunderstanding instead of summoning arguments to protect our position, we might find that what our friend is actually saying is not what we thought we heard. Or we might find that the anger being expressed is the residue of an earlier argument, or is really aimed at someone else and has nothing to do with us.

But whether or not another's argument or criticism is valid, we will always be better off asking questions and exploring the feelings behind the case being made. In that way we learn about ourselves and, at the same time, we honor our friend by showing acceptance rather than rejection. Listening to a different point of view shows respect for the friendship and, notwithstanding the conflicts that are inevitable in all relationships, will help it deepen over time.

Harmony—not wisdom—tells us never to welcome disagreement. It's almost always painful and usually requires that we make change. But developing trusted friends and establishing relationships that will last a lifetime, depends on our not being afraid of opinions at odds with our own.

Part of being human is realizing we may not be perfect all the time. We don't have to assume an argument is an attack on our worth as a human being; instead, we can use it to determine if our behavior or thinking might need adjustments. It has been aptly said that "We learn more by welcoming criticism than by rendering judgment." Where judgment can destroy friendships, our willingness to listen to another honestly and openly helps to deepen them.

WEEK SEVEN : LAW B

Life is ten percent what you make it and ninety percent how you take it.
P. Dorman

Johnny and Ann attend the same school and both recently lost their fathers. Johnny's dad died from cancer and Ann's dad from heart complications. They both did all they could to make those last, difficult months as worthwhile and pleasant as possible. Because his dad enjoyed sports, Johnny watched televised games with him and read the sports section to him. Ann's dad had been a college professor before becoming too ill to work and he was an avid reader until his eyesight began to fail. Ann spent hours reading books to him and exchanging ideas and thoughts about the contents. It would seem as though Johnny and Ann were very much alike in the responsible way they cared for their dying fathers. Yet after their fathers died, they showed very different attitudes.

Johnny felt he had done the right thing in giving so much of himself to his dad. He took on much of the burden of the funeral, knowing it would help his mother and two younger sisters get through those difficult days. But then Johnny decided he had "done his duty." Two things began to happen. First, he became bitter and felt betrayed because the one who had supported the family and guided them, the one who had handled the heaviest chores, had been taken from him. Secondly, Johnny started living his own life again with a vengeance. His sports activities and social life took first place. He felt he deserved his time for himself. He had little left for others.

Ann responded very differently. Although she resumed many of her favorite activities, she also continued to give of herself. Her father had been a great source of comfort to her and her younger brother, especially in helping with their education. Ann missed his patience and the way he could make the most difficult problems clear. But because she felt her kid brother would be affected even more deeply by his loss, Ann did her best to help encourage Tommy scholastically and to explain anything he didn't quite understand, just as her father would have done. Ann was also aware of the progress that had been made in treating heart patients, and she felt that helping to raise money for heart research projects would be a wonderful way to honor her father. She took part in a walkathon to raise money. She became a volunteer in the hospital where her father had spent a great deal of time. She also started a support group in her school for young people whose parents were seriously ill or accident victims. In other words, she used her experiences not only to make her own life richer and better, but also she touched in a positive way the lives of many other people.

WEEK SEVEN : LAW C

When the one great scorekeeper comes, he counts not whether you won or lost but how you played the game.

Grantland Rice

Much emphasis is placed on winning in today's world. We've been taught that everyone loves a winner and, as the former baseball manager Leo Durocher put it, "Nice guys finish last." In professional sports, winning is everything. In business, striving for the top rung of the ladder is a constant goal. Nations compete with other nations to win control of markets. Companies spend millions of advertising dollars to help win over the consumer. The saying, "It's not whether you win or lose, it's how you play the game," seems a worn shibboleth judged by current competitive standards.

But, while winning is a good thing, placing an inflated value on being first can be destructive. There is a mistaken assumption that you will be a better and happier person if you always come in first. But the fact is, many who hold the top seat in their sphere of expertise prove to be remarkably unhappy and insecure on a personal level.

What does coming in first actually mean? It simply means you outperformed someone else on a given day. Your next performance may be completely different, as new and eager talent zealously vie for your position. You can be certain that your position on the top rung will not go unchallenged. If your self esteem rides on your ability to outmaneuver, outwit, or outsmart someone else, you will have a great deal riding on a very shaky foundation. Approached in this way, competition becomes a means of survival, a weapon used to destroy those who threaten to depose your vulnerable empire.

That's not to say that competition can't be a positive force in our lives. In fact, it is a necessary part of our social and economic development, of its continuing vigor. On a personal level, pitting yourself against another in sports or business provides you an opportunity to sharpen and expand your skills. In addition, it brings into focus those areas that need further development. You can gather a tremendous amount of useful information quickly either by engaging in competition or observing others competing.

The problem is not competition but our attitude towards it. In the heat of competition, we often measure our self-worth by how well we do against our opponents. If we lose the game, we believe we're losers. If we come in second, we feel we're second-rate. It's important to remember that productive competition with another serves as a yardstick that measures our performance, not our value as a person. Win or lose, we come out on top each time we can allow ourselves to learn something new.

Life is a game, and the way you choose to play it is the key to being a winner or loser. Coming in first does not make you a winner, any more than coming in last makes you a loser. If you work toward making each performance a little better than the last one—and if you find your sense of life steadily expanding and improving—you will definitely emerge a winner.

We tend to find what we look for: good or evil, problems or solutions.

Reality is often a matter of personal perception, as much as objective fact. The way two people respond to the same incident reveals this almost every time.

Imagine the following scene. Friends are having dinner at a restaurant. They overhear the couple at the next table talking excitedly. Neither speaks of it until later. Then one woman says: "Could you believe the nerve of that man, telling her what to eat? Why he treated her like a child!"

"I think he was helping her with her order," her companion responds. "The menu was completely in French." We have one event with two entirely different interpretations.

"Life is the movie you see through your own unique eyes," Denis Waitley writes in his book *The Winner's Edge*. "It makes little difference what's happening out there. It's how you take it that counts." Ask any professional athlete what is the attitude that allows one man to win and another to lose; what separates those who try and fail from those who try and succeed, and the answer is likely to be belief. Belief in the vision of what can be accomplished. Belief is the athlete's own internal vision of himself as a winner.

"Men are disturbed not by things that happen but by their opinion of the things that happen," Epictetus said over two thousand years ago. How many times have we over-reacted in a situation because we misinterpreted what we thought was happening?

Take jealously for example. If you often find yourself feeling jealous in your relationships, it's probably because you haven't learned to trust yourself. You may be projecting unfaithful behavior onto your mate because you question your own ability to be faithful.

"I know I'm not seeing things as they are, I'm seeing things as I am," says the singer Laurel Lee. And truly, our interpretations of events tells as much about ourselves as about those we are describing. "A loving person lives in a loving world. A hostile person lives in a hostile world.

Everyone you meet is your mirror," Ken Keyes writes in *Handbook to Higher Consciousness*.

Each morning when we awaken from sleep, we begin anew to tell ourselves stories about the events of the day. "A noisy bird woke me up this morning!" you might complain upon waking. Another might respond, "The most wonderful singing bird was in the window this morning!" Same event, but a different story. And ultimately, a different life.

"Thought are like boomerangs." Eileen Caddy writes in *The Dawn of Change*. They come back to us. If we believe in a positive unfolding good, then that is what we will see in the events around us. Even in the dark clouds, we will search for the silver linings, because we are committed to a way of thinking that involves growth. Negativity and pessimism are blocks to embracing the part of ourselves that already knows the answers.

In the end it may come back to the simplest of cliches and adages, one that encompasses the wisdom of every age, one that you can tape to your refrigerator, "When you have lemons, just make lemonade."

WEEK SEVEN : LAW E

Fill every unforgiving moment with sixty seconds of distance run.
Rudyard Kipling

Imagine answering the telephone and hearing a voice announce: "Congratulations, you have just won $1,440! You can spend the money any way you like, but you must spend it within twenty-four hours. You cannot save any of it nor can you give any away."

What should you do with the money? Would you put it in your savings account? No, because the contest conditions state that it will be gone forever if it's not spent in a day. Do you try to give some of it to your friends? No, Because this prize cannot be shared with others. You decide to spend it but to spend it wisely, knowing it can then be turned into something valuable.

Life awards all of us with something very valuable, 1,440 minutes each day to spend as we choose. And spend it we must, for it cannot be saved nor given away. These minutes can either be used wisely or wasted.

Many people do not discover the truth of Ben Franklin's proverb until they are older and remark wistfully, "I wish I'd gone to college when I was younger" or "I regret never telling my father I loved him now that he's dead." Because lost time is lost forever, right now is the best time to do the things that are important to you. As the poet Horace said, "Seize the day!" Do something new and interesting that you have never done before. Travel to a place that you've never visited. Read a new book, make a new friend, or start a new hobby.

Even if you're very busy you will find your daily routine enhanced by using your time wisely and efficiently. You will achieve more success at whatever you set out to do by asking yourself each morning, "What am I going to do with my time, and what can I do to reach my goals today?"

You can begin an exciting new project or finish a term paper ahead of schedule. You can join a club, play a sport, earn money from a part time job, or plan your college career. Whatever projects are exciting and important to you, whatever pursuits and dreams you are passionate about, seize the day!

A woman was tending her garden and thought "Should I plant some roses?" She kept putting off the decision until one cool day she realized it was too late to plant them. Sadly she said: "I should have planted them right away and not wasted my time. Now my garden will be without the beautiful sight of roses for another year. I wish I had the time back."

Are you passing up the opportunity to use your 1,440 daily allotted minutes wisely and well? Act now and plant some roses in your garden of life! You will be glad you did. *Seize the day because lost time is never found again!*

WEEK EIGHT : LAW A

Every ending is a new beginning.
Susan Hayward

Nature demonstrates that almost everything occurs in cycles. The earth rotates on a daily cycle. The moon revolves around the earth on a monthly cycle and the earth around the sun on an annual cycle. Within each year the four seasons take us from cold to warm and again to cold as plants and animals go from a dormant to an active stage and then, as another winter approaches, once more to dormant. Within nature, every beginning has an ending and all endings herald a new beginning. Every day tides go out and then come in. As each day ends a night begins, followed by a new day, followed once again by night. When winter ends, spring begins. And so it goes. Every ending is followed by a beginning: life out of death.

And our lives have seasons and cycles as well. Each one of us ex-priences an endless flow of beginnings and endings. Every season of our life has a beginning and an ending that leads to a new beginning. Childhood ends and adolescence begins; adolescence ends and adult-hood begins; young adulthood ends and middle age begins; middle age ends and old age begins.

We generally like beginnings—we celebrate the new. But we resist endings and attempt to delay them. Very often we don't feel the joy of a beginning, knowing that in each beginning are the seeds of the end. Although endings can be painful, they are less so if, instead of resisting them, we look at time as a natural process of nature: as leaves budding in the spring, coming to full leaf in the summer, turning to red and gold in autumn and dropping from the trees in winter. It is a comfort to comprehend that we are an integral part of the great scheme of nature.

Much of our resistance to endings stems from our unawareness of each new beginning, from our inability to realize that we *are* one with nature. Indeed, we may even doubt that there will be a new beginning! The more we can allow ourselves to trust that every ending is a new beginning, the less likely we are to resist letting go of the old. The less resistance we have, the less pain we will experience in making the jour-ney through the many cycles of our lives.

Imagine you are a caterpillar. You have this strange urge to spin a cocoon around your body—certain death! How difficult it would be to let go of the only life you have ever known, a life of crawling on the earth in search of food. Yet if you are willing to trust, as caterpillars seem able to do, the end of your life as an earthbound worm will be the beginning of your life as a beautiful winged creature of the sky.

The powerful potential behind change lies in the possibility that each new beginning will bring us greater joy and freedom than we have ever known. Whether or not that actually happens—whether or not we continue to grow throughout the cycles of our lives—is largely up to us. We play a part in what happens by choosing how we see our changes, our beginnings, our endings. We can see each ending as tragedy—lament it and resist it—or we can see each ending as a new beginning, a new birth into greater opportunities. What the caterpillar sees as the tragedy of death, the butterfly sees as the miracle of birth.

WEEK EIGHT : LAW B

The only way to have a friend is to be a friend.
Ralph Waldo Emerson

A friend has been described as a gift we give ourselves, another part of ourselves, a mirror reflection. Friendship not only involves us, it begins with us. The attractive force of friendship has its source within the individual's actions. What does a friend do? How does a friend act? What does a friend require of another friend? The answers to all these questions revolve around the word "love." A friend loves.

When Paul defines love in his letter to the Corinthians, he lists the attributes of a true friend. "Love is always patient and kind; it is never jealous; love is never boastful or conceited; it is never rude or selfish; it does not take offense, and is not resentful. Love takes no pleasure in other people's shortcomings but delights in the truth; it is always ready to excuse, to trust, to hope, and to endure whatever comes" *(1 Cor. 13:4–7)*.

Reaching out to another with love means reaching within to find the love we want reflected back to us. When we love ourself, when we are a friend to ourself, we are in a position to attract a friend to us. As our own best friend, we have that gift to give to another.

When healthy friendship reaches outward to involve another human being, it becomes a two-way street, one that may include an occasional detour when opinions differ. No road is completely smooth. Relationships are never consistently smooth. However, even with differences, a true friend does not demand more of us than he would of himself, nor lead us into harmful ways. A friend treats us in the best way possible without trying to control us. We are treated the same way we want to treat ourselves.

What friends have in common is the best interest of each other. Friends seek to coexist, complement, and grow toward greater good with each other. One example of such a friendship is the relationship between Ruth Eisenberg and Margaret Patrick, pianists who have played to audiences in Canada and the United States. Because of the effect of strokes, one woman plays piano with her right hand and the other with her left. Together they produce the mutually harmonious music they both love because each woman is willing to share the best of herself.

Friendship begins when we learn how to be our own best friend. Once we feel solid in self-friendship, we are in a position to offer the gift of friendship to another. As Emerson put it so well, "The only way to have a friend is to be a friend."

WEEK EIGHT : LAW C

Man is what he believes.
Anton Chekhov

There is a story about a woman who dreamed she was being chased by a large, ugly and terrifying monster. Everywhere the lady ran, the monster would always be right behind her, drooling, making ghastly noises and breathing down her neck. In an attempt to get away, the woman ran into a canyon that proved to be a cul-de-sac. She was trapped. With her back against the tall mountainous wall, she watched as the monster came closer and closer. When he was within inches of her she cried out, "What horrible thing are you going to do to me?"

The monster looked at her and said: "That's up to you. It's your dream!"

At that point, she could decide to be devoured by the monster or have the monster turn into a handsome prince or even choose to have the monster disappear. It was her dream and she had the power to determine how it would play out.

To a certain extent, many of us create monsters out of our self image. We come to view as wrong those aspects of ourselves that are different and unique and spend most of our lives trying to hide those "bad" qualities from the world around us. We try to run away from who we are because we feel there's something about our natural selves that isn't right.

Our lives are very much like our dreams. We have control over our thoughts and can view our lives anyway we choose. If our thoughts have created a monster out of a certain aspect of ourselves, then our thoughts can take control of the monster and turn it into something that will create a positive self image.

Every person will appear to others as he appears to himself. If you believe a part of you is wrong, is a failure, is not all that it should be, and those beliefs cause you to dislike any part of yourself, then that's how you'll present yourelf to the world and the world will react in kind.

Nature abhors sameness. Every tree, every flower, every blade of grass is magnificently and magically different. Instead of thinking negatively about your differences, accept the challenge, the joy and the wonder of variation. Each of us tends to become what we think we are, and if we present to the world a person who we honestly believe is "okay," the world will respond to us positively and with acceptance.

The dark of night is not the end of the world.

The ancient peoples thought that the earth was flat and, if one ventured too close to the edge, he would fall off. "The end of the world" is a place where there is no solid ground for us to step upon. It is as if the earth stops there and only emptiness lies beyond.

We all have times when there seems to be nothing solid on which we can walk, stand or even rest. Our world, then, seems to be crumbling under our feet and we wish we were anywhere but where we are. We are certain our family doesn't understand how we feel; we are unable to convince those close to us how serious our state of mind is; there seems to be no way to find outside help in making our decisions.

A mystic, Saint John of the Cross, called this crisis "the dark night of the soul." If you have been wakeful during the pre-dawn hours when the world is still sleeping, you know how lonely it can feel. There is no one to talk to; it's almost as if you are the only person alive in the world. The night seems endless and it is easy to believe that morning will never come.

Our crises are like that, seeming to be endless and without hope of a good outcome. At such times, we might begin to believe that life is not worth living. Perhaps we think, the world (the family, the school, the job, the relationship) will be better off without me. However, this is never true! You have a reason for living; each person in the world has a reason for living. You have a part to play in the life of every other person in the universe. You *do* matter.

What we often see as "no reason for living" is, in truth, a situation in which we can learn a valuable lesson for becoming a whole person. The most stressful event can be a gift in the form of a learning experience that will help us to grow in wisdom and understanding of life's true meaning.

When involved in a situation that feels like the end of the world, picture yourself standing at the beginning of a stairway. If there is no light, you cannot know there are steps that will support your weight.

If you ask for light, you will be shown that there is indeed a stair, each step leading you from the problem to the solution.

There is a part of you that knows the right action for any problem that might arise. Remember: even if you have tried many things that haven't worked, there are always more ways to attempt a solution. There are no insoluble problems, only those we haven't yet learned how to solve. Not knowing how to solve a problem doesn't make you a worthless person. You are a valuable and a valued being.

After the darkest night, the sun always rises. What you are experiencing is only a cloud hiding the face of the sun. Let the power and warmth of the sun within you burn away the cloud that blots out your inner light. Let the sun of belief in life and energize you as you climb.

WEEK EIGHT : LAW E

Revenge is devilish and forgiveness is saintly.

At some point in our lives, most people will have to deal with something that seems hurtful or unfair. It seems to be part of the human experience. How you handle these events is a major determining factor in your life. It makes all the difference to your happiness and your health, physically, mentally and emotionally.

Some people experience hurt or apparent injustice, but manage to find their way through it and maintain their stability. Others take their problems hard and hold on to them; these individuals suffer a great deal. They may believe that someone has dealt them a blow from which they won't recover, not realizing that this is their own decision, not their fate. Or it might seem a kind of strength or toughness to maintain a grievance, as if to say, "They can't do that to me and get away with it!"

Holding on to your troubles can often destroy peace of mind, interfere with clear thinking and insight, and lower the body's energy, resistance and strength. Blame, resentment and self-pity are not comfortable or healthy emotions to carry around inside. Like acid, they sour and corrode the human system. Many physical ailments are associated with an unforgiving attitude, because disharmony in the mind naturally creates disharmony in the body.

The severity of the offense makes a difference in our ability to forgive. Say a friend borrows your favorite shirt and loses it. Someone makes an unkind remark to you. Your friend made plans with you but goes off with someone else instead. You are abused mentally or physically. A careless accident or an aggressive act causes you injury or takes a loved one's life. Certainly there is a range of injury that affects the amount of time and effort it takes to forgive. But even if something appears impossible to forgive, the person who's unwilling to even try will inflict greater suffering on himself than on the other person by making that decision to harbor his misery. He might as well say: "I don't want to feel better. I don't want peace of mind. I don't want to be happy."

He has chosen to place his ability to be happy in someone else's hands. Holding onto a grudge is a decision to suffer, whether the grievance is small or large. The laws of life do not change according to circumstances; their effect is consistent.

The willingness to let go of anger is an important start, but forgiveness means much more than a cooling of emotions. It means the relinquishment of any sense of blame, including blame held toward yourself. When you fully forgive someone, you release any feeling that they owe you for the wrong done. You release the wrong itself. There is no longer the question of whether they should make it up to you. They are free in your eyes.

You have set them free to live up to their highest potential. Within each person is a scale that can help them seek out and measure a proper course of action. Your forgiveness releases them to find that balance. It may be soon, it may be later. You may see it, you may not. But proof to you that they understand what they did is not what matters and it isn't necessary. None of us has the wisdom to be another's judge.

Without walking in another's shoes and seeing the world through that person's eyes, it's impossible to accurately judge him. But there is something crucially important you *can* do. Letting go of the grievance is a decision to deal with your own feelings in a healthy and responsible way, and then to move on. It is a decision on the side of healing, freedom, and peace of mind.

Helpfulness, not wilfullness, brings rewards.

Are you willing or willful? Do you work well with other people's ideas and direction or do you demand to have your own way? When we exert our will in every situation we may be forming a log jam that blocks the flow of good in our lives. When we allow others to express their ideas and to share in planning and direction, we open ourselves to the flow of life.

After trees are cut down for processing into wood products, they are sometimes floated downriver to the mill. Occasionally, logs will become stuck on a rock or other obstruction. More logs will become entangled until virtually all of them are caught in a massive log jam. The only way to untangle the mess is to use dynamite to remove the block and to start the flow down stream once again. Although the dynamite removes the block, it also literally blows what would have been usable lumber into an unusable scattering of mulch, a tremendous waste of raw materials.

When we are willful—when we are full of our own will—we may be blocking the flow of good in our lives, just as the log jam blocks the flow of logs. And what happens when we are stuck in our own willfulness? Just like the lumberman who uses dynamite to break up the log jam, life will come along with someone or some event that will blow us out of our stuck place. The result can be destructive. The more we resist, the greater the potential for an unpleasant occurrence. The more logs that are piled up in the jam, the more dynamite is necessary to get it unstuck.

Science has made us aware of forces in nature that, because they are greater than ourselves, we may never overcome. Some call these forces God or Mother Nature or Tao. Whatever they are called, our lives are much more enjoyable and fulfilling when we learn to work with them. Willingness means being willing to work with the mighty forces of nature, the forces or laws of life.

Too often we tend to take the facts of our lives for granted. We have learned to work within the self-imposed limitations we've experienced in our development. We have developed the habit of just floating from one log jam to another, letting the forces of life blow us up and reduce our potential for inner greatness.

We have the ability to work with the forces in our lives in a new way to experience a greater expression of who we are and what we're capable of being. This requires the willingness to take a new look at our current attitudes; it requires that we be willing to change our minds, to think again, to make new choices, to subordinate our willfulness in favor of willingness. We can begin again from where we are right now. We can choose to work with and not against the forces of life and to experience all the good that is there for us to experience.

Birds of a feather flock together.

There was once a small boy named Sam who felt lonely and bored after his family moved to a new city. He wished dearly to have some friends. After scouring the neighborhood for several days, he finally found a group of boys who accepted him into their group. At last he felt as if he belonged! Unfortunately the group which had befriended him was not one of which his mother approved. One day, Sam overheard her talking with a neighbor. His mother sighed: "Well, I guess my son's just not the boy I thought he was. After all, you know what they say: 'Birds of a feather flock together.'"

The small boy was devastated. He did not want to displease his mother, so he immediately stopped playing with his new friends. Fortunately for him, he found another group of boys, of whom his mother did approve. From then on, however, the boy interpreted this law of life the following way: If you hang out with the "bad" crowd, then you are a "bad" person.

Although this could be a wise and useful interpretation, it does leave something to be desired. Who is to say who is the bad crowd and the good crowd anyway? Just because Sam's mother disapproved of Sam's friends, were they really a "bad" crowd? Interpreting this law of life as Sam did often can lead to some decision-making that is based more on opinions that facts. Given this possibility, should we just throw out this law of life altogether? Of course not. Often we do search for groups that are like ourselves, and by joining these groups fulfill this law of life, by showing that indeed birds of a feather do flock together. The point here, however, is how can we use this law to help us grow in life? Perhaps we can interpret this law differently. We all learn from role models.

Often the way we talk, eat, and work comes from role models. Thus, if we want good role models, it would make sense to associate with a group of people that provided them for us. Rather than trying to judge whether a group of people is desirable or not, we can decide what type of role models we want and then find a group of that type of people. The difference is subtle, but very important.

Albert Einstein interpreted this law of life in a similar way. Although many regard Einstein as a peculiar and solitary eccentric, this is not really the case. While Einstein was working on his first theory of relativity, he often invited many friends to his home, where they discussed physics, philosophy, and literature. Einstein wanted to be someone who knew lots about these things, so he managed to center himself in a group of people who knew lots about them. Thus, Einstein never wasted his time deciding whether it was good to be in one group or another. Instead, he formed his own group full of people he admired and could use as role models.

Perhaps, we are not in a position to put together our own group, but we can still learn from Einstein's lesson. Like the genius scientist, we can decide which feathers will complement and support us and create our own flock. Tired of wasting your time deciding whether one group or another is an "acceptable" one or not? Then simply decide what type of role models you want, find individuals who fit this description and have a fine time flying together to new heights of success.

WEEK NINE : LAW C

Crime doesn't pay.

You know that crime doesn't pay. But do you realize how *much* crime doesn't pay? We all know that most people who commit a crime are arrested sooner or later, and we know that a person who is found guilty can receive a sentence that can forever change his life. However, there are many other ways in which crime doesn't pay.

For example, once you've committed a crime, you will start worrying. In the back of your mind you'll worry that maybe someone did see you or that you made a mistake. You may think you're safe but when you read a story about someone arrested for a crime several months after it took place, all those inner fears will return to haunt you. When the phone rings or the doorbell sounds, you'll jump. You may have to find excuses for avoiding a person or place because of what you did. Sleep may come with difficulty; you'll find yourself tossing and turning. This is guilt even if you refuse to think so, and it's a horrible way to live.

There are so many ways you can pay for committing a crime. One of the hardest punishments can be when your family finds out. They will probably continue to love you; most likely they will forgive you. But it will never be the same.

How about your relationship with friends? Can you honestly handle facing them once they learn about your crime? What if you're arrested? Do you know that means being questioned over and over? Being fingerprinted? Having your picture taken? Do you know what it's like being locked in a cell? Even a holding cell can be a painful and humiliating experience. The conferences with your lawyer are absolutely nothing like those you've watched on television. What if it ends in a court trial with people staring at you?

Even probation presents problems. You can be checked at any time unannounced, and teachers or employers may be questioned about your progress. There are understanding employers, of course, but there are also those who prefer not to have "someone like you." Teachers and employers, friends and even family will watch you more closely. Some of those who were in your life may now choose to drop you. A new friend may change and turn cool when informed about your past.

It's not a happy situation. Although you can prove yourself and over-come it, the better way is to simply never commit a crime in the first place.

You can make opposition work for you.

Is something or someone bothering you? Is there a troublesome person or difficult situation you would like to be rid of? How about in your past? Is there something you wish had never happened? How about your future? Are you facing an imminent and difficult situation that you wish would just go away?

A story from the life of Abraham Lincoln affords a wonderful lesson for living. During Lincoln's presidency, there was an appointee who was always finding ways to challenge and disrupt whatever the president tried to do. If Lincoln was in favor of an issue, you could just bet that this fellow would be dead set against it. After this had been going on for quite some time, a friend of Lincoln's asked him why he didn't have this person replaced by someone more agreeable. Lincoln answered by telling his friend the following tale.

It seems that Lincoln was walking down a country road one day and came upon a farmer plowing his field with a horse-drawn plough. As he drew near and was about to give a greeting, he noticed a big horsefly on the flank of the horse. As the fly was obviously biting and bothering the horse, Lincoln made ready to brush it off. As he raised his hand, the farmer stopped him and said: "Don't do that, friend. That horsefly is the only thing keeping this old horse moving."

As you reflect on your own life, you may recall times when you couldn't see the value of some person and were tempted to brush him or her off. It takes hindsight to recognize that the very situation you were seeing as an irritating bother turned out to be a blessing in dis-guise. Wouldn't life be a much more enjoyable and meaningful experi-ence if we all had the ability to look at the seeming bad things—the difficult people, the irritating situations—and see some blessing there instead? In fact, as we look at them more deeply, we might see them as problems that motivate us to grow and change for the better. Like the horsefly, they may well be what keep us going.

We need to remember that it's up to us to determine how we respond to life. A wise person once said it's not what happens to us in life that's important, it's how we *respond* to what happens to us. This wonderful law of life can be practiced and perfected. As a start, it's important to realize that there's good in everything and everyone. Let's take the time and effort to find it. Before we brush away troublesome people and difficult situations, take another, closer look. That troublesome person or difficult situation may very well be a blessing in disguise.

WEEK NINE : LAW E

Small attempts repeated will complete any undertaking.
Og Mandino

When we entered the first grade many of us experienced great fear. The objectives were monumental in comparison to anything we had been challenged with up to that point. But, with the help and support of our parents and teachers, we steadily progressed and accomplished mastery of many basic skills.

For first graders, learning the strange figures of the alphabet may be initially overwhelming. They have never had to draw on their memory to that extent before. However, with practice in writing each letter over and over and repeating the sounds aloud, each child learns his ABC's. This accomplished, the young students are next asked to pull out certain letters from the alphabet, mix them up, and put them in a special arrangement to form words. When they have learned how to form words, they begin working on making sentences, then paragraphs, and eventually, by the end of the first year, each one is able to write a story. With practice and repetition, undertakings of increasing complexity have been completed, and what at first seemed an impossible task has now become routine. Every person who learns to read and write takes a giant-sized problem and, through daily practice and persistence, works away at it until he masters it. In school, every grade presents us with new problems. As we learn how to solve those problems, we progress on to a higher grade with ever more difficult problems.

Life is a process similar to the one we experience in school. As we go through life and attempt to improve ourselves, to become better people, to expand our awareness of who we are and what life is all about, we encounter new problems. Every time we try something new, attempt to discover a new insight or to implement change, there is always a challenge to face.

Learning how to improve ourselves and discovering better ways to live, is not much different from the studies we undertook in school. Whenever we're confronted with a new problem, it's like learning a new alphabet. There are new factors, new considerations and certain adjustments that we must incorporate into our lives. If we don't become overwhelmed by the magnitude of the problem but proceed steadily and with confidence, we can complete almost any undertaking that comes our way.

Life seldom presents us with challenges we can't meet, with obstacles we can't overcome or with problems that can't be solved. We simply have to approach each problem with a positive attitude and know that it's only a matter of persistence and time before we arrive at a solution, just as, in the first grade, "small attempts repeated" finally overcame the problem of learning how to read and write.

WEEK TEN : LAW A

No one knows what he can do until he tries.

Robert the First, King of Scotland, struggled to protect his kingdom against the invasions of the English. There came a time when he was driven from his castle and was forced to flee to keep from being taken prisoner. He took refuge in a cave where he suffered from great depression and uncertainty about what course to follow. He felt that everything was lost.

As King Robert sat in the cave contemplating his next move, he spotted a tiny spider spinning its web. Time and time again, the spider would remain still for a few moments before it put forth another effort. Finally after repeated failures, the spider succeeded and the web was completed.

King Robert observed three outstanding characteristics of the spider: its tremendous patience, its tremendous tolerance and its tremendous perseverance. No matter what, the spider never gave up.

King Robert cleared his mind of all anxious thoughts. He became still and quietly waited for all the conflict and confusion within him to go away. He began to concentrate more objectively and logically on the current state of affairs that had plagued him for so long. Lastly, he became determined never to quit trying to regain his kingdom. He would persevere and continue moving toward his dream. Eventually, King Robert consolidated his position and forced the English to recognize Scottish independence in 1328.

Each of us possesses the same three characteristics that King Robert observed in the spider. When faced with a difficult or challenging situation, we can utilize our strength to become calm, wait patiently for confusing and conflicting thoughts to pass and persist with another well-planned attempt.

If at times you feel the world is conspiring against you, try to be tolerant of your conditions. If there is an obstacle preventing you from realizing a dream or desire, accept the obstacle as it is. Remember that instead of trying to change the obstacle, it is much easier to go around, go over or go under whatever stands between you and the realization of your goal. Lastly, use your inner strength to persevere. Let no ordinary setbacks stop you from continuing on toward the successful accomplishment of your dreams. You have within you a strength that is equally matched to your potential and your creative imagination.

When you feel defeated and your dreams seem in danger of never being fulfilled, think of the predicament of King Robert and the observations he made that allowed him to recapture his kingdom. And always keep in mind that "no one knows what he can do until he tries."

'Tis the part of the wise man to keep himself today for tomorrow, and not venture all his eggs in one basket.

Miguel de Cervantes

Helen Keller once said, "I do not simply want to spend my life, I wish to invest it." For many people throughout the ages, human life was simply spent in doing what was necessary for survival. The hand-to-mouth existence of our prehistoric ancestors precluded their deep consideration of the future; to live through a single day may often have been an accomplishment.

As human civilization mastered survival, life became more refined and the pursuit of a life to be spent in comfort, ease, and physical pleasure preoccupied many people. In the developed state of our world today, most of us have the guarantee of an extended life-span and the assurance of luxuries undreamed of a hundred years ago. If we choose to, we can spend our life doing a moderate amount of work to obtain a maximum amount of comfort. Yet, those persons who are on the leading edge of human evolution realize, as did Helen Keller, that the greatest happiness in life comes, not from the comforts and pleasures that money can buy, but from the investment of the days of our lives in a purpose which transcends our purely personal interests.

Each of us has a purpose for living beyond our own survival and pleasure. Every individual is like a strand in a web, with a vital contribution to make, not only to the sustenance of life as we know it, but in the creation and development of more beneficial expressions of life. Investing, rather than spending, our lives involve the commitment of our resources—ideas, love, talents, time, energy, money—to those activities which support this larger purpose. The return on a wisely made investment is happiness and satisfaction.

Investment of resources can be exciting. When you watch a worthwhile organization or project in which you have invested yourself succeed, you can share in the success, knowing that in some way it might not have happened without you. When you see your investment joining with others to make a positive difference in the world, you can feel the power like-minded individuals have to effect change in the world. The return on a successful investment is a tremendous motivation to invest again and again.

While you may be delighted with the success of an initial investment, the advice of the experienced investor is that you not concentrate in only one area, but share your resources with many deserving organizations or people. The wise investor follows a simple rule based on the law of life, "Don't put all your eggs in one basket." For, as Mark Twain said, if you put all your eggs in one basket, you'll have to watch that basket!

Dependency in an investment or any kind of human relationship breeds a watchful concern based on a fear of the loss of that in which we may have invested a great deal. If you have only one friend to whom you devote all of your energies and affections, don't you come to expect a lot from that one? And what if your friend, for some reason unrelated to you, cannot give you what you expect when you need it? If you are like most people, because of your disappointment, there will be a resentment that grows between you. Ultimately, your investment will not return any good to you. If, however, you invest yourself in several friendships, when one friend cannot fulfill an expectation, there will be others who continue to support and nourish you. Because you do not depend on any one, you are free to enjoy them all, and reap the reward of all your relationships.

Writes the author of *Ecclestiastes:* "Cast your bread upon the waters, for you will find it after many days. In the morning sow your seed, and at evening withhold not your hand; for you do not know which will prosper, this or that, or whether both alike will be good" (*Eccl. 11:1*). Investment in those endeavors which fulfill a higher purpose is vital to achieving happiness in life. You have much to give, so give it to many.

WEEK TEN : LAW C

Thoughts are things.
Charles Fillmore

Thoughts are things. Thoughts make things. Thoughts shape things. Thoughts are real. The invisible process going on inside our heads that we call thinking can produce objects as real as the ground we walk on or the food we eat.

Consider that nearly everything we use or come in contact with each day was originally a thought, an idea, in someone's mind. For instance, the paper this is printed on, the machine that made the paper, the saw that cut down the tree from which the paper was made, all were originally thoughts, ideas, theories, dreams. Similarly, the car we drive and its motor, tires, seats and steering wheel as well as its thousands of other parts came into being as thoughts in someone's mind.

All of the material things we take for granted in life and that make living easier or more pleasant—pencils, ballpoint pens, chewing gum, magazines, textbooks, candy, ice cream, telephones, television, radios and VCR's, houses and apartment buildings, schools, churches, and so much more—started as thoughts, as ideas.

An outstanding intelligent girl began thinking in the sixth grade about becoming a registered nurse. Her mind was filled with dreams of entering nursing school. She saw herself helping others, assisting at deliveries, caring for sick people, training people in rehabilitation programs. She studied hard so that her grades would be high enough for her to be accepted into nursing school. Today, because of her thoughts years ago, she is a registered nurse associated with a top hospital.

There are two reasons why we fail to realize how important our thoughts are: First, because thoughts are invisible, we aren't aware of their tangible existence. Second, the material manifestations of thoughts may come hours, days, months, or even years after their inception as ideas.

But it would be a mistake to underestimate the power of the mind. Our thoughts make us the kind of people we become. Our thoughts are as important as our behavior; in fact our thoughts are a *form* of behavior. If we think negative thoughts, we become negative, reactive and uncreative. But if we think positive thoughts, and try to see the good in every situation, our attitude reflects those positive thoughts, and we become noted for having a sunny and pleasant disposition.

Never forget that thoughts shape not only the material objects we use every day, they also shape our minds, our faces, our dreams, our daily activities, our very being.

Thoughts are indeed things. They make us the people we are.

WEEK TEN : LAW D

As within, so without.

A cartoon shows Sally Bananas sitting behind a desk covered with untidy stacks of paper. She is saying, "I'm gonna get organized just as soon as I find my calendar!" We all have days like that. We can't work because neither our desks nor our minds are ready to work. Often there is something else claiming our attention.

There is a saying, "As within, so without." It means that what appears in our outer world—friends, jobs, school, career—reflects what is going on inside ourselves. If our minds are cluttered and unfocused, our immediate surroundings will tend to be cluttered. If our surroundings are neat, everything in its place, chances are *we* are focused and energized—as long as we don't overdo it to the point of obsession.

Neither attitude is wrong unless we stay in that mode all the time. For example, a screwdriver is great for fastening the plate on a light switch and it can also be used to pry the lid off a paint can. An emery board smooths torn fingernails and it can also smooth rough wood on a chair or sharpen a wooden pencil in an emergency. There is the original purpose and the one determined by circumstances.

If a person with a cluttered mind needed to remove the lid from the paint can, the thought that the screwdriver would do the job might not get through the clutter. The person with the "perfect" mind might never think to sharpen a dull pencil with an emery board because "that's not what they're for."

The most effective mind is one that keeps a good balance between two tidy and too messy. Take a look at your working space. Is it so perfect it resembles a furniture advertisement? Or does it look as if E.T. might come crawling out? Now, think of how well you get things done. Do you have to hunt for supplies before you can finish your work? Do you become frustrated and angry if someone has moved the things in your room out of place?

You can be so much more effective when the energy you've spent in the past on hunting for a lost item, or being angry when someone carelessly moves an item, is put into finishing your work. Think of the extra time you can spend on more pleasant and rewarding projects. The secret is living consciously and with a sense of balance between too lax and too rigid behaviors.

All of us live with habits and routines until something happens to make us want to change. Examine your working space and determine if there's anything you would arrange differently. Sometimes the right change can set your life on the course you want it to take.

WEEK TEN : LAW E

A stitch in time saves nine.

We all know the wisdom of sewing a button back on when it first falls off. If we put it in our pocket we may lose it and will have to buy another. And, of course, the exact button may not be available, which means that all the buttons will have to be replaced with new ones.

A young woman named Melissa once failed to take that crucial "stitch in time that saves nine." On the way to her parents' home for a family gathering at Thanksgiving, she stopped at a self-service station to fill the car with gas. But she was in such a hurry that even though she remembered it was time to check the oil and water, she refused to take the time. She had promised herself to check the oil and water at least every three or four times she filled up; she had even written herself a note that she kept attached to her gasoline credit card. But it seemed that remembering was only part of the problem; she also needed to take the time and energy to actually act on her own commonsense advice.

She started off on her journey full of the excitement of a joyful holiday with her loved ones. About halfway to her destination, as she began to climb a steep grade, the car began to heat up. She still felt rushed and decided that surely the car would be all right once she reached the top of the hill. Being in a hurry, she pressed the accelerator to the floor. The temperature gauge continued to climb. Finally, the car stalled. Now she was stranded on the freeway on Thanksgiving morning with a disabled car.

The car had to be towed to a garage, where the mechanic was off for the weekend. No work could be done until the following Monday. And it turned out that the valves had to be reground; they had begun to disintegrate because of the heat that built up in the engine when it ran dry.

This may be a dramatic story about a stitch in time saving nine; yet how often do smaller-scale versions of it happen to each of us? And they happen not only in the handling of external circumstances such as Melissa and her car but also in our inner lives. What about the times we feel tired or hurt or confused or angry and neglect to mend those "stitches" in a timely fashion? The time we feel the "stitch" is the time to respond to it. As we learn to deal with the problem of the moment *at the moment it arises,* we will avoid many unnecessary—sometimes even major—disasters.

We live in a "self-service" world in which we need to check our own oil and water levels if we want to protect our engines. We can tend to ourselves, our friends and our loved ones with the same degree of care. By tending to ourselves when one stitch will do the job, we will learn to save those other eight stitches.

Perseverance makes the difference between success and defeat.

A despondent man who had lost his job and had completed more than a dozen interviews without finding new employment was given the advice to continue looking forward to his next rejection. In amazement, he questioned such advice. Why should he try again? In reply he was told that with every rejection he was moving a step closer to the perfect job that was waiting for him. He continued to persevere.

Imagine a goal you strongly desire resting at the summit of a steep and slippery mountain. Next, imagine a heavy stone placed on your back just before you begin to climb. How do you feel the higher you climb? Excited? Tired? Frustrated?

If you fail to reach your goal the first time or even the second, what keeps you going? The answer may include many qualities, but at least one of them is perseverance. To persevere is defined as the ability to persist in or remain constant to a purpose, idea or task in the face of obstacles or discouragement. Removing obstacles in the path leading to your goals can be difficult and frustrating, leaving you with the desire to abandon the goal and to abandon the energy and belief required to achieve it. Perseverance is the voice within, constantly urging you that "if at first you don't succeed, try, try, again."

Reaching a goal may require repeated attempts, each one bringing you closer to achieving the objective while in the process of reaching other goals as well. Among these may be personal redirection or the achievement of a greater good not initially planned.

George Washington Carver, born about 1864, had a dream of enriching the depleted soil of the southern United States. He persevered in getting an education when to do so was extremely difficult, especially for a black man. Rather than give up, he continued with his efforts, and in 1896 earned an M.S. degree from Iowa State University. Afterwards, he persuaded southern farmers to plant soil-enriching peanuts and sweet potatoes in place of cotton. After achieving his initial success, he went on to discover more than 300 uses for the peanut, thus encouraging a steady market for the crop.

At the age of twelve, Thomas Alva Edison became a railroad newsboy, and at age fifteen earned his living as a telegraph operator. He studied and performed experiments in his spare time. Although he fathered many useful inventions, it cost him more than $40,000 in unsuccessful experiments to produce the first incandescent lamp in 1879. In fifty years he filed for 1,033 patents. He continued to try, and try again.

With the kind of effort exemplified by George Washington Carver and Thomas Edison, we not only come closer to our goals but, in the process, we also learn about ourselves. Through perseverance we discover virtues we may not be aware of in ourselves. At the same time, we may discover areas in our personalities that need further development before our goal can be reached. We gain satisfaction as we master tasks that lead to success. In the process of persevering we increase our inner strength. We develop our spiritual muscles when we continue working faithfully toward the desired end that we label success.

Only in the dictionary does "success" come before "work." Though failure seemed to be his constant companion, Abraham Lincoln never stopped reaching for his dreams. Many of his detractors found little in his background to suggest that as president he could bring the Civil War to a successful conclusion. Here was a man who had faced a series of failures:

> Death of his mother and sister when he was a child.
> Death of his sweetheart.
> Suffered a nervous breakdown.
> Death of three of his young sons.
> Defeat as a candidate for state legislature, 1832.
> Failed business partnership in a general store.
> Large debt to be paid off after a partner died.
> Defeat as a candidate for Congress, 1843.
> Defeat as a candidate for Congress, 1844.
> Lost nomination as commissioner of the general land office.
> Defeat as a candidate for the Senate, 1855.
> Defeat as a vice presidential candidate, 1856.
> Defeat by Stephen Douglas for Senate seat, 1858.

When asked how he had overcome so many personal defeats and failures in his life, Lincoln attributed his success to his undying faith. He said, "Without the Divine Being, I cannot succeed. With that assistance, I cannot fail." Lincoln found solace and comfort from his belief in God and from reading the Bible.

Thomas Edison was not a religious man but believed in a "supreme intelligence." Faith in oneself may be stretched to the limit when others tell you you'll fail. Lincoln had very little schooling and was described as a "wandering laboring boy" who grew up literally without education; Edison had only three months of formal education. One of Edison's teachers called him "addled," so his mother pulled him out of school and taught him at home. Later he said that formal school bored him.

Dedication is another attribute of success. Edison said, "Genius is one percent inspiration and ninety-nine percent perspiration." He was never discouraged when he didn't get results even after countless experiments. When a friend consoled Edison after his repeated failures to make a storage battery work, he said: "I have not failed. I've just found 10,000 ways that don't work."

In his later years, when asked how his developing deafness was affecting him, he said, "I find it easier to concentrate now."

When we pursue a goal, we sometimes encounter setbacks. There are many men and women throughout history who achieved incredible success only after trying, then trying again and again. And we can do the same.

WEEK ELEVEN : LAW B

The secret of a productive life can be sought and found.

We hear so often nowadays of the increase in teen suicide and read about the rise in suicide rates among the elderly population. While mental health professionals attempt to deal with this alarming situation, we may gain fruitful insight into a solution from the Plains Indians who lived on the North American continent hundreds of years ago.

The Plains Indians believed that each person had an important part to play in the life of their tribe. At an early age they would go through an activity known to us now as "vision-seeking." They believed that, through proper preparation, individuals could receive a special vision of their life purpose. The Plains Indians fasted and prayed and meditated and spent long hours in solitude. They practiced the ceremony of the sweat lodge. They performed these rituals to discover their true connection to life.

In our contemporary world, we go off to school at a very early age and become educated to varying degrees. This process of education seems to operate on the theory that information must be added to us and that, when enough facts are added, we are then ready to be of service and productive in our world.

By following the philosophy of the Plains Indians, we would learn to view the child as a person who has come to us with a special gift to give instead of as a product of the educational system. Rather than trying to make this person into "something-out-of-nothing" through a hit-or-miss method, we would use the educational process to bring out the special gift that each child already possessed. We would help to discover and then to develop that special gift.

When we look at life and people in this way, we realize that everyone, no matter what their age or condition, has something to give. There have been many examples of famous people who have discovered their gifts late in life. Mahatma Gandhi was in his fifties when he realized that non-violent resistance was his special gift to the world. Cervantes was in his sixties when he began to write.

Are you struggling with a sense of unfulfillment? Do you have a feeling that you're here on earth for reasons that presently elude you? Perhaps, as you begin to practice your belief that you do have a significant part to play and begin actively to try to discover what it is, you may find your sense of joy. Perhaps the suicide rates will begin to lower as we encourage one another to discover our own special gifts and to give the greatest gift that any of us can give—the gift of who we truly are.

WEEK ELEVEN : LAW C

Enthusiasm breeds achievement.

Enthusiasm—that state of exuberance in which all things seem possible. *Webster's Dictionary* defines it as "fervor" and "ardent zeal or interest." Its root word is the Greek "entheos/enthous" meaning possessed by a god or other superhuman power.

Quite a definition to live up to, isn't it? But all of us know that feeling. It's as though we were drunk on the wine of life, high with the power of a feeling within that is bursting to be shared with others.

It's how you feel when you're in love. It's how you feel when you have found something so profound in your heart that you want to share it with others. It's how some people feel about their work, or a magnificent piece of art, a book or a poem that has moved them, or a religious experience.

Enthusiasm is like the fuel in the tank of a car. It's the moving kinetic energy which inspires us to pursue something we love and demands to be shared—if only with the object of our own passion.

And behind the enthusiasm is usually a belief, a belief in something greater than ourselves, something that has uplifted and connected us to the Divine within. How does that come about? What is the spark that could lead us to have enthusiasm in every part of our life?

"Expansion in love is an action available to every human being all the time," writes Thaddeus Golas in *The Lazy Man's Guide to Enlightenment*. "Anything can be experienced with a completely expanded awareness." And isn't that what happens when we feel enthused about something or someone? We open to the world, and anything seems possible.

Just how does this apply to greatness, you might ask? "Greatness after all, in spite of its name, appears to be not so much a certain size as a certain quality in human lives," wrote Phillips Brooks, the author of "O Little Town of Bethlehem." Greatness is indeed a quality of being. It encompasses love, vision, belief, hope and a generosity of spirit. Greatness is a way of being which then allows a certain set of actions to come forth.

"Some are born great," Shakespeare wrote, "some achieve greatness, and some have greatness thrust upon them." Yet greatness almost always involves a vision of possibilities greater than those that currently exist in the lives of those around them. Greatness goes about its work with quiet authority. Greatness may speak softly. Or greatness may lie in the courage and fortitude of a child undergoing major illness or personal tragedy.

Greatness belongs to many unsung heroes. Greatness is a way of being that knows its own strength and leads others into discovering theirs. Many mothers without fame or name have learned the lessons of a selfless greatness, and gone down into the dust of time without the world singing their praises. Many prisoners have given years of their lives in prison cells, sustained only by their desire to set freedom loose in a world of political oppression. These are the great ones, who fear as the rest of us fear, yet act in the face of that fear.

Greatness rarely boasts of itself, for it is fueled with a light that knows enthusiasm like a brother. The road of the great man or woman is often littered with obstacles. Certainly their road is no easier than that of the common man. In fact, often it is harder. Adversity and discomfort are the fires that the master blacksmith uses to temper the metal he would use. And when one's choices seem harder than the average person's, we must remember it is because they are aligned with values that the world has usually forgotten.

"Good sense travels on the well-worn paths; genius, never," Cesare Lombroso wrote in *The Man of Genius* in the early 1900s. "That is why the crowd, not altogether without reason, is so ready to treat great men as lunatics."

How often have any of us stood at a crossroads and asked ourselves why we should choose the harder path, when we knew our friends would tell us to take the easy one? How often have each of us known the speaking of the inner voice that demanded we not "cop out" or "drop out" when that was the simple choice, the one that most people would take.

That voice, which is always aligned with integrity and honor, and ultimately the higher principles, is the one that great men and women follow. "It is a rough road that leads to the heights of greatness," Lucius Seneca, a 1st Century philosopher said. And often he has been right.

So what sustains us in these difficult times of decisions? Perhaps it is the belief in the vision—the fuel of enthusiasm which reminds us of who we really are, and that the dreams we believe in matter. "Nothing great was ever achieved without enthusiasm," wrote Emerson. And, for the great man or woman, the enthusiasm and vision are often all that sustain him in his or her time of greatest darkness.

That Roman philosopher Seneca perhaps said it best, "Live among men as if God beheld you; speak to God as if men were listening." Then all you do or say will be with honor and the dream that inspired you will never die.

When Charles Fillmore was more than ninety years old he wrote, "I fairly sizzle with enthusiasm as I spring forth each day to do the things which ought to be done by me."

WEEK ELEVEN : LAW D

The way to mend the bad world is to create the right world.
Ralph Waldo Emerson

"Let there be peace on earth and let it begin with me" are the opening words to a famous song. But what do the words mean? How can being peace-filled inside oneself lead to peace on earth? We are, as a race, coming to understand that we are all "one" in spirit. Each one of us is like a pixel; just as a hologram is make up of numerous pixels, each one containing all the information that can be found in the total image, so each person may be a tiny particle of all life, containing all the data that is present in the sum total of existence. Then peace and harmony may not exist in our world until most of us commit to it internally.

The way to create a better world is for each of us to be better people. There are certain laws of life which, when followed, can make life sweeter, more harmonious, prosperous, healthy and free. When we choose to abide by these laws, we reap the benefits of living in harmony with the universe; when we don't, we risk experiencing sickness, war, economic insecurity and unemployment. The 70s and the 80s were called the "me" and "have" generations. This will change only when each person makes a conscious decision to act and think for the good of all.

Personal motive is always our best guide. Ask yourself "Why am I doing this?" and that inherent wisdom should provide the true answer. If your motives are pure, good will come of them. This could be termed being "on beam" with life. Pilots often fly using a radio beam as a guide. As long as they remain "on beam," they are safe. If they get off beam, they're in danger.

Man, too, has an inborn "beam"—a conscience. While we are in tune with the way things were designed to be, we are "safe." When we are out of tune, we show it in the form of greed, fear, sickness, addiction and jealousy. Many of us experience a lifetime of having flu each winter, allergies in the fall, headaches, indigestion and all the so-called minor ailments that we accept as a part of life. Maybe it need not always be so. Each of us has within us the power to encourage health, happiness and serenity; we are capable of reeducating our bodies and our thinking.

By thinking and acting always with good in our hearts; by becoming responsible for ourselves and, as an old Irish saying has it, "If you see a job that needs doing, that means it's yours to do," we can begin to change our wrong world into a right world. It's time to stop saying that "they" need to be changing things around here. There is no "they"—there is only "I." When we start saying *I* need to be giving life a helping hand, we then start to benefit all of life.

It has been well said that a journey of a thousand miles begins with the first step. Let's make it count. Let's each one of us take that step.

WEEK ELEVEN : LAW E

It is better to praise than to criticize.

"I feel like saying 'thank you, thank you, thank you,' I feel like saying 'thank you' to this world of mine!" This is a line from the kind of song you might enjoy singing from time to time. It would be the perfect song to sing when you really mean it, when things are going great and you feel on top of the world. But sometimes it's the right song to sing when you *don't* feel the words, when things are not going so well and you can't see daylight for the darkness. Either way, the song won't fail to leave you feeling better about yourself and about life.

The reason is that praise is a powerful tool. We may be involved in a situation that is very challenging to us and feel we're just not up to the task. But what happens when we begin to praise our own abilities? What happens when we begin sincerely to give thanks for our wonderful minds and our strong and healthy bodies? It's not at all difficult to believe that our own senses of confidence and self-worth are actually activated and strengthened by this kind of praise.

Through the ages, the wise and thoughtful among us have said that there is good in everything and everyone if we just take the time to look for it. We have all experienced how wonderful it feels to receive praise and gratitude from others. Children who are praised and encouraged achieve better results in school and play than those whose accomplishments are ignored. Although some people might argue whether there really *is* good in everything and everyone, few would doubt that looking for the good leads to greater happiness and well-being. To look for the bad just to prove a point seems a waste of time if we're sincerely interested in our happiness and the happiness of others.

As wonderful as it is to praise and give thanks for others, it may be even more important to praise and give thanks for our own talents and abilities. There is not often much praise to be had from others in this world. How wonderful to look for and find the good in ourselves! As we are blessed and uplifted we cannot help being a good example for the world.

We should try to cultivate the art of praise. We should work at seeing the good in ourselves and in others. Let's encounter every situation with the wonderful truth that there is something good awaiting us. As we learn to praise ourselves and our world, we will begin to blossom in ways that are wonderful to behold. The attitude of gratitude!

Let's practice right now: "I feel like saying 'Thank you. thank you, thank you. . . .'"

Laughter is the best medicine.

When the United States entered World War II in 1941, patriotism was at a high point and young men by the thousands rushed to their recruiting places, eager to serve their country. Movie stars of Hollywood were no exception, although some who applied were not accepted, comedian Bob Hope among them. The country's leaders felt he could serve a better purpose with the U.S.O., entertaining the troops. He protested vigorously that he didn't want preferential treatment, but the government stood firm. They could not possibly have known at the time what a wise decision that was.

Hope and his troupe logged millions of miles and performed thousands of times for troops in Europe and the Far East. They risked their lives many times by performing in combat zones. They visited the hospitals where the wounded were treated. Always the positive entertainer, Hope didn't dole out sympathy or pity. He would ask a wounded serviceman questions such as, "Did you see our show, or were you already sick?" The therapeutic value of laughter was never questioned by those who received his visits.

When a person laughs, many good things happen. Muscles relax, the breathing is deeper, the bloodstream is more fully oxygenated. Pain and gloom are forgotten or at least put in proper perspective. It's difficult for a person who is shaking with laughter to think negative thoughts. For children confined to a hospital, a visit from a clown is therapy. The good effects of such a visit can last for days.

Those who bring laughter also seem to be beneficiaries. Minnie Pearl, Red Skelton, George Burns and Bob Hope are all well past eighty with George Burns pushing one hundred and going strong.

Although we can't all be professional comedians or clowns, we can share our laughter and good humor with everyone we meet. We can visit hospitals, convalescent centers and homes for the aged. The people who live in the homes are often terribly lonely. They feel forgotten by the ones they love, and visitors are always welcome, especially those who bring moments of healing laughter.

For those who feel unsure of themselves as natural wits or stand-up comedians, there are books and video and audio tapes that can be shared. The sharing is the important part. It can brighten a lonely person's life, it can improve your relations with those close to you. The reward for bringing laughter is extremely high. It consists of love, cheer and the gratitude of those you help and entertain.

Progress depends on diligence and perseverance.

One of the most precious resources we have is our time. According to *The Wall Street Journal's* book, *On Management: The Best of The Manager's Journal,* the single most important aspect of being a role model and leader is how we handle our own personal time. The book described the importance of information-gathering and its influence on decision-making, and states that we must consider seriously the impact of our own work habits on those around us.

In order to manage time effectively, we must be able to prioritize our activities on a daily basis. One of the keys to time management is the quality of endurance. In most athletic competition, it's not always the most talented player who wins but the one who's the best finisher. As expressed in the book of *Ecclesiastes,* chapter 9, "The race is not to the swift, nor the battle to the strong," and as the actress Helen Hayes once said, "Nothing is any good without endurance."

The ability to endure is probably the most important ingredient in realizing personal success, in business as well as in other areas of our lives. All too often, we resolve to exercise regularly, lose weight, spend more time with our family, eat more nutritiously. But all too often that commitment is forgotten, because over the long haul we fail to demonstrate the endurance needed to reach our goal.

There are so many avenues of opportunity where we can develop our own unique talents and abilities. Whether it's a career in the arts, sports, business, or the professions, the only way to perfect our skills is through diligent practice and study on a consistent basis. This means making the commitment to develop our self-discipline and to persist and endure until the goal is met. This commitment to "finish the race" is never easy for anyone. There are times when we're tempted to spend valuable time pursuing those interests that give pleasure while neglecting our long-range priorities.

In order to realize the wonderful feeling of accomplishment that comes with meeting our goals, the ability to endure hardship is essential. "No one ever said it would be easy" is no less true for being a familiar saying. If we truly want to be all that we're capable of being, we must be committed and we must prepare ourselves to endure—to be a strong finisher in the race of life.

WEEK TWELVE : LAW C

Humility like darkness reveals the heavenly light.
Henry David Thoreau

If you walk outside on a clear dark night and look into the sky you can see thousands of stars. Did you ever consider that if it were not for the darkness of space the starlight would never be revealed to us on earth?

We tend to think of anything dark or black as bad, not as valuable as white or light. Or we perceive black as nothing at all for it has no color, it's the absence of light—it could be called an illusion or invisible. But every time you go to a movie, you know how important it is for the room to be very dark, for that's when the picture can be seen most clearly.

Perhaps the heavenly light within each one of us, our divine purpose of potential, also has a dark background against which it becomes illumined, not a destructive or negative darkness but a necessary foundation of strength. And perhaps this darkness is humility: our ability to admit we can never know everything or be all things to all people.

Humility is not self-deprecation. To believe you have no worth, or were created somehow flawed or incompetent, is foolish. Humility, rather, is wisdom. It is knowing you were created with special talents and abilities to share with the world, but that you are one of many, each with an important part to play in life. Humility is knowing you are smart, but not *all*-knowing. It is accepting that you have personal power but are not omnipotent.

Just as a tree needs a strong root system to grow tall, or a skyscraper needs a deep foundation to hold strong against stress, we need the strength of humility to reach our greatest heights. It is what we possess inside, that which will serve as our foundation and will help us challenge life and take risks. We have unlimited potential to create, but it must be rooted in the knowledge and understanding of the limits of our personal power.

A humble attitude is a flexible one. Just as the tree and the building must sway with the wind, our agility in dealing with whatever life throws our way will be our strength. Inherent in humility is an open and receptive mind. We not only don't know all the answers but sometimes not even the right questions have been revealed to us. Humility is a strength that serves us well; it leaves us more open to learn from others and to refuse to see issues and people only in blacks and whites.

The opposite of humility would be arrogance—the belief that we are wiser or better than others. Arrogance tends to promote separateness rather than community. It looms like a brick wall between us and those from whom we could learn. An example would be Virginia Smith, a young woman who was about to graduate from college with honors. She had a very high opinion of herself and visions of greatness. As she came down from the podium in her cap and gown, she was carrying not only her diploma but an air of intellectual smugness. Out of the crowd stepped an old woman. We can call her Wisdom of the World. She spoke to the young woman in a casual way, "Well, who have we here?"

"You evidently don't know me," said the young woman in an annoyed tone. "I am Virginia Cordelia Smith, A.B."

"Well, my young friend," said Wisdom of the World with a chuckle, "come with me and I will teach you the rest of your alphabet."

This graduate undoubtedly had a bright light to shine on the world. She had great potential for doing good, but she had yet to understand how much of life would be a mystery to her. If she could only gain humility, her "heavenly light" would surely shine.

WEEK TWELVE : LAW D

Love conquers all things.
Virgil

Many fables and fairy tales depict the same vicious dragon, spewing his fiery breath and destroying white knights, fair maidens, and complete villages. He always seems to be in a rage.

As much as we might hate to admit it, we all have our inner dragons. None of us escapes occasional feelings of anger, sadness and grief. The big question is, what do we do with these beasts when they attack us?

In the world of fable and fairy tale, the knight in shining armor was always trying to steal the dragon's head, or an army would pierce the beast to death with their tiny arrows. But it seems that no one ever tried to tame the dragon with understanding and compassion.

Can you think of times you have felt angry and either lashed out at someone or tried to "kill" your angry feelings? Have there been times in your life when you could feel understanding and compassion for yourself when you were angry and upset?

Being compassionate might mean taking your anger out on a pillow instead of your best friend, or going out for a run instead of letting your feelings smoulder and fester inside. Being understanding means knowing you have a right to *all* of your feelings—even the negative ones—and that you're not a bad person for feeling the way you do.

Another way to tame with compassion is to talk about your feelings with a trusted counselor or friend. Sometimes it's enough just to have someone hear you. You might even want to tell the listener that you don't need anything from him or her but a listening ear.

Sometimes your angry feelings are delivering a message you should pay attention to: "I don't want to do this anymore" or "I don't like the way this feels" or "I've got to understand my anger and be kind to myself, and then the bad feelings will go away."

So the next time you feel a dragon breathing down your neck: (1) See what he's trying to say to you; (2) give him a pat on the head; and (3) take him where he can't hurt you or anyone else and let him blow off his steam. Once he learns he can trust you to love him, you'll never need to fear him again.

WEEK TWELVE : LAW E

If you do not know what you want to achieve with your life, you may not achieve much.

Those who don't set any goals in their lives drift aimlessly through the average three score and ten years, often complaining that "life's not fair." They often say, to paraphrase the Rolling Stones, "I can't always get what I want." But, on the contrary, in keeping with an important law of life, they are getting exactly what they are prepared to give. Many of us are quite clear about what we *don't* want in our lives but how many of us are prepared to do the inner work that will lead us to what we *do* want? Once we know what we want, we're in a position to set goals and work toward achieving them.

If we were asked to give someone directions on how to get from A to B, we would not say: "Well, first you don't go down this road 200 yards and then you don't turn left by the gas station at the corner and as you go over the hill, you'll see a supermarket. Well, don't make a right there nor do you turn left at the second stop light. . . ." Instead, we would tell them in which direction to drive and the correct turns to make. Our lives are run on the same principle, yet the majority of us insist on working from the premise of what we don't want rather than what we do. You may have experienced that yourself with your friends when discussing which movie to go and see. "Well, I don't want to see *Benjie Goes to the Seaside,* and I've seen *Rambo 9* so I don't want to see that again." It's only when you start talking about what you *do* want to see that you end up in the theater with a tub of popcorn in your hands.

By setting goals, we give ourselves the opportunity to develop our full potential. We have a vision in our minds of an ideal, and the more we dwell on it and work toward it, the closer it comes to reality. Some people find it helpful to put their goals and dreams in writing so they have them in black and white as a reminder. Some people make a "treasure map," cutting out pictures from magazines and making a collage of the things they would like to see successfully fulfilled. And this goes beyond the material to such areas of life as emotions, family and relationships.

Most of us know the story of the little red engine, climbing the hill, who kept saying to himself "I think I can, I think I can." As a result of this, he accomplished the seemingly impossible climb. He had a goal and a vision of himself doing it, and he achieved what he pictured in his mind.

Napoleon Hill said, "Whatever the mind of man can conceive and believe, it can achieve."

WEEK THIRTEEN : LAW A

The greatest gift you can give another is the purity of your attention.
Richard Moss

There are times when we reach out to friends in their times of need. We want to help them move through their crises quickly and successfully. Sometimes, though, our help is ineffective because we give what is not really needed and fail to give the gift that would make a real difference.

There are times when our first reaction is to swamp our poor friend with our own life experiences and a barrage of advice that may not relate to his problem. We remember when we had trouble with our boss; we recall that difficult period when we felt rejected by our spouse. We're ready to tell our friend exactly what we did in those situations. And even though our advice may be quite good, the person may not be ready to receive it or it may not apply to his case. He may be faced with a complex problem and may need time simply to adjust to what is happening. Until he's had time to get his emotional bearings, our advice may prove useless. It might actually confuse our poor friend rather than help him.

Let's say he has lost his job and has been moping around for a month. It's clear to us that he needs to get out and start living again. We are quick to point out solutions, but how can we be certain that our advice even applies to him? We can only have an approximate idea of what's going on in his mind and heart. No two personal crises are the same and each individual's way of dealing with them is different. Our advice about our friend's job loss could be completely in error. Not because he won't listen to it, but because we are not him: We cannot fully grasp the situation from his point of view and know what is the best solution for him.

And yet, he's a friend and we want to help him through a difficult time. When we see him suffer, how can we sit by and do absolutely nothing? He may be a person, however, who needs solitude to work things out. The most important thing we can do is continuously remind him that we're there for him; we can let him know that even if he wants to be alone, we're still there if he needs us. We can let him know that we're not trying to hit him over the head with advice, but that we're there to listen to whatever he has to say. We want to be his supporter, not his dictator.

Sometimes, the best we can do for our friends is to listen to them and support them in their own decisions. Remember that "the greatest gift you can give another is the purity of your attention."

WEEK THIRTEEN : LAW B

Everyone and everything around you is your teacher.

Ken Keyes

Would you like to find the greatest teacher in the world? The one who could teach you exactly what you most need to learn at this moment? You can, and it's easier than you think. Just look around you. Your teachers are everywhere. Your life is set up to teach you exactly what you need to learn. Whether you recognize it or not you posess an inner wisdom that is capable of showing you who your teachers are and what they have to teach you.

To find those teachers, look at those closest to you—your family, your friends, you co-workers. The people you spend the most time with can tell you much about yourself. How? One way is that, very often, what we see in others is, in some way, a reflection of something within ourselves. What we admire most in another may be a quality we possess but have failed to recognize.

Conversely, what we dislike most in another may also reflect some trait within ourselves that we weren't aware was there. This is especially true when we have very strong feelings, positive or negative, about someone. Other people can be our teachers, not necessarily because of what they themselves know or do, but rather because of the way we react to them. In other words, you can use other people as mirrors to teach you about yourself!

The way people respond to us can add to our self-knowledge as well. This doesn't mean that if we aren't popular we're "bad," or that if a lot of people like us we're necessarily "good." How people respond to us is certainly their choice; yet we can use their reactions to learn something about ourselves. This is especially true when we see several people responding to us in a similar manner.

Another way we can learn from others is to simply look at the characteristics of the people we choose to associate with. Again, this is not a matter of judging anyone good or bad, but rather recognizing that there is something within ourselves that is attracting us to these persons, and them to us.

It's also helpful to look at those activities you spend the greater part of your time pursuing. What do your time priorities tell you about yourself? Also examine yourself in other areas: How do you spend your leisure time? On what do you spend most of your money? What thoughts do you most often hold in your mind? What feelings do you experience most often?

All of these things—indeed, everything in your life around you and within you—can teach you a great deal. The truth is, you are teaching yourself, and as you use your life and the world around you as your "textbook" and your "classroom," you can become your own greatest teacher.

WEEK THIRTEEN : LAW C

Hitch your wagon to a star.
Ralph Waldo Emerson

A young woman who had recently graduated with honors from a good college aspired to write novels, but her ideas kept ending up as short stories. The thought of such an ambitious project as a novel seemed to overwhelm her. One day she confessed to a friend how discouraged she was, and he told her she needed a bigger vision for her work; he suggested she outline a whole series of novels that would carry forward all the powerful stories and characters she had already created in her imagination. The outline, he said, should be a plan that would cover several years, or perhaps even her lifetime.

Following his advice, the writer built scenarios of the years to come and how the novels would flow one after another. It was a design for an exciting and successful career. When the plan was completed, she could easily see her work in a larger context, and realized where she needed to begin. The first book was very clear in her mind. She started to write, and, by the time the first novel was published, she was well into the second.

It was a wise friend who helped her realize that her problem was not with her writing ability but stemmed from a limited vision of who she was and what she could accomplish. Ralph Waldo Emerson understood the importance of looking at life from the highest possible vantage point when he said, "Hitch your wagon to a star."

The German philosopher, Goethe, explained that "the greatest thing in the world is not so much where we stand as in what direction we are moving." We need to think big and aim high when planning our goals; we need ambition to sustain us—with our thoughts and hopes up in the stars—while struggling along the path toward success. And there *will* be a struggle. Many famous and successful entertainment stars, whose names and faces we now see everywhere, spent years in clerical or restaurant jobs, waiting for an opportunity to express the talent they were convinced they had. People successful in business may have tried many ideas and failed before they hit on the one that worked. Many of the innovations that have changed our lives were once the dreams of inventors who at first came up against seeming dead ends and sometimes the skepticism of family and friends.

But these successful entertainers, business people and inventors had one quality in common: To realize their dreams and ambitions, they managed to see the bigger picture of their lives. They believed in themselves and aimed for the best. They understood, with Emerson, that to set a mighty goal and stick to it is to "hitch your wagon to a star."

WEEK THIRTEEN : LAW D

The price of greatness is responsibility.
Winston Churchill

Winston Churchill's comment that "the price of greatness is responsibility" has been proven to be true again and again by the actions of people who have helped shape the world for the better. Both the climb to greatness as well as the time spent there require taking on large responsibilities and handling them with diligent skill.

If you hope to accomplish great things, you must begin by accepting responsibility for the smaller things facing you today. The student who fails to do homework assignments or to take on extra research in each subject may well lack the ability and the knowledge needed to be successful as an adult. The young person who fails to act caringly and responsibly at home and with friends, will often fail in crucial relationships, professional and personal, later in life because compassion and understanding were too long left to others. A business may fail because the record keeping and other areas of exacting work have been neglected.

The words of Winston Churchill need not refer only to future greatness. They can apply to what you accomplish today. Tom, a senior in high school, was interested in working in a summer program as a crossing guard for an elementary school. He felt that would be a worthwhile activity as well as one that would be a credit to him. But, after a few days, Tom became careless. He would talk to a friend who dropped by to see him and just glance at the traffic. When a small girl was nearly struck by a car, Tom was removed from the program at once. And when the article was published that year about the program, it noted that the record was marred by one student's lack of responsibility. Embarrassed and hurt, Tom learned a very important lesson, one for which he paid a high price in humiliation.

Sarah wanted to be a nurse. She greatly admired a neighbor who was a head night nurse at the local hospital. This nurse had been honored many times for her service, always above and beyond simply doing her job. Sarah aspired to be like her. She decided a good first step would be to sign up as a candy-striper at the hospital. Sarah became even more convinced that nursing was for her because being a candy-striper was such fun. She chatted with her girl friends, enjoyed breaks at the commissary and was often slow in performing her responsibilities. When patients complained about long waits for fresh water because Sarah was watching something interesting on the patient's TV, she was first warned and then dropped from the program. Her record made her acceptance into a school of nursing more difficult and, to a greater extent than her classmates, she had to prove herself capable of handling responsibility.

No matter what our age, we must start being responsible today!

Good words are worth much and cost little.
George Herbert

There always seems to be a grouch in every crowd. He's the one who never has a good word for anyone. He recounts his tales of woe to anyone who will listen, telling about what's currently going wrong in his own life, or about the latest tragedy he saw on TV or overheard on the street. For the grouch, the world is a place of doom and gloom, filled with bad guys ready to pounce on him and rob him of his rightful due. He arms himself with a sharp tongue and a bitter temper in order to keep everyone at a distance, even those who might care about him. He paints himself into a corner of anger and contempt where he stands alone.

The grouch often is unemployed, in debt and emotionally bankrupt. But there's a way he can get rich quickly. And it won't cost him one cent of his money. He has to find the commodity that's in greatest demand and buy lots of stock in it. When most people are plagued with pessimism, words of understanding and hope can be rare as gold bullion. Good words are money in the bank—the more of them you can accumulate and put to work, the richer you will be. Invested liberally in all your conversations, good words of encouragement, compassion and support will earn you interest from the vast treasury of good will that is always at your disposal and tax-free. While no one wants to spend time with a grouch, everyone enjoys being with the person who expresses enthusiasm, care and concern.

Constructive and uplifting words pay big dividends. In times past, when one person looked another directly in the eye, shook hands firmly and gave his word, a matter was settled as securely as if a dozen lawyers had drawn up a fifty-page contract. A person's word was his promise to bring the best of all his capabilities to bear in fulfilling the agreement between the two parties. Sensitive words of love and understanding are like such promises; they help to create new ways of being in the world. Good words bear the promise of a more enriching life for both the giver and receiver.

Perhaps the grouch got to be a grouch because there were few good words spoken to him when he was a child, or because he was hurt deeply by an intimate friend who broke a sacred trust. Acceptance and forgiveness of past events will free him now to open a trust fund account of good words in his own name. This gift to himself and to the world will be compounded daily. It is important to remember that: "Good words are worth much and cost little."

You can never solve a problem on the same level as the problem.

Emmet Fox

The prophets of Old Testament times, esteemed in leadership positions, assumed two major roles in their society: as advisors they had an aptitude for solving the problems that confronted the ancient Hebrews; as seers they had the ability to anticipate the outcomes of various plans the "Chosen People" considered as their culture developed. Today, seers are sometimes called research analysts because they anticipate outcomes. Advisors are known as doctors, lawyers, merchants, business executives and others who also anticipate outcomes and solve problems in their area of expertise.

Emmet Fox, a twentieth-century author and problem-solver, wrote that the only way to solve a problem is to "lift your consciousness above the level where you met the problem." A problem appears as an obstacle that cannot be seen accurately because it dominates our mental landscape. From the meadow the forest may appear ominous and troubling; all the trees seem to block our journey to a desired destination. A lifted consciousness, however, functions like a hot air balloon—when it gets up high enough, the forest is revealed in its entirety, and shown in proper relationship to all its surroundings. Distance and height provide an encompassing perspective that is helpful in showing us how to cope with challenging circumstances.

A successful problem-solver is one who creates a new context in which to view the problem. He does this by directing his attention away from the distracting details of the difficulty. From a detached perspective, he examines the situation in a new or different light and, after exploring information and options, chooses an appropriate course of action.

King Solomon was noted for his wisdom. As an aid in solving the problems that were presented to him, he examined the inner motivation of the participants in order to gain perspective. His decision in the case of two women who claimed the same child has become legend and illustrates how he used his wisdom and imagination to get inside of people's true feelings. Solomon examined the motivation of each woman by suggesting that the infant be divided in half so that each woman could have an equal share of him. The true mother begged him not to do so, preferring that her child should live, even if with the other woman, rather than be destroyed so that she could have her fair share. Solomon easily determined the rightful parent by her concern for the child.

Prophets are perhaps most widely acclaimed for their ability as seers. But prophets are not the only ones endowed with the capacity to anticipate outcomes. Each one of us possesses the ability to discern, that is, to make choices. Each one of us can examine the appearance of a situation, look at motives, and then make an informed decision.

Some judgments or choices must be made based on information from the five senses—touch, taste, smell, sight and hearing. Other judgments yield more beneficial results when made at the level beyond what is readily available as fact. This kind of discernment can sometimes be recognized through a hunch, and whoever follows it is deemed truly wise.

The Old Testament prophets understood higher judgment. They used it; they anticipated outcomes and solved problems. They were the leaders of their day. The ability exists today in you, as it did in the ancient prophets, to rise above the problem, examine motives, look at options and make choices.

WEEK FOURTEEN : LAW B

Happy relationships depend not on finding the right person, but in being the right person.

Eric Butterworth

In the fairy tale, "The Sleeping Beauty," the heroine is saved from her seemingly endless sleep by a kiss from the handsome prince, who whisks her away to his palace where they live happily ever after. This same idea is portrayed in "Snow White" and in countless other stories. Even in the 90s, many films and novels continue to follow a similar plot concept.

The majority of us grow up believing the false information given to us by television, radio, film and the printed word that something or someone can rescue us from our mundane lives and turn us into all that we want to be. Even our parents give us the impression that the right person will make everything just fine. Young women dress up like fairy princesses in white lacy dresses on their wedding day, propagating this myth even further.

Why, then, do so many people seem discontented in their marriages and relationships? Why do people divorce and then often remarry to someone who resembles their previous partner? This is because they remain the same within—and like attracts like. So, they will go on and on attracting the same unsatisfactory relationships for as long as they continue to live with the same old attitudes.

When a person begins to work on changing himself from within, he will start to attract different types of people into his life. The junkie who is still using drugs is going to associate with other other drug users. When he reforms himself and starts to change his attitudes, we notice him associating with a different sort of person. This is because *he* is changing from within.

Most people think of love as some sort of power outside of themselves that will "take them away from all this." Sadly, that is not the case. Love exists only within our own hearts and to have happy relationships, we must first become truly loving people. And as we fill our hearts with love by expressing love toward all people in thought, word and deed (faking it till we make it happen, if necessary), then that love will heal our own lives, help to solve our problems and enable us to feel good about ourselves. The need for a partner to rescue us will disappear; instead, we will attract whole, loving people into our lives and when the time is ripe for a relationship it will be one between two whole, emotionally healthy people coming together to give to each other rather than to take from each other.

In his famous prayer, St. Francis asks that he may seek rather "to love than to be loved. For it is by self-forgetting that one finds. It is by forgiving that one is forgiven." So, too, it has been our experience that it is by loving that we are loved; it is by being the right person that we find the right person.

WEEK FOURTEEN : LAW C

We receive freely when we give freely.

Each year thousands of people hang a "Gone Fishin'" sign on their doors and trek to mountain streams and deep placid lakes to pursue a great American sport. Armed with the most sophisticated rod, reel and fancy tied flies, or with a simple bamboo pole, string and a worm, the afficianado casts his bait on the waters. Employing a curious mixture of intuition, skill and perseverance, the fisherman lands his catch, and soon is savoring his success as it sizzles to golden delicious perfection.

Chris Hartley is in the fishing business. He is a young man with his own boat who lives in some of the best fishing territory in the world. The clear, turquoise-green waters of the Bahamas teem with many varieties of fish; charter boats abound that will take visitors on fishing trips out of Nassau. However, Chris doesn't fish from his boat, and neither does he allow others to fish from it. Furthermore, he will not eat fish that anyone else has caught. You might think such a fisherman would have a hard time running a successful business, but Chris is thriving in his endeavor. He has a different kind of tourist fishing business, based on the universal principle that as you give freely, you will receive freely; his enterprise profits by using this principle.

Chris loves to be underwater; he seems to be in his element there. Capitalizing on his affinity for the sea, he procured a boat and some equipment which allowed him to set up "Hartley's Underwater Wonderland," a boat excursion to a nearby coral reef. There, tourists in diving helmets walk along the sea floor fifteen feet below the surface, while Chris introduces them to the flora and fauna of the sea world.

Halfway through the tour, on perfect cue, a big black and white striped fish swims up to Chris, who pets Harry the Grouper as he would a cat or dog. Harry then swims to each of the underwater guests, allows himself to be touched by each one, and poses for photographs that Chris later sells to the tourists. One year Chris dressed Harry up with a Santa Claus hat, snapped his picture and made a unique Christmas card souvenir.

If you're wondering why Harry performs so well for Chris, it's because of Chris' practice of giving and receiving, the law of life he lives by. When he began his business, he realized that a tame fish around the coral reef would be a great attraction for tourists, but most fish were afraid of people and stayed away out of an instinct for survival. Chris realized he would have to give to the fish an assurance that they wouldn't be killed, that he was coming to them as a friend. Chris began to bring food to the fish, food for them to eat, not bait on the end of a hooked line. And although Chris had no guarantee the fish would respond, they did by flocking around the coral reef every time his boat appeared. Given freely of Chris' love and food, the fish responded with their friendship and Chris had benefited tremendously by sharing that friendship with his customers.

Perhaps you've been led to believe that to profit and gain in an enterprise, someone must lose—that for you to win this game we call life there must be a loser. What Chris Hartley demonstrates is that you never lose by giving, whether it's food for fish, or love for friends. For in giving freely without guarantee of return, you set into motion an irresistible momentum of goodness. When we give, everyone is a winner.

WEEK FOURTEEN : LAW D

The truth will make you free.
John 8:32

"You will know the truth and the truth will make you free." But how can knowing the truth make anyone free? It may seem as if your freedom can come only by a change in external circumstances. It may appear that your boss or your bank account have more to do with your freedom than anything you know or believe.

We tend to see freedom, or lack of freedom, as the result of something outside of ourself, and so it may appear. Once, a volunteer from a nightclub audience was hypnotized and told that he was chained to his chair. He was then instructed to try to get up and walk around. No matter how hard he tried to pull away, he could not break that invisible chain that bound him.

Was the chain real? It would not be to you and me, yet it was absolutely real to the man who was hypnotized. Anyone in the audience could get up and leave if they wanted to, but this man could not because of his belief, a belief that kept him in bondage. Because the observers knew the truth they were free to move about as they pleased; the man in the chair could not become free until he too knew the truth.

A person in a hypnotic state is highly suggestible to the hypnotist's commands. What he says goes unchallenged, accepted by the subject's subconscious mind as the absolute truth—accepted so deeply, in fact, that what the hypnotist tells the subject is what he or she will see. Convinced that "seeing is believing," the subject's eyes will confirm what he or she is already certain is true.

Everyone is suggestible to a certain extent, which is why advertising is effective, and why it is important to examine your beliefs from time to time to see where they originate. How much of what you believe is the result of what others have told you? How much of what you believe about yourself comes from what others believe about you?

What if someone grew up being told that he was very bright but not very attractive? The chances are this person would accept these statements as true and would act accordingly. This person would be just like the man who was chained to the chair because someone told him he was. This person would be in bondage because of something he believed, and whether it was true or not would not make the slightest difference.

The truth really *can* make us free once we realize that much of what we believe, especially about ourselves, is not necessarily the truth, but is instead a "hypnotic suggestion" we have accepted from others. Struggle to become aware of what you believe about yourself, others, and the world around you. Ask yourself, "Is this really true or could it be an illusion or a lie?" If your beliefs are limiting your options in life by keeping you in bondage, they probably do not represent the truth. When you know the truth about who you really are, you may indeed be free!

WEEK FOURTEEN : LAW E

If you would find gold, you must search where gold is.

William Juneau

In the 1930s, television had not been invented, and radios were scarce, because so many people were very poor. Movie theaters were available, but again, many people were too poor to pay the 25-cent price of admission. People entertained themselves most of the time by singing songs, telling stories and playing games.

Occasionally, a circus or carnival would come to town, and the people who had a bit of money to spare would attend these. There was another kind of entertainment that came to town two or three times a year. It was called a "Medicine Show" because the carnival owners put on a vaudeville type of entertainment—admission free—and made money by selling patent medicines, soap and candy. Their main product was a tonic they claimed would cure any disease ever heard of, including dropsy and the vapors, neither of which is heard of nowadays. That was their internal medicine, composed to a great extent of grain alcohol flavored with licorice, cinnamon, or cloves. They also had an external medicine. It was a fiery liniment guaranteed to cure arthritis, gout, and all kinds of skin conditions.

The entertainment was not high quality, but it was free, so medicine shows were popular. In one of the skits, an actor would come out on the stage and conduct a thorough search of the area. A second actor would enter and ask, "What are you looking for?"

"I dropped a dime a few minutes ago," the first would reply.

"Did you drop it at the front of the stage, or at the side?" the second man would ask.

"Neither place. I dropped it around behind the wagon," the first would say.

"Then why don't you look for it back there?"

"Because there ain't no lights back there," was the punch line.

All of us can appreciate how humorously ridiculous the comedian's logic was; yet we see people every day searching in the wrong places for the things they desire. Too many of our fellow humans try to find peace and happiness in drugs, alcohol and sensual excitement, but they don't find what they want because they're searching in the wrong place. If you want peace, the first place to look is within yourself. It's not an external condition so much as an internal one.

If you want the company of good people, try going to the places where good people go—churches, charity functions, community picnics. Good people will not be found where gangsters and thieves hang out.

Those in search of an easier, softer way to obtain the important things of life often find cheap imitations or nothing at all. The miner who searches for gold on the beach because the digging is easy will certainly find lots of sand, but he'll never find gold. Sometimes we must dig among stones and hard clay to find the treasure we seek. And when we do, we will know our efforts have not been wasted.

WEEK FIFTEEN : LAW A

Habit is the best of servants, the worst of masters.

J. Jelinek

Everyone has habits. Getting up in the morning, doing the things that create order in your environment, eating nutritious meals, exercising your body, practicing good hygiene, getting enough sleep. These habits enable you to function at full strength both at work and play. Good study habits enable you to organize your thinking and use your time for effective learning. Habits of courtesy create natural good manners that make others comfortable. Consistent practice habits enable you to develop a skill or talent like music or sports, painting, crafts or writing.

A habit is a pattern of behavior we have acquired that has become so automatic it's difficult to modify or eliminate. Most habits become unconscious and we no longer have to think about where, when, how or whether to do things—it's almost as though they're done outside of our conscious will.

Habitual behaviors can certainly be helpful. We rarely need to think about the way we use our bodies to walk, run and climb stairs. We are robotic about the way we hold a pencil, fork or a cup. Drivers get into the habit of operating the accelerator, brake and turn signal efficiently, never giving the process a thought. Habits of politeness such as saying "hello," "please," "thank you," "you're welcome" and "excuse me," promote harmony as we communicate with each other in our daily routines.

Hygiene habits also aid us in our journey through life. Keeping ourselves clean, brushing our teeth and eating nutritious foods in the proper amounts contributes to sound bodies. Keeping our clothing and living quarters clean and neat are habits that promote self-esteem and success. Once learned, these good habits become unconscious ones.

The habits of doing routine things in a certain order can sometimes assure completion. For instance, putting everything you need for work in the same place near the door before you go to bed each night can help you get a smooth start the next morning. If before you leave the house each day you form the habit of taking a few seconds to visually scan the room and think about what you need to take with you, you will save yourself time and embarrassment. Thinking about what needs to be turned off (like stoves) or unplugged (like curling irons) will help keep your home safe.

Still, not all habits are helpful to us, and the bad habits can become cruel masters that sabotage our well-being. Smoking, drinking and taking drugs can rapidly develop into habits that can ruin our health and our relationships with others. While the dangers of addictive drugs are becoming more obvious each day, sometimes habits that are much more subtle can be just as detrimental to our development into successful individuals.

The habit of thinking negatively about ourselves and our opportunities is self-destructive, as is the habit of day-dreaming instead of concentrating on our work. Procrastination is an insidious and self-defeating habit that has ruined many lives. Blaming other people or circumstances for our failures can become a habit that prevents us from moving forward toward the completion of our goals.

By the time a behavior pattern becomes a habit, it feels so familiar that it seems to be a natural part of us, but, in fact, habits are learned and practiced. Just as we have learned them over time, so too it's possible to unlearn them. By observing yourself you can become aware of the habitual ways you think and act that do you harm. When you're conscious of a habit you want to change, you can unlearn it by replacing the automatic behavior with a different, more thoughtful response. You may make mistakes, or slip back into old ways, but it's important not to give up. Just correct your behavior as soon as you're aware that you've slipped back into the old habit. Determine how to be the master of your habits, so that your habits can be useful servants to you.

Man cannot discover new oceans until he has the courage to lose sight of the shore.

The eagles that live in the canyons of Colorado use a special kind of stick with which to build their nests. A female eagle will sometimes fly as many as two hundred miles in a single day in order to find a branch from an ironwood tree. Not only are the ironwood sticks as strong as their name suggests, they have thorns that allow them to lock together so that the nest can set securely on a ledge high up on the canyon. After building the nest, the eagle pads it with layer upon layer of leaves, feathers and grass to protect future offspring from the sharp thorns of the ironwood.

In her preparations, the female eagle goes to great lengths to promote the survival of the birds she will hatch. This interest in their survival extends well beyond their birth, although the expression of that interest changes. As the young eagles grow, they begin to fight for space. Their demands for food eventually become such that the mother eagle cannot feed them what they need. She instinctively knows that in order to survive, her brood is going to have to leave its nest.

To encourage the young eagles to fend for themselves, the mother pulls the padding out of the nest so the thorns of the ironwood will prick the birds. As their living conditions become more painful, they are forced to climb up on the edge of the nest. The mother eagle then coaxes them off the edge. As they begin to plummet to the bottom of the canyon, they wildly flap their wings to brake their fall, and end up doing what is the most natural thing in the world for an eagle—they fly!

Human beings often find themselves in a similar situation. When our lives can no longer provide us with the growth we desire, and change must take place, we may need to leave safety and familiarity behind. But just as the baby eagles are reluctant to leave the nest, we also may resist change. Even though conditions are not pleasant, we may try to tolerate the increasing discomfort because we're afraid of the unknown.

Many times unpleasant conditions in our lives tell us we are ready to move on and experience new areas of our potential. While our fear of the unknown might temporarily increase our tolerance of an uncomfortable situation, circumstances are likely to get thorny enough that, like the growing eagles, we'll be coaxed into moving on.

When the time comes to venture out and accept new challenges, try to remember that everyone has the ability not only to survive but to prosper. We are all designed to achieve high levels of success and to enjoy fulfillment and satisfaction in life. This means we never have to settle for less than we're capable of.

Within each of us are resources that can be realized only when we climb to the edge of the nest, slip off into the air—and fly!

WEEK FIFTEEN : LAW C

Men are punished by their sins, not for them.
Elbert Hubbard

There once were two sisters who quarreled constantly. The older sister often stayed in the bathroom so long the younger one had to go downstairs to get dressed. One day, when they were home alone, the younger sister locked her sibling out of the bathroom just as they were getting ready for school. Big sister was furious. As pounding and hollering didn't work, she lay in wait until little sister opened the door and then rushed in and tried to force little sister out. In the struggle, she bashed her over the head with her hand mirror. It broke into small pieces and fell on the floor.

When mother came home, each told her side of the story. Mother gave the following assessment: "Big sister, you take more than your share of time in the bathroom so you can't blame little sister for locking you out. Little sister, you were getting even instead of trying to work out an agreement that would be good for you both, so you were actually encouraging the fight.

"The two of you have suffered from what happened—one has a knot on the head, the other broke a precious gift from Grandmother. You both need to think about how you can work together rather than fight."

Most of us grow up knowing we'll be punished for our bad behavior, and often, we are. But the truth is, we are hurt far worse by the results of what we do than by the spankings and groundings other people impose on us.

We suffer from misdeeds even when no one finds out. Many a young girl has been sure she could have sex with her boy friend without taking any precautions, only to find herself pregnant.

As in the case of the sisters, many people are hurt by the reckless behavior of the boy and girl. The young lovers have had their lives drastically changed in a way they neither anticipated nor wanted. The baby they've made has a right to stable, loving parents who can provide for its needs. Their parents' and brothers' and sisters' lives are affected by something they were not responsible for.

There are many examples of what the world calls "sins"—stealing, extortion, and taking illegal drugs are all too common—and they carry penalties of prison and heavy fines that are meant to discourage their practice. A better deterrent, however, is our recognition of ourselves as worthy of a better fate. No one deserves to go through life with a scrambled brain or a family to support without enough education or financial security to do so comfortably.

If you are tempted to do something and feel even a shade of reluctance, ask yourself, "If I do this, how will it affect my life in six months, two years, five years?" See yourself as a vital part of the world, interdependent and affected by the actions of every other person on the planet. Ask yourself: "Will this be good for me and for everyone?" Asking the right questions is a step in the direction of finding the right answers.

WEEK FIFTEEN : LAW D

Accentuate the positive; eliminate the negative.

"You gotta accentuate the positive; eliminate the negative; latch on to the affirmative; don't mess with Mr. In-Between!" So sang Johnny Mercer in the mid-1940's. It's still a good message for us today.

When something is going wrong, it's tempting to believe that everything in our lives is wrong. Unfortunately, when we have this attitude we act in ways that tend to cause more "wrongs" to happen to us and we overlook the positive parts of our lives.

Have you ever gotten up late, found the shirt you planned to wear that day is dirty, there's no cereal for breakfast, and your brother beat you to the bathroom? Whether or not the day goes downhill from there depends on how you feel about what has already happened. Are you angry at yourself for not setting the alarm and not laundering the shirt the night before, at the person who failed to do the grocery shopping, and at your brother for beating you to the bathroom?

We often tend to blame others for our misfortunes. But instead of wasting time and energy on anger and accusation, it can be far more productive to focus on solutions and move away from the problem and into your day in a positive frame of mind. "Accentuate the positive; eliminate the negative." It can work for you!

Anger feeds on anger. If brother is criticized or yelled at for staying too long in the bathroom, he is apt to stay even longer, which won't get you out of the house on time. Refusing to argue with him and using the waiting time to prepare for your day, not only keeps peace but maintains your schedule. If you discuss your needs and ask him to agree to a time limit, you both have the opportunity to "eliminate the negative."

Learning these lessons early on will stand you in good stead throughout life. You will continue to have times when you'll want to cry, "It's not fair," but feeling sorry for yourself will not solve the problem. Better to think: "This is how it is. Now, what can I do about it?" Remember, anger is an emotion and emotions don't solve problems; they are more likely to create new ones.

As you practice thinking in this way you will find that your life becomes smoother, with less tension and anger. You will begin to manage your feelings, instead of allowing outer circumstances to manage them for you. You will be able to shift your thinking and react positively, while releasing negative thoughts.

Pleasant, productive days will result from your new way of thinking. Your mind tells you how to feel about what is going on because it holds all your memories. It remembers past events and how you felt about them and, when a similar thing happens today, it sends a message, "We feel angry about this." You can give your mind new messages and choose whether you will feel anger or whether you will solve the problem in an affirmative way.

When you control your mind and emotions, you control your life. Outer circumstances have less effect on you and you exert a positive effect on everyone around you.

WEEK FIFTEEN : LAW E

Forgiving uplifts the forgiver.

A young woman named Sue had a puppy she frequently scooped into her arms and showered with kisses. "Oh, I'm *so* thankful to have you in my life," she would coo. But she rarely took him for walks and often forgot to feed him. She may have felt she was thankful for the gift of the puppy's friendship. True thanksgiving, however, is a way of expressing gratitude and love through positive action.

Love is not just a feeling. It is a way of setting a course through giving; it is a letting go of fear. True thanksgiving transcends fear and frees us to live in the here-and-now where we can feel free to express our giving and forgiving natures. Most of us understand giving, but some of us are still confused about the meaning of forgiveness. Forgiveness is not something granted to us by another. True forgiveness allows us to rid our thinking of rigid ideas; we develop the flexibility to change our minds and our behavior, and thus find greater freedom. Many people go through life in a groveling mode, mistakenly believing they have to receive forgiveness from others.

As a child, when caught doing something inappropriate, Sue would cry and beg to be forgiven although she had no intention of changing her behavior; she simply was upset that she'd been caught and her pleas for forgiveness were a way to avoid the consequences of her behavior. True forgiveness would have had to come from Sue herself and the scenario would have then gone something like this: "Yes, what I did was wrong. I realize that and I know you have to ground me for a week. I guess that will be a good lesson for me." Not many young children can accept and reason this way, but as we mature, if our role models have been adequate, we can learn and grow from our mistakes rather than repeating them.

Forgiveness is about loving oneself enough to be honest, open-minded and willing to move on in life. It is about learning to be grateful, not only for our own mistakes but for all our experiences, even if they appear to be bad or are painful. It is about knowing that although we may have to experience pain, we don't have to suffer. When we give thanks for our challenges, the faith expressed through thanks dissolves the appearance of the bad and the good then appears. By giving thanks we learn not to resist the changes that truly come to bless us.

No one is saying it's easy to let go of old ideas; even though we may know they're self defeating, we may still struggle to hold onto them because they are familiar. Growth, however, is not intended to be a struggle but rather a surrender. One of the things that can block the development of our true potential is the fear of giving up the good for the better.

Through giving and forgiving, the old ego structures that have been built up over a lifetime start to crumble. Only when that wall comes down are we free to build healthy structures in our minds and, when the mind is strong and healthy, then our world reflects strength and health. During this process, there may be the appearance of chaos, turmoil and confusion from time to time. But let us remember that it's thanksgiving that sustains this wonderful, self-perpetuating, positive cycle not only in our lives but in the larger scheme of things.

WEEK SIXTEEN : LAW A

The light of understanding dissolves the phantoms of fear.

Ellie Harold

Most of our fears are no more real than the eerie ghosts that haunt the houses of Elm Street on Friday the 13th. These phantoms of doubt, confusion and pain are the fabrications of our minds. They may cause us to run away and hide or to scream with fright, but when seen in the light of understanding, our fears dissolve.

There once was a woman who was terribly upset when she returned home from a trip to find her beloved cat missing. She spent the entire day searching the neighborhood, calling her cat by name, asking the neighbors if they'd seen her pet. Between heaving sobs, all she could say, over and over, was, "I know she's out there starving somewhere. Or else dogs have killed her. She can't protect herself—she's a house cat, she has no front claws." In her mind, she visualized all sorts of horrible things that had happened to her cat. Twilight finally drew her away from the search and the grieving woman went into her house and began to unpack. As she started to hang up a dress, deep from within the closet came the cry of her hiding cat. The poor woman nearly fainted with relief.

By letting her thoughts run wild and unchecked, the woman created her own worst-case scenario. As Job lamented, "The thing that I fear has come upon me, what I dread befalls me." When we let fear overwhelm us, scenes involving the worst possibilities flash before our minds. Perhaps it's an instant replay of some disaster from the evening news, only personalized to involve our children or our parents, or a nightmare from childhood. Thoughts, stained by fear, cannot perceive reality accurately. It's like trying to study objects through a clouded lens. Nothing is seen clearly for what it is; everything is reduced to diffused and shadowy images. Sometimes we may be paralyzed by our fear; other times we react defensively because doom seems so imminent. Like the woman who thought her cat had been destroyed by dogs only to find it safely hiding in her closet, we often put ourselves and others through a lot of anguish only to discover that the facts don't support our worst fears.

Cases have been recorded of individuals whose hair turned completely white on receiving tragic news about a loved one, only to learn later that the report was unfounded. In other difficult situations, people have received horrible news and have emerged, after great pain and despite their loss, with a strong sense of wholeness. The difference between the two groups lies in how they received bad news rather than in the bad news they received. The first group succumbed to mental imaginings that were ultimately proved incorrect, while the second faced their fears and dealt with reality.

Fear is also FEAR (*False Evidence Appearing Real*)—a famous acronym that sheds the light of understanding on those phantoms of fear. There are at least two false premises regarding fear. First, is the belief that things are as they appear to be. Increasingly scientists are discovering evidence to the contrary. For example, what seems to be solid matter is in fact composed of patterns of sub-atomic units of energy. Second, the fearful individual assumes that he or she lacks the resources to handle a tragic situation. The truth is, courage belongs not only to heroes and heroines but is developed within you as you meet life's challenges. As Eleanor Roosevelt wrote, "You gain strength, courage and confidence by every experience in which you really stop to look fear in the face." When you look fear in the face you may see right through it, if it is only a phantom after all.

WEEK SIXTEEN : LAW B

It's better to lead than to push.
William Juneau

Some of comedienne Minnie Pearl's funniest stories are about her brother, and that's what she calls him, Brother. On the surface, Brother doesn't seem to have enough sense to come in out of the rain, but sometimes, hidden in the humor are nuggets of wisdom.

One story Minnie Pearl tells has Brother walking along the road near

Grinder's Swith, their home town, pulling a chain behind him. As he passes a neighbor's house, the neighbor asks why he's pulling a chain. Brother answers, "Did you ever try to push one of these things?"

Anyone who ever worked with livestock or even pet animals knows they're much easier to lead than push. Humans are not much different. Someone who possesses good leadership abilities can accomplish much more than one who pushes.

Positive leadership can set an example of the proper or desirable way to do what needs to be done. A good boss shows up at the job ahead of the time that others are required to report and he works as diligently as is expected of them. Workers develop a negative attitude toward a superior who seems to have little to do except watch them, and they resent an employer whom they perceive to be trying to exploit them.

There is a computer company in a small midwestern city, fairly new to the area, where good leadership abounds. It reveals itself in the attitude of the people who work there. They smile a lot, and they get an amazing amount of work done. The company is expanding rapidly and showing an excellent profit.

It's easy to see why. There are no "unimportant" jobs or people in this organization. The supervisory personnel let all the workers know how important they are to the company by giving them good pay, safe working conditions, excellent medical and other benefits and, most important of all, respect.

How can they afford to pay better than similar companies? How can they afford better medical insurance, and give sick leave and vacation time? The answer is simple. Satisfied workers produce much more than unhappy ones. They take better care of the company's buildings, equipment and customers, because they know it's in their own best interests to do so. That's what positive leadership can do—it can lead people willingly to an attitude to which no force on earth could have pushed them.

Make yourself necessary to the world and mankind will give you bread.

Ralph Waldo Emerson

Take a look at the world around you, and you will see many people whose work fills an important social function. Farmers grow the food we need, wholesalers bring useful good to the stores, doctors heal our bodies and teachers expose us to knowledge. However, if you look deeper into some of those lives, you'll find they're not all happy with their vocations. Some of the business people would rather be writing poetry, some of the teachers are better suited to an outdoor occupation and some of the doctors dream of being athletes or cabinet makers. They are the ones who wonder how they can earn a living and yet use their best talents.

Ralph Waldo Emerson, in many of his masterful essays, pondered this question. He was expected to follow in the steps of his father and grandfather as a Unitarian minister. Although he did become an ordained minister, he was not content to "minister" in the ways of his forefathers; he knew that he had a different gift. On fire to reveal his ideas on morality, self-reliance and the soul, he began to write. His ideas were new to many, and his audience began to grow. Before long he met with success, and today his essays can be found in almost any bookstore and library. Emerson was true to his own formula: "Make yourself necessary to the world and mankind will give you bread." He bravely stepped forth and created a need for what he had to give the world by offering it.

We hear a lot today about unemployment. Yet what if all of those seeking work simply started doing the thing they're best at? For some it might be child care; for others, the making and refinishing of furniture; and, for still others, the creation of special desserts. A few years ago, a group of unemployed artists banded together to form a business called The Starving Artists. Today they sell their paintings all over the United States. Wally Amos, who created Famous Amos Cookies, began by baking a good chocolate-chip cookie. His friends enjoyed the taste and wanted more.

These innovative people believed, with Emerson, that if you produce that special thing you have to give the world, the world will supply your needs. Think of a way people can benefit from what you have to offer, then offer it. You might find, as Emerson, Famous Amos and the artists did, that all it takes is a taste of something good—something you have to offer the world—and people will find themselves hungering for more.

Love is something if you give it away.
Malvina Reynolds

Perhaps you've seen the bumper sticker that begins, "If you love something, set it free," and ends, "If it doesn't come back, it wasn't yours to begin with." The truth is that unless we learn to love openly and generously, we can smother the object of our love and affection from the disease of our over-dependency. Love that grows and lasts thrives on healthy nourishment, on give and take between equal partners in a relationship. It is truly love "set free."

There can be very little love in our lives if we're so afraid of being hurt or rejected that we never give love or kindness to others. It is only through giving that we can create a space to receive substance. If we allow our love to be freely given and expressed to others, we will experience love in return as it multiplies and flows to us from others.

Not that it's appropriate to run around hugging everyone you meet. There may be better ways to show your love for others. A good way to start is to just be there for another, to listen without interrupting, without feeling the need to "fix" whatever is wrong in the other person's life. Loving others can also be expressed by being positive in your comments, finding the right, kind words that say, "I care" or "I know what you're going through; it's going to be all right." Doing something for someone else without the need for recognition or gratitude will benefit the giver as much as, or even more than, the receiver. When you act out of love, get ready to receive more love than you ever possibly imagined.

There is an old saying that "he who lives with acceptance, friendship and love will find those very qualities everywhere he looks." Give freely; give without thought of return; and your supply of love will never run dry but will expand and be constantly replenished.

Thoughts held in mind produce after their kind.
Charles Fillmore

Twenty years ago, comedian Flip Wilson made famous the phrase, "What you see is what you get." While this is a common belief, it would perhaps be more accurate to say, "What you *think* is what you get!"

Our thoughts, like seeds, sprout and blossom according to their variety, and the thoughts we cultivate create our experience of life. Just as a seed planted in fertile soil produces healthy fruit, our mind is lightened or darkened depending on the type of thoughts we plant in it. If we plant apple seeds and nurture them, we will get juicy apples. If we plant thistle seeds, we will get prickly thistles. The same holds true for the mind. Positive thoughts get positive results, whereas negative thoughts lead to negative results. Understanding this cause and effect relationship can help us think into being the kind of life we wish to have.

The personality, ever in a state of change, creates itself anew based on ideas that move through the inlet and outlet of the thinking faculty. It is important, then, to monitor the traffic since thoughts held in mind do produce after their own kind. It may take practice, though no more energy, to direct the active, zealous, impulsive thinking faculty to retain thoughts that build one's world according to a wise pattern.

Each of us is born with the freedom to choose the thoughts we want to direct our lives. We choose the path we want to walk down, so to speak. We have the power to choose the pace at which we will travel and also what we wish to carry along the way.

Napoleon Hill, the bestselling American author of *Think and Grow Rich,* was born and raised in a one-room log cabin in the mountains of southwest Virginia. Young Hill's home was so isolated that he was twelve years old before he saw his first railroad train. Adding to his impoverishment was the loss of his mother when he was eight.

Dr. Hill, in his later years, remembered the day, a year after his mother's death, when his father brought home a new wife:

"My father introduced her to each of the relatives. When my turn came, I was standing in the corner with my arms folded and a scowl on my face. I was all set to show her how tough I could be.

"Father walked up to me and said, 'Martha, here is your son, Napoleon, the meanest boy in Wise County. I won't be surprised if he starts throwing rocks at you by tomorrow morning.'"

All the relatives roared with laughter.

"My stepmother walked up to me," Hill recalled, "put her hand under my chin, and lifted my head upward so she could look squarely into my sullen face. 'You are wrong about this boy,' she said. 'He is not the meanest boy in Wise County. He is a smart boy who has not yet learned how to make the best use of his wisdom.'"

With his stepmother's encouragement, Napoleon Hill traded his rifle for a typewriter. She taught him to type, to research information and to express his ideas in writing. When later he said: "There is but one thing over which man has complete control. That is his own mental attitude," it was his own experience speaking. For when Napoleon Hill replaced the belief that he was mean with the seed-thought that he was wise and could do great things, he became the great person he was meant to be. He went on to advise kings and presidents and to inspire millions through the power of the written word. His book *Think and Grow Rich* is still a bestseller after some thirty years. It is Hill who wrote these famous words: "There is but one thing over which man has complete control. That is his own mental attitude."

Just as fruit generated from the best kind of seed is the most delicious and pleasing, so, too, the life most worth living is cultivated from the best, most loving thoughts. Before we can utilize the positive power of our thoughts, we must become aware of our current pattern of thinking. We may not have a stepmother who was as helpful as Napoleon Hill's in pointing out negative thought patterns. Nevertheless, in quiet times on our own, we can observe our habits of thought, and begin to weed out those that do not suit the higher purpose.

We can train our minds to nurture positive and loving thought patterns, and through them, we can develop a deeper, richer personality that will be the fulfillment and fruition of our greatest creative potential.

Try making friends with the most powerfully good ideas that are available to you as a human being. Try giving them your attention and belief. Instead of filling your mind with aimless chatter or with fears and negativity, work at filling your mind with the presence and instruction of positive ideas. As you do, you will not only be blessed but you will become a blessed representative in our world of the life-transforming "law of good ideas." You will slowly and surely grow from negativity and limitation to an abundance of usefulness and happiness.

<hr>

WEEK SEVENTEEN : LAW A

Progress requires change.

We all suffer from a broken heart at one time or another during the course of a lifetime. Most of us will experience the loss of a loved one, or the diminishment of physical or mental health, or the loss of a job that provides much-needed income. Even reaching out toward a goal that for whatever reasons never materializes can cause a broken heart.

Everything changes; in fact it's been said that change is the only constant in our lives. And if we don't know how to handle change, it can be heartbreaking. Relationships end. Loved ones die. We grow old. Some of our cherished goals will go unrealized. How do we deal with the pain of loss that is bound to come to us all?

When a seed falls into the darkness of the earth, the seed's outer shell must break so that new life can emerge. Jesus said: "Unless a kernel of wheat falls to the ground and dies, it remains only a single seed . . . But if it dies, it produces many seeds." When our outer shells break in pain, when our hearts are broken, it is important to learn the lesson that Jesus set out to teach us: whenever we lose something we always, in some way, gain something at the same time.

We can then come to understand and appreciate that life offers unexplainable experiences that will not always make rational sense. This understanding is a precious gift in and of itself. We often think that if we could just do everything "right" we could keep ourselves from pain. But life is more complicated and mysterious than that.

There is a gift right in the midst of the loss. The very pain we experience is the shell of our understanding, our wisdom, our maturity and compassion, breaking forth its gift, its new life.

This understanding is not a drug to dull or deny the pain but, rather, a means to open ourselves to pain's mystery, to what it has to offer as well as what it takes away. Next time you feel that shell breaking in your heart, feel it fully and deeply and take comfort in knowing that living with and through pain can help you become a more understanding and compassionate person toward yourself and others. Adversity can be a rich and educational gift. Adversity can be a milestone in your spiritual growth.

WEEK SEVENTEEN : LAW B

Chance favors the prepared.

By the time Dean began his second year of college, he was considering a career in education, so he scheduled a session with his counselor and the education department of his college to plan his course of study for the next three years. His advisors convinced him that he should work toward a master's degree and perhaps even a doctorate. But realizing that many valuable lessons could not be learned in the classroom, Dean began to consider the kinds of extra-curricular activities and part-time work that would best prepare him for his chosen career. He became active in the Student Education Association and other campus activities geared for education majors, but he wondered what his part-time job as a salesman in a department store had to do with education.

But he liked his job and his employer was very supportive of Dean's commitment to get an education. He worked out a schedule which allowed Dean to earn the money he needed and yet have the time he required for study. Another benefit of the job was his ability to buy shoes and clothing at a discount. His salary was on a par with other jobs available on a part-time basis, and he decided that the support of his employer was worth a great deal, even though his actual work seemed to have little to do with his life's goals.

Dean pondered what he could do at work to forward his career. He noticed that as new people were hired, they had no idea how to use their time when they were not busy with customers. He knew from his own experience that the owner tried to train them well, but he had many other priorities. The new clerks were quickly left on their own to learn the hard way. Dean created a checklist of items that would have helped him when he was new. He made notes of questions new employees asked and listened closely as they dealt with customers.

In a few short weeks, he had pages of notes, and recognized he had the bare bones of an employee training manual. He presented his boss with a rough draft of the manual, asking him to read it through and make suggestions and comments. Dean proposed that he write the book, which would then be printed and circulated to all new employees. His boss enthusiastically endorsed the plan and gave him a raise. Three years later, when Dean was applying for graduate school, it was his employer's sincere and strong recommendation that was the deciding factor in Dean being granted a substantial scholarship to a university that was preeminent in the field of business education. Dean's good fortune was not a matter of luck or fate as many of his classmates thought. It was a clear result of his applying his interest, skill, and energy in every part of his life. Dean had used all the resources available to him; consequently, he was given the chance to be successful.

WEEK SEVENTEEN : LAW C

A good reputation is more valuable than money.
Publilius Syrus

By the time he was eighteen, John was saddled with a very poor reputation. He often lied. He would make promises to his friends he failed to keep, no matter how important those promises were to the other person. He had even been arrested for shoplifting. Because John's father was very comfortably off financially, John thought he had everything. He lived in a fine house, wore the latest fashions, had his own car and plenty of spending money.

But he did not have everything—far from it. He did not have a good reputation. That summer, between his high school graduation and the start of college in September, John tried for a summer job in the field of his planned future career. But he didn't get the job; his poor reputation cost him the position. Then, for the first time, he fell in love. But because of his well-known reputation, the girl refused to date him. Fortunately, John came to realize that money is not so important in your life if it's joined to a poor reputation—that your reputation, not money, is the most valuable currency of all. He began to change, but several years passed before people completely accepted the "new" John.

What you do every day of your life affects your reputation. It is up to you, and you alone, to make the right decisions. You can heed advice, learn from the experiences of others and study the laws of life. But only you can decide how to use the knowledge you acquire. Friends, parents, clergymen and teachers can help you, advise you, stand by you, but they cannot act for you. If you take the time to think about what any action will mean and make your decision based on that, you will earn a good reputation. It doesn't matter if you're rich or poor, a good reputation increases your chances of leading a life rich in meaning and happiness. This doesn't mean you will never make a mistake. Everyone makes mistakes. It is important, however, to admit your mistakes when you make them and do what you can to right them. This will keep your reputation intact.

When you have a good reputation, you feel good about yourself. And remember, you have to spend every single moment of your life with yourself, you and you alone. If you don't like and respect who you are, it's going to be very difficult for you to like or respect anyone else. Work to build that good reputation. Money cannot buy it, but hard work can earn it.

Your life becomes what you think.

With modern scanning equipment, we can see the brain, but we cannot see the brain working. We see only the results of the brain activity; the mind, which is invisible, directs the thinking process. It tells the brain how to sort experience and fact, and how to give shape and form to new ideas.

Have you ever had an original idea and wondered where it came from? It's as if your mind planted a seed of the idea in the brain. Your brain recalled your experience and knowledge and developed the idea in a way that could finally be expressed by you coherently and persuasively. The idea probably improved as you tested it under various conditions.

In the same way, the mind can tell the brain what to think about. It's tempting to believe that we have no control over what comes into our heads, but we do. If a thought comes to you that is not in your best interest, you can, with very alert practice, begin thinking something else, so that the undesirable thought will go away.

Sound hard? Try the following experiment. Don't think about bananas. Pause for a few seconds. What's happening? I know you are thinking about bananas! So telling yourself to stop thinking something doesn't do much good, does it? Now, try thinking Valentine hearts. Once those two words are planted in your mind, bananas may pop back in from time to time, but if you just recognize that bananas are back, think Valentine hearts again and add "with white lace and arrows through them" or any additional thing you can think about Valentine hearts. Soon the bananas will go away.

When you face an unpleasant task, such as mowing the lawn, it can be tempting to complain about it. However, when it's in your best interest to finish the job, why not make it more fun, now that you know you can?

Do you like the color of your lawn mower? Then every time you catch yourself thinking "I don't like mowing the lawn," think instead, "I like my red lawn mower." Ask your family to help you. If you say something negative about mowing the lawn, they can wink and smile and say: "Oh? What color is your lawn mower?"

It's important for you to find something that is true for you, however insignificant it may seem, with which to replace the negative thought. It could be that you like the fresh air, the sunshine, being outside, the smell of newly mown grass, or that you may get to visit with a friend over the back fence.

Anything to change your negative thought to a positive one will change your attitude and, as a result, your experience around it. Your grass will not only get mowed, but you will feel better about yourself too.

Try to be kind to yourself in this process. If you've worked at changing your thoughts and the negative ones seem to keep roosting there, laugh at yourself. Accept that you're doing your best, and go back to thinking your replacement thought. As you get better and better at controlling your thoughts, your positive, good thoughts will change your life for the better.

WEEK SEVENTEEN : LAW E

To err is human, to forgive is divine.

Do you currently blame anyone for a wrong you believe has been done to you? Do you hold any resentments toward someone for your present situation? Is there a part of you that says "If only so-and-so hadn't done thus-and-such to me, I would be feeling happier and more successful"? In one way or another, we all can find a scapegoat for a lack we feel in our lives.

But we need to be aware of the price we pay for holding grudges and resentments. We need to understand that we are the ones who suffer from this unforgiveness. It takes a lot of energy to hold onto a grudge, energy that could be better spent. We may feel justified in our attitude, but in the long run what does it really matter? Why would we punish ourselves even further by dwelling on negative thoughts and emotions? A tremendous cost in sickness of mind and body may affect those who cling to feelings of unforgiveness.

It has been rightly said that "to err is human, to forgive is divine."

The highest and best qualities we possess urge us to get on with our lives and to stop making excuses for our failures. We do ourselves a disservice when we blame our failures on someone else rather than choosing to learn and grow from our experiences.

Complete and total forgiveness is a sure way to health and happiness and to new energy and enthusiasm. It is a sign that we are taking responsibility for our lives. No one can stop us from experiencing success and fulfillment unless we give them our permission. Once we realize that we're in the driver's seat, we can move swiftly and surely to greater and greater good.

WEEK EIGHTEEN : LAW A

What is of all things most yielding can overcome that which is the most hard.

Imagine a majestic mountain, its granite peaks towering thousands of feet into the sky. Nothing would seem to be more invincible than this giant fortress of solid rock. Yet, in time, certain forces will reduce this mountain to tiny pebbles. Ironically, the forces that wield such power are among the softest, most yielding elements of nature—water and air. The blowing of winds and the flowing streams will ultimately conquer the mightiest of mountains.

This fact is just one example of this universal law: "What is of all things most yielding can overcome that which is the most hard." This statement is taken from the *Tao Te Ching* which is the sacred writing of the Chinese religion of Taoism. This law works not only in the physical universe but also in man's world.

"Victory comes through surrender" is another statement from the *Tao Te Ching*; and Jesus said, "The meek shall inherit the earth." What does all this mean? And what does it have to do with us here and now? Actually, it has a great deal to do with us today. "Yielding, surrendering, meekness," all relate to an attitude of mind wherein we recognize that our "battles" are won not by personal strength alone but by allowing a higher power to work through us.

What is this "higher power?" Some call it God; some call it "the Self"; some call it "Universal Intelligence." It really doesn't matter what we call it, it's always present; it's present whether or not we even believe in it! This mighty power is always present but will never interfere with our personal will. It is necessary that we surrender our personal will and *allow* this power to work in our life.

How do we allow it to work? In part, by believing in it. In part, by surrendering, by yielding to it. In part, by not resisting the obstacles that appear in our lives and by seeing the higher power as the wind or the river that wears away all such obstacles without effort or struggle.

For example, if you have a problem in your life (which most of us do!) you can attempt to overcome this problem through personal willpower and force. It may work. Most likely it won't and, even if it does, the basic problem may show up in some different form. (Most of our personal struggles are with symptoms and not with the actual cause of the problem.) Another alternative is to do what you can do without resistance and struggle and then turn your attention to the higher power and surrender to it. Allow this universal intelligence to work through you. Let go of all personal intentions and trust that the higher power is bringing about a solution that is far greater than you could achieve, or even imagine, through personal willpower and struggling to solve the problems "your way."

<hr>

WEEK EIGHTEEN : LAW B

The seven deadly sins are: pride, lust, sloth, envy, anger, covetousness and gluttony.
St. Gregory

Although theologians differ in their definition of sin, most would agree that it is the nature of sin to distort the gift of life as it has been given to us to live. When someone "misses the mark" with an error in thinking or behavior, life itself doesn't change, but the individual's relationship to it does. A sin is deadly, therefore, because it diminishes the sinner's potential of living a life full of peace, joy, happiness and usefulness.

The sinner, out of step with life's truest and highest aims, fails to see life's infinite potential for good. He becomes deadened to life's possibilities for fulfillment and attempts to find a sense of fulfillment the best way he knows how, through further distortions of life's reality. The "seven deadly sins" are seven common ways many people continue to deaden themselves to life's goodness. They use pride, lust, laziness, envy, anger, covetousness and excess in an effort to get satisfaction and fulfillment where it can never be found.

"Pride goeth before destruction, and an haughty spirit before a fall," the proverb says, which in turn recalls the adage, "What goes up, must come down." An inflated sense of importance is like a hot air balloon that is bound to cool down sooner or later. If we don't feel good about ourselves as we are, we often try to find ways to make ourselves look better than someone else. We may try to make others seem wrong in an attempt to appear more righteous. But when we come to understand that we are all equal as human beings, that there is no basis in reality for either extreme shame or pride, the balloon of our vanity will deflate. In order to keep our world from crashing down around us, we will need to come to rest in a balanced and realistic view of ourselves as the equal of others. We can then hope to find true contentment in expressing the unique and valuable qualities we do possess.

If we were to judge from television and other contemporary media, we might come to believe lust rather than love makes the world go around. Some of us may wonder how lust found its way onto the list of deadly sins; we might reason that perhaps St. Gregory was simply a prude. On the other hand, we might look more closely at some of the present day consequences of indulging our lustful passions. The AIDS epidemic, unwanted teenage pregnancy and drug addiction all suggest that the instant gratification of all our desires is not the answer. And there is much to be gained from the delay of such gratifications; truly intimate, healthy relationships, and a deeper experience of our own emotional reality may result if we can set aside our craving for excitement and enjoy the blessings life brings to us from self-control.

Although the term sloth is no longer in current usage, we are familiar with its synonymous cousin, laziness. We've often heard that a little laziness never hurt anyone. While this may be a common belief, it fails to take into account the damage it can do to our aliveness. Psychiatrist M. Scott Peck observed in *The Road Less Traveled,* "In the struggle to help my patients grow, I found that my chief enemy was invariably their laziness." He noted the universal reluctance of all humankind to "extend to new areas of thought, responsibility, and maturation." Laziness, which, as Peck suggests, may be fear in disguise, limits life by giving full license to inertia. Many times we may feel a task is just too much trouble to complete. Even when it's in our own best interests to persevere, our laziness prevents us from doing it. Meeting our fears and overcoming our lazy resistance, however, is an enlivening experience.

When we feel envy or covet another's possessions it is a sure sign that life is inviting us to grow into new forms of self-expression. The fact that we see a quality of personality in someone else we would like to embody is not a deadly sin. By believing ourselves incapable of expressing that quality, we decrease our sense of well-being and aliveness and *that* is a sin. When we see someone with a good quality we want and believe we can't create, we may be distorting the truth about our own potential. When we make ourselves miserable comparing ourselves to what others are or have, we're wasting time and energy that could be better spent mobilizing our own inner resources. Real life is found in using the unique gifts we've been given. And the more of ourselves we give to life, the more life gives back to us.

Everyone is tempted by anger from time to time. When things don't go according to plan, when we're hurt by someone we love or frustrated in some way, it's likely we will feel at least a spark of anger, if not an explosion. The temptation itself is not a deadly sin; it's what we do with it. Many times we project judgment and blame onto the person whose behavior triggered our reaction rather than take responsibility for our own anger. When we project blame in this way we often feel the need to punish the perpetrator by denying them our friendship. Since much of the time we're triggered into an angry response by those closest to us, we frequently endanger our most important friendships. We miss the mark when we fail to see both sides of a dispute and to realize others too are trying to do the best they can with what they have in life.

Greed is deadly in its opposition to the natural, abundant flow of life. The greedy person is the one who tries to dam the stream and keep all the water for himself. He doesn't realize it's not the water in the river that's really important; it's the love and activity the flow of the water brings into our experience. As old King Midas learned the hard way, a self-centered life based on greed is really no kind of life at all. Desperately afraid, the greedy person builds guarantees for his material well-being, which, in fact, cut him off from the true prosperity of sharing, giving and loving.

The sinner is the one who tries to dam the river. The river, however, will find its way around all obstacles, including the ones that would try to prevent its flow. Whether engaged in one or the other of St. Gregory's "seven deadly sins," the sinner, over time, becomes frustrated and discouraged at the waste of his own life energy spent uselessly blocking the inevitable flow of the river. At some point it is hoped he will accept the forgiveness that is always available, and simply let go and enter the flow of life.

Never do anything that you'll have to punish yourself for.

Have you ever noticed that when you cheat or lie or don't support a friend, and then realize what you've done, it can set off an inner alarm system—a kind of moral wakeup call? What if your friends knew what you did? How would you feel if your parents found out? If your best friends found out? If the person you looked up to most in the world discovered you had let him down?

Hiding a cruel or unloving act deep down inside doesn't make it go away. Often it festers and you begin to feel guilty and full of shame. Even if no one knows but you, those bad feelings can come back to haunt you whenever you think about them.

Unfortunately these bad feelings about ourselves rarely go away without some kind of self-examination. And it's only by experiencing the emotions and accepting what you've done, that you can begin to accept and change yourself. Once you realize you've done something you shouldn't, there are several ways you can come to terms with yourself.

First, you can admit the truth, even if it's only to yourself and one other person. That way you're being honest and you have a chance to forgive yourself. Secondly, if it's something that can be corrected by telling the truth, then do so. That will clear the emotions of shame and guilt, and perhaps deepen your friendships in the bargain, because the friends you share your burden with will appreciate the courage it took for you to be honest.

Lastly, you can choose to make a contract with yourself to do only deeds you will be proud of in the future. This contract is a commitment to live in your own integrity, regardless of whether others around you choose to live in theirs. Try to remember that in the end, it is you who must benefit by living in honor and integrity. It is the key to good health, good relationships, and self esteem.

WEEK EIGHTEEN : LAW D

It is better to light a single candle than to curse the darkness.
Motto of the Christophers

Darkness is one of the first things we fear. Darkness holds the unknown and the undefinable. When we wake in the middle of the night from a nightmare, we are in the darkness. We may stay there, paralyzed by fear, and do nothing but curse our situation. Or we may reach for a nearby lamp and switch it on, thus freeing us from the terror. Problems affect us much like the darkness does. When we are faced with it, we are too scared to move, but only curse our horrid situation, rather than do anything about it.

Is there anything to be gained by cursing the darkness? Nothing has changed. The darkness is still there, totally unaffected by our outburst. Still, something has indeed changed, our perception of the darkness. We have acknowledged that we have a problem. To a degree, this is essential. We cannot solve a problem until we recognize it. But recognition is enough. By going further and cursing the darkness, but excessively complaining about our problems, we make things worse. We end up focusing our minds on just how bad things are. This makes our situation appear even less solvable than it did before. Thus, when we complain about a problem, we have done nothing about it, except to make it worse.

It is possible that the darkness may be beyond our control. Alone, we may not be able to solve a particular problem we face. In other words, we may need others' help. Certainly if we curse the darkness, others will realize that we are faced with a problem. Yet, unless they see us trying to solve the problem and failing, they do not know we need help. Even people who want to help, will have a difficult time helping someone who does nothing for him or herself but complain about a miserable situation.

We must face simple facts. A problem cannot be solved by merely complaining about it. We can curse the darkness till we are blue in the face, but it will still be there. Until we make an active effort to solve our problems, they will not go away. Once we make a small active effort, even if this effort fails, we are closer to exiting the darkness. By attempting one solution, we may see other better solutions. Others may recognize our effort and consequential failure and try to help us. In general, once we take the attitude that the problem can be solved, the darkness becomes much less terrifying, and much more manageable. Some would go as far to say that it is no longer a problem, but a challenge.

Thus, cursing the darkness is to no avail. It does nothing but magnify the problem. It pushes others away from us who may have the power to help. Only by trying to do something about a problem can we expect to solve it. To curse the darkness may be our first reaction, but hopefully it will be our last.

WEEK EIGHTEEN : LAW E

To be forgiven, we must first forgive.

Roy Masters, in his book, *How Your Mind Can Keep You Well,* says that we ought to be grateful when someone offends us. They are doing us a favor, he suggests, because when we forgive those who have offended us, it erases some of the self-destructive effects of offenses we may have caused others. In this way, we learn a valuable lesson: "To be forgiven, we must first forgive."

The person who cannot forgive often becomes physically, mentally, emotionally or spiritually ill, as the story of Kathy so convincingly demonstrates. Kathy had hated her father all her life and felt justified in her extreme feelings. He had repeatedly abandoned her, her mother and six other children. Each time the mother became pregnant, he would disappear until the new baby came. When he returned, the sad process would repeat itself. And while he was home, he would physically abuse everyone, even occasionally beating the mother with a horse whip. She and the children were terrified of him. None of them ever knew when he would lose his temper and turn violent. Kathy sometimes hid under the table or bed in fear. Many would agree that she was justified in hating her father.

The problem is that her anger hurt no one nearly as much as it hurt her; her chronic state of anger violently affected her life and affairs. Like her father, Kathy would lash out at those around her with only the slightest provocation. It cost her job after job and many strained and unhappy relationships.

The hatred and bitterness finally ate away at her health. She suffered from headaches, stomach problems and eventually developed arthritis. She fell victim to every germ that came along in spite of all that doctors and medicines could do. By her twenty-fifth birthday, she looked middle-aged.

She knew she would be better off if she could learn to forgive her father, but she just couldn't do it, nor did she want anyone else to forgive him. "He's just a terrible person," she would cry as she relived the miseries of the past. "Look at what he's done." But Kathy's inner guidance kept reminding her that "To be forgiven, you must forgive." We have all done things for which we need forgiveness, and Kathy was no exception. She wanted to be relieved of things she had said and done. She wanted to be forgiven. So she started the forgiveness process with a statement that went something like this, "I forgive you, you sorry so-and-so."

At first it was difficult and she felt dishonest because she didn't feel at all forgiving. But as she persisted, the statement became softer. Soon she was able to drop the "you sorry so-and-so." As she came to understand how her father could have acted so violently, she began to feel pity for him, then compassion, and finally real love.

When she learned to forgive her father, she began to forgive and actually to love herself. Eventually, her physical problems cleared up and her life was transformed for the better. Through experience, she discovered that forgiveness benefits both the forgiven and the forgiver.

WEEK NINETEEN : LAW A

Reverse the word EVIL and you have the word LIVE.
P. P. Quimby

Why do bad, or evil, things happen to good people? That question has perplexed artists, philosophers and religious thinkers throughout the ages. When accident, disease, financial misfortune, or other personal tragedy happens to the morally responsible, it piques our sense of justice, especially when those with less than honorable behavior often live problem-free lives, at least on the surface. It seems only fair that those who are upstanding should be rewarded with an existence unmarked by tragedy. Instead, we hear repeatedly how some innocents are victimized while some oppressors go free. What flaw in the order of the universe, some people ask with no small amount of bitterness, allows misfortune to plague the existence of good people?

Although bitterness is not an unusual response, it is only a superficial one. We have to move beyond bitterness and understand that we can learn from our "bad breaks." In the fullness of time, the pain of personal catastrophe can give way to new understanding and inner growth.

Evil is typically experienced by the victim as a destructive reversal of fortune that causes unnecessary suffering. An honest, hard-working political candidate is undermined by her opponent's slanderous remarks in the media. A star football quarterback is made a paraplegic in an accident caused by a drunk driver. These are two examples of gratuitously evil acts that invite the beginning of transformation for the victim. From these tragedies can emerge the possibility of a deeper, more meaningful life. Evil, transformed and reversed often can indeed spell *live*.

The passage of a good person through a painful experience can mobilize inner resources and open doorways into a new and more expanded life. In the Old Testament story, Joseph was cast into a pit by his jealous brothers and abandoned to die. He was saved by traders who sold him into Egyptian slavery, where again he incurred the wrath and jealousy of some people he met. He was jailed, once more an innocent victim. But instead of destroying Joseph, the prison experience served as a new beginning. He learned to channel his dreams toward constructive ends and eventually he was able to serve the Egyptian people. To his brothers who sought his forgiveness, Joseph granted it, telling them, "You meant evil against me; but God meant it for good. . . ."

Evil multiplies and triumphs when good people become resentful and bitter over misfortunes but, just as surely, evil is often overcome when they find it within themselves to transcend despair, forgive ignorance, heal betrayals, love everyone and go on with a life of spiritual growth. In fact, as was true with Joseph, such transcendence is the hard road good people can travel to become great people.

Great people refuse to be victimized by circumstance. Instead, they often use even the most traumatic event as a springboard for a creative and helpful response to life. From his wheelchair, the paralyzed quarterback mobilized his leadership skills to help handicapped children. The victimized politican spoke her simple truth and thus gave an example in humility to millions. Those who grow in stature through adversity have learned to reverse the word EVIL to the word LIVE.

WEEK NINETEEN : LAW B

He who has a *why* for which to live, can bear with almost any *how*.
Friedrich Nietzsche

In his book, *Man's Search for Meaning*, Austrian psychiatrist Dr. Viktor Frankl documents the profound power that a life purpose exerts over an individual under even the worst of circumstances. Frankl, who survived the Nazi concentration camps, described how prisoners who felt they had nothing to live for succumbed, while those who perceived themselves as having a mission to complete, struggled to survive. Deprived of all external supports that might give life meaning, these survivors came to realize that, in Frankl's words, "It did not really matter what we expected of life, but rather what life expected from us." Their sense of an inner purpose pulled them through the most horrible physical and emotional experiences so that they might make their unique contribution to the world.

Everyone has a purpose in life beyond one's immediate interests and gratifications, though that purpose frequently goes undiscovered. Many people devote their entire lives to the pursuit of greater ease and pleasure. Those who had not found the "why" that gives meaning to existence may achieve material success, yet the real goodness of life will elude them. The true meaning of life lies in sharing our particular qualities of greatness with others.

There is a simple way you can discover your special purpose in life. Draw up a list of all the qualities you value in yourself and that other people admire in you. If you're a humorous person, you have the ability to uplift and entertain. If clear thinking is your strong suit, and you're skilled at developing ideas, accept this as a gift that can benefit those around you in many ways. Since we sometimes think poorly of ourselves, it's important to dig a little to unearth those skills and talents that may lie hidden.

Next, examine the ways in which you interact with other people and make a list of those ways that work the best. Does it excite you to teach someone a skill that will help him? Do you enjoy simply listening while someone shares a problem with you? Are you happiest when organizing a group for a project, or when encouraging someone who feels hopeless about himself?

Finally, imagine what the world would be like under the best of all possible circumstances. Would it be clean, peaceful and productive? Form a mental picture of the world you'd like all your loved ones to live in and write down that vision in as much specific detail as possible.

Your mission in life is to have a "why" to live for, to use your best qualities in the service of the kind of world you want to live in. That is your purpose. That is what life expects from you. And when you live according to your purpose, setting goals that support it, you'll find the pieces of your life drawn together into a strong internal whole. Then, no matter how difficult life's experiences may prove to be, you will be able to endure and even prevail.

WEEK NINETEEN : LAW C

If at first you don't succeed,
try, try again.

When Thomas A. Edison, working in America, and J. W. Swan, working in England, invented the electric light bulb, the end seemed to have been reached in that kind of experimentation. A safe means of lighting streets and buildings now existed. What further uses could there be for the electric light bulb?

But, after a time, researchers developed new types of bulbs that made use of ultraviolet rays and infrared heat rays. Still others were developed that killed bacteria in the air and before long these were produced in numerous styles and sizes for use in hospitals, schools, homes and even in chicken coops. New blessings are halogen bulbs and fluorescent bulbs.

These are only a few of the uses discovered for what at first seemed to be a simple and self-contained invention. To this day researchers continue to search for new and better ways to make use of the electric light bulb. There is a lesson here that can be applied to our own lives. Often, when we reach a high level of performance, or achieve a breakthrough in our profession, we're so proud of ourselves that we rest on our laurels. We quit trying to do better.

Beau, who has always suffered from minor learning disabilities, is making a C average in college. "That's okay," he says. "I'm just average and I've never had an easy time in school. I'll just settle for that ol' C."

Ashley is making A's. "I worked pretty hard to pull my grades up, and now I can relax," she says.

"I just got a big raise for selling the most advertising pages on our magazine," says Greg. "I can afford to coast now and take a few extra days off."

And so on.

True, Beau, Ashley and Greg, and others like them, have achieved something, have made some progess. But have they accomplished all they're capable of? Have they made full use of their abilities?

If Beau is a C student, chances are that, even with his problems, he could go beyond a C, if he were willing to try a little harder. Or at least he could strengthen that C so it would mean more to him later on.

And Ashley's A average shouldn't be an end in itself. If she doesn't continue doing good work, those A's could take a quick tumble. She may need to find new outlets for her considerable intellectual endowments—develop a personal reading program, learn a new language or make a contribution to the community.

And Greg must realize that he succeeded by working harder than most others, and that continued success will demand the same level of hard, conscientious work.

Success is based on a high level of striving, day after day, in everything we do. It's important to understand that we never actually arrive. Success isn't a destination, but a journey. It's a journey of seeking and learning in each situation, trying to better ourselves as human beings. Like the researchers who continue to find new ways to use electricity, we must struggle to perform at maximum capacity even though we will sometimes fail and make mistakes.

Ask yourself what areas of your life could stand improvement. Are you being sensitive enough in your friendships? Are you spending enough time—quality time—with your family? Are you putting enough honest effort into your job?

It's helpful to remember that "If at first you don't succeed, try, try again."

WEEK NINETEEN : LAW D

The family that prays together stays together.

"The family that prays together stays together" is a saying most of us have heard so many times that the words may have become meaningless. Yet, there must be some truth to this statement because it has helped so many. What images come to your mind as you think of a family praying together? It might be a family of pilgrims giving thanks that their table is full or a modern family in the face of a crisis. But how can the average family apply this principle to their lives and why would they want to?

Let's take a new look at this old adage. We'll begin by examining prayer. What is it? Many of us have an image of kneeling by our bedside petitioning to an old man on a throne or sitting at a table asking grace. Webster's dictionary gives one definition of prayer as to entreat or petition. This implies communication, knowing what we want and need, and learning to ask for it. Charles Fillmore speaks of prayer as entering the silence. He says, "There is a quiet place within us all, and by silently saying over and over, 'peace be still,' we shall enter that quiet place and a great stillness will pervade our whole being." So to pray could mean to go into the silent place inside ourselves and commune with something wise within us, the result of which will bring peace.

The silent communion will look different to each of us. Some of us commune with an inner wisdom when we are with nature. Some of us feel the silent place when we hold a new puppy or sit quietly with someone we love. It isn't so important how we enter the silence, as it is that we do.

When we enter the silence with our families, whether they consist of our parents, brothers and sisters, or a family of our closest friends, we are going together to a silent place of wisdom and peace. It is an experience that can mend hurt feelings, calm anger, encourage love and forgiveness, and help us to remember how important we are to one another. If this is a new idea to you, you might be wondering how it could possibly apply to you and your family. You will probably be surprised to find you have prayed together.

For a family, prayer can happen when there are no longer words to speak. If you've ever come home from school feeling hurt or afraid and someone has quietly held your hand, you have entered the silent place together. Maybe, when you were a child, you sat with your brothers and sisters on Christmas Eve, feeling warm and safe together or, when you were older, took a quiet walk through the woods with a favorite friend. These are ways of communing together in the silence of prayer.

As a family begins to consciously make the choice to pray together in their own way, conflict begins to resolve itself and love increases. Entering the silent place of peace together in the storm of conflict provides a neutral place to find solutions. What are some ways your family has "prayed" together in the past? How can being in the silence together benefit your current problems and conflicts? With your parents or children? With your boss or friends?

WEEK NINETEEN : LAW E

There's as much risk in doing nothing as in doing something.

Trammell Crow

What is the risk in doing nothing? Perhaps it's not exciting but isn't it safe and harmless? But is water or air that does nothing harmless? No, it becomes stagnant. It's not part of any flow or current of movement. It not only contains no fresh, renewing activity, it's the breeding ground for germs and disease. In the stagnant human being, the disease is often guilt and depression.

Why guilt? Certainly the choice to do nothing is your own business. But deep inside, every one of us knows we're meant to be active, and we know in what directions that activity should be aimed. Life shows us, day by day. You'd have to live in an isolation chamber to be unaware of opportunities for doing. Instinctively you know that doing nothing is resisting and avoiding the natural flow of life, because it's not the nature or design of the human being to be inert. You have too much power, too much energy in mind, body and spirit for that to be true. Unused, those gifts are wasted. So if you do nothing, never start, never step forth, never try, it's not going to be easy to remain at peace with yourself for very long.

A life without activity becomes sluggish and dull. A mind never fed with new ideas or experiences becomes stale and apathetic. There is no personal growth or change. And the more you do nothing, the more you are caught in inertia, the lack of inclination to motion, exertion or change. The longer you do nothing, the more you procrastinate, and the harder it is to talk yourself into doing anything positive and worthwhile. And the greater grows your fear of doing something, of departing from the dull but safe status quo. You become increasingly afraid of the unknown, afraid of the world, afraid of yourself.

This does not mean the kind of "doing nothing" you often experience at the end of a busy day or week. It's important to give the mind and body time to rest and relax. It's neither necessary nor wise to be constantly doing something. And some people who don't appear to be doing much outwardly are actively engaged in their minds, considering, exploring, weighing, planning. "Doing nothing" here refers to never getting started.

What is the risk in doing something? You might not do it well. You might not like it. You might be wrong; it might not work. It might turn out to be a useless idea or effort. You might look foolish. You might waste time, energy, money. You might fail. (Fear of failure is a paralysis!)

Even if these things happen, you're sure to learn something from what you did. You might see a better way to do it from having tried what didn't work. Everything you do helps you to do it better the next time. Or you may learn that this just isn't for you, but now that it's done, you can see what you really *do* want to do. You might find courage and determination you didn't know you had. You might discover a new interest, a skill, or a new friend just from having been involved and exposed to something different.

Even if you try and fail, you will generate energies in the process that can create a new perspective for you, give you a new way of seeing things. Your experience gives you new knowledge and wisdom, and that is never wasted. Once you've experienced something new, regardless of the result, it's impossible to ever again see life exactly the same way, for a new dimension has been added to your vision, your mind, your feelings, your body. If you take piano lessons, your understanding and appreciation of music will forever be enhanced, even if ultimately you decide it's not for you and quit. Once you've climbed a mountain, even if you didn't enjoy it, you'll never forget the view.

And, you know? . . . you just might succeed. Even if you're nervous or afraid, go ahead and *do* the thing and see what happens. Say to your fear: "Yes, I know you. But I'm going to do it anyway." You've started down the road, and your momentum will gather. "Life sends thread for the web begun." So start with your present idea and do something. More ideas will meet you on your way, and you will find yourself living fully alive!

Lost time is never found again.
Benjamin Franklin

Oh my darlin', oh my darlin'
Oh my darlin', Clementine,
You are lost and gone forever.
Oh my darlin', Clementine.

Like the sweetheart in this old ballad, time is a precious resource that will be lost and gone forever if we let it carelessly slip away from us. When the moments that make up our lives go unappreciated, we find our capacity to experience and enjoy diminished. It is *our* own life that is passing away, as slippery and elusive as mercury.

To understand time is to be aware of how it operates in our lives, for time is a subjective experience, different for everyone. We've all experienced how each minute seems to stretch interminably when we're unhappy or the task at hand is unpleasant; yet we're also aware how fast time races by when we're engaged in a creative and useful project. Most people have also had those moments of total absorption when the clock's minute and hour hands are frozen—all reality compressed into the experience of *now.*

While it's true that we all have the same twenty-four hours available to us in each day, we can manipulate our perception of time in order to alter our relationship to it. Dead and boring time can be revived by the creation of a deadline; and the pressure of an unyielding deadline is often relieved by the promise of a vacation to follow.

Time, like money, is valuable precisely because it *is* limited; we are all allotted a finite amount of it. Gold would have little value as a standard for currency if we could pick it from trees. And even if, like old King Midas, everything we touched turned to gold, we still wouldn't be truly happy unless we could pursue our lives—all of our minutes and hours—in creative and productive ways. Even if our time on earth were unlimited, we would still need to use it well in order for it not to lose its value. Only by putting the limited time we have to good use, can we find success and satisfaction in our lives.

Time is like the tons of cement that turn over and over in a concrete mixer. The cement exists only as potential until the operator opens the chute and lets it pour out into a form where it can harden into something useful. Time wasted is the concrete that never gets poured or that gets poured from the chute but finds no form to contain it. We can prosper to the extent that we learn to shape our lives within the limitations of time, because it is only in the good use of time that we are able to take charge of ourselves—and to express the genius that is within us in tangible ways that will help other people and bring joy and satisfaction to our own lives. In learning time management skills, we discover strategies for developing new commands and responses that give us more hours in every day.

One of the best strategies for giving form to our time is to establish long- and short-term goals for ourselves. What is it we hope to accomplish? What steps need to be taken today to fulfill tomorrow's goal? Each day, make a list. Use every minute because if you don't, you'll lose it! And the time you lose today, like darling Clementine, is gone forever.

When you rule your mind, you rule your world.

Bill Provost

Selling is a business that depends on a positive mental attitude for success. According to most experts in the field, a positive self-image is a key element of good salesmenship. One sales expert in the real estate field, Floyd Wickman, states that believing in yourself is the most important link in the chain of success. It can be simply stated in the words: "If anyone can, I can."

A positive attitude toward life is difficult for some people to accept. To some, it seems unrealistic. These sceptics find it hard to believe that positive thinkers can do most anything they set out to do. However, the real essence of the concept of self-belief is that with a positive attitude everything can be done better. This means that your chance for success in any situation is greater if you focus your mind on the positive, if you look for solutions rather than allowing negative thinking to affect your decision-making. As another sales expert, Zig Ziglar, says: "Your business is never really good or bad out there. It's either good or bad right between your two ears."

In our interactions with others, we are all involved in being a salesman practically every day of our lives. Our "customers" are family members, teachers, co-workers, and friends. Often we must "sell" someone close to us on an idea or a request, and its frustrating when we fail to sell our point of view. The challenge is to learn how to win and get what we want, thereby maintaining control of our world.

Zig Ziglar describes the most essential component of successful selling as the ability to understand and meet the other person's needs. "You can get everything in life you want if you will just help enough people get what *they* want," he says. However, to be able to listen to the needs of others and properly interpret them depends to a great extent on the right mental attitude. We not only need to feel good about ourselves, we must be willing to want to help other people and give them what they need.

Mary Kay Ash, founder of Mary Kay Cosmetics, is probably one of the most remarkable success stories of our time. Since 1963, her company has grown from a modest storefront beginning in Dallas to an international multimillion dollar operation with a sales force numbering over 200,000. Her approach to management is based on meeting the needs of others, or as expressed in the Golden Rule, to "Do unto others as you would have them do unto you." With well-grounded Christian values contributing significantly to her business philosophy, she also asks everyone in her organization to focus on meeting the needs of others as their top priority.

It's essential to control the impulse to ask "What's in it for me?" before taking action. Selfishness overlooks a key principle to success as a salesman: that of helping others. By observing and analyzing what makes successful people successful, a clear pattern emerges. First of all, they meet the needs of others because they are sold on themselves. Then, by subordinating their own selfish motives to others' needs, they are able to successfully negotiate whatever it is in life they choose. Just as with the successful men and women we study, our success will be proportionate to the number of people we have helped to grow and prosper. And by following the Golden Rule, we will not only attain whatever we wish but in the process we are bound to enrich the lives of everyone around us.

WEEK TWENTY : LAW C

Happiness comes from spiritual wealth not material wealth.

Years ago, there was a television series called "The Millionaire." Every week some deserving person would receive a cashier's check for a million dollars from an unknown benefactor. The recipient of the check could keep the money and spend it any way he wanted on the condition that he never revealed the source. Each week the recipient faced many challenges to his agreement with the benefactor. Quite a few times the recipient had to return the money.

Hollywood has made movies demonstrating that true happiness does not come from material wealth. The movie "Money Grows on Trees" concerned a family that suddenly became rich when they discovered that one of the trees in their yard grew money. In the course of the film, the family faced many difficulties because of the money tree.

These are fictional examples of people who did not find happiness from the acquisition of great wealth. But what about real life? There have been accounts of people who have become instant millionaires by winning the lottery. When asked how their lives had changed since winning the money, some of them responded that life had become more complicated. They had all the money they could desire, but instead of finding happiness, new problems had arisen.

In all of these accounts, fictional and real, there seems to be a missing link. If spiritual wealth has not been developed, no amount of money will make us happy. Spiritual wealth gives us faith. It gives us love. It gives us wisdom. Spiritual wealth leads to happiness because it guides us into loving relationships; it helps us restore friendships that have been damaged.

It is easy to determine how wealthy we are materially. To determine how wealthy we are spiritually, we need to look at our lives. What are our relationships like? Have we learned how to accept others for who and what they are without reservation? Have we learned how to forgive and forget wrongs done to us? Do we value life—all life and the many forms it assumes? The answers to these questions give us a fair estimate of the quality of our spiritual wealth.

Spiritual wealth leads to true happiness because with it, we have a resource that will never run dry. Material wealth is dependent on many factors that sometimes are outside our control. Spiritual wealth is totally within our control. We are the ones who determine how much or how little we have of it in our lives. If we take inventory and find ourselves lacking in spiritual wealth, it is up to us to draw on that great resource within us to replenish the supply. We have within us all we need to make our lives prosperous and happy; we have the ability to love and to be loved; we have the ability to enjoy life to the fullest no matter what is going on around us.

Not that material comfort can't be a positive force in our lives. With it we never need to worry about going hungry or paying our bills or educating our children. If the economy is strong, we can depend on our material wealth to be our security. But by working to develop our spiritual wealth, we never need to worry about our inner security. Spiritual wealth is always there to serve us. It is our "blank check" that will be honored anytime. If we need wisdom, it is to that bank we go. If we lose all our financial resources, our spiritual wealth will help us recover and recoup our losses. With spiritual wealth as the foundation and security for our lives, we gain a deep, abiding peace that can't be obtained with material wealth alone. In the process we gain true happiness.

WEEK TWENTY : LAW D

Once a word has been allowed to escape, it cannot be recalled.

Many times we say something in anger and then wish we could take it back. But unfortunately, once spoken, words can never be erased. Anger is an emotion that often leads to sadness, hurt and even violence. And anger is most often vented in two ways—physically and through words. A boy, angry over what should have been a simple difference of opinion, told a close friend "I hate you." Once he calmed down, he regretted having told his good friend he hated him; he realized that people have a right to different viewpoints. The trouble was, even though his friend accepted his apology, their relationship had lost something. They were no longer completely relaxed and happy in each other's company. The element of total trust was no longer there.

Sometimes something we say is overheard or repeated. This can cause a great hurt, both to the person directly affected by what you said and to you yourself. It might be something you consider minor. "Carol's new hairstyle looks terrible on her" may be an idle opinion, not meant to do harm. But what if Carol is told what you said? She may be hurt. She may worry that her friends and classmates think her new hairdo is unattractive. You've made a friend miserable. She may be so unhappy she'll wear her hair in another style even though she loved the one you disliked. If only you hadn't made that unkind comment! If only you could take it back! But you can't. It's too late. The damage is done.

You can avoid this type of situation, however, by following one very simple rule: Always think before you speak. Think about the words that are about to issue from your mouth. When a friend asks, "Do you like Carol's new hairdo?" take that important pause to think out your answer. You don't really care for the style. And you don't want to lie. So you smile just a bit, and say: "I'm not used to it yet. Ask me in two weeks." You haven't lied nor have you said a hurtful thing.

Get in the habit of thinking before you speak. You'll never regret it.

WEEK TWENTY : LAW E

By giving, you grow.

After serving for more than eighteen years in the U.S. Army, Sam was dishonorably discharged for drinking and fighting. Depressed and unable to even imagine himself holding a steady job, he soon exhausted the little he had managed to save during his Army career and became a "street person."

"Living on the streets was worse than Vietnam," Sam recalls. "At least in Vietnam you usually knew who your enemy was. On the streets, you never knew who might knock you out and steal your shoes right off your feet!"

Early one afternoon, while waiting for lunch to be served at a church-run center, Sam answered a call for volunteers to help move some furniture and roll up a rug that needed replacing. It was the first time he'd done anything for anyone but himself in quite some time. It felt good.

As he was leaving the building after lunch, Sam noticed a heavy growth of moss on the roof that threatened to damage the shingles. He volunteered to remove it. "You're welcome to help, but you know we can't pay you," the supervisor said. Sam went ahead with the work anyway, again experiencing an unexpected good feeling.

Sam developed the habit of offering his services whenever he heard of a job he thought he could do. It wasn't long before the center needed a volunteer typist. Sam had learned to type in the Army and offered his services if someone would help him purchase a pair of reading glasses. Money was found to pay for the glasses and Sam became an enthusiastic office volunteer.

Soon after he began working in the office, Sam moved from the streets to a spare bedroom in the home of one of his co-workers. Then, without his asking for it, the manager of the center offered Sam a small salary and increased his responsibilities in the office. Another co-worker offered Sam a good used automobile for a reasonable price, with payments he could easily afford.

Today, Sam manages a community food closet operated by the same organization to which he first volunteered his services. He rents his own apartment and is planning to marry.

Sam believes that the positive changes in his life started when the people at the center began to believe in him. Others believed in Sam, it's true, but it seems clear that Sam was the one who took the first step. With his first gift of willing service, Sam began to establish himself in the creative, prospering flow of abundant life.

We can all experience a similar reward, regardless of our circumstances. No matter how well or how poorly our lives seem to be going, we can always become part of a greater flow of good and increase our awareness of our own worth by doing something more than we have to do—by giving of ourselves.

WEEK TWENTY-ONE : LAW A

Enthusiasm facilitates achievement.

George Joe was a high school student in a town in Northwest Central Texas, an area famous for its love of high school football. In small schools, there aren't enough players to field separate teams for defense, offense, and special teams so they must do double or even triple duty. George Joe did quadruple duty. He was the quarterback on offense, running and passing the ball expertly; a corner back on defense; kick returner on receiving teams; and punter on kicking teams. Even more remarkable was the fact that he was usually the smallest man on the field, standing barely five feet six inches and weighing no more than one hundred forty pounds. He didn't possess great speed, although he was quick and agile.

How did a small boy hold so many jobs on a team that had a history of winning year after year? He had a great love for the game and competition and he had great enthusasm. He put every ounce of his energy and ability into every play and he did it joyfully; he was fifty percent inspiration and fifty percent perspiration and a thrill to watch.

The story is told of a young boy who wanted to be a radio announcer and entertainer, but he stuttered so badly it was painful to listen to his attempts to carry on a conversation, let alone hear him perform in public or in a broadcast. It seemed impossible that he could make a career in radio, and no one gave him much hope but he was not to be denied by the lack of confidence of others. He had read that a very famous person in history with a similar problem had gone to the beach, filled his mouth with pebbles and shouted into the surf until he overcame his disability. Although this young man had no beach or pebbles near at hand, he filled his mouth with marbles and worked day after day until he, too, overcame his problem. Dedication and enthusiasm overcame the difficulty he faced and today he is a successful entertainer on national television.

One of our most respected and famous former presidents, Theodore Roosevelt, had a vision of American ships being able to go from the Pacific to the Atlantic ocean and back without having to make the arduous trip around the tip of the South American continent. There were many difficulties to overcome. First was the opposition of his own countrymen who lacked the vision to foresee what a great boon to shipping the proposed canal would be. Then there was the opposition of other world leaders who didn't wish to see the United States in control of such a project and the South American leaders who opposed the intrusion of the United States in their domain. Teddy Roosevelt was not deterred by any of those problems. He negotiated with the governments of Columbia and Panama and gained the right to build a canal across the Isthmus of Panama from Colon on the Atlantic coast to Panama City on the Pacific coast. The problems did not end there. The whole effort was almost brought down by mosquitos carrying yellow fever.

Teddy tackled the problem in typical fashion. Medicine was found to fight the disease and insecticides to fight the insects. He wanted the canal to be a showplace to attract tourists as well as shipping and he realized that people will not visit places where their health is at risk. When it was completed, the Panama Canal was a model of sanitation, a tribute to the enthusiasm and determination of Theodore Roosevelt.

The boy who loved football, the boy who dreamed of becoming a radio announcer and a president of the United States understood, and profited from, an important law of life: that enthusiasm facilitates achievement.

You have the most powerful weapons on earth—love and prayer.

In the New Testament, Jesus admonishes his followers to "become as little children" and to "love your enemies." There are probably no two commands more difficult to follow in today's world, confronted as we often are with our own negative thoughts, whether in business, within our family, or among friends.

It's so easy to look at the bad example set by others and shrug off our Christian responsibility to "love one another," even as God has loved us. We use the excuse that if no one else follows Christian principles, why should we? And yet, throughout history, it is impossible not to notice the success of those who have acted on the courage of their convictions to "love thy neighbor as thyself."

There are some in modern times who, if asked how to handle a difficult relationship, respond by saying, "Just tell them you love them." Mother Theresa, as she lives out these spiritual principles of love in her own life, declares that "love for God is love in action." She states that "loving Him through words is not enough," and has shown her love for God through a lifetime of dedicated work with the poor.

But what really sets the Mother Theresas of the world apart is their ability to enjoy the "fruits of the Spirit" as described by St. Paul after his conversion to Christianity on the road to Damascus. Albert Schweitzer wrote in 1929, in *The Mysticism of Paul the Apostle,* that the highest proof of the Spirit is love.

As the anthropologist, Margaret Mead, states in her book *Twentieth Century Faith,* each man is indeed his brother's keeper and the need to love our enemies ought to be given new scientific meaning. Only if we are able to love those who are our enemies, in the sense of cherish and protect, can we hope to protect the lives of men and the life of the world.

Once we understand how to express this love to others through our own lives, we will be better able to direct our prayers to make God's priorities our own. As we learn to share and give and care, love can only multiply. A person who knows how to love is never lonely or alone. In this sense, the power of love is a true weapon against harm. As a friend of mine is fond of saying," Love given is love received," and happiness is a by-product of that kind of love. This law of life, when put to use through prayer, can guide us in fulfilling our every aspiration, as well as enriching the lives of those around us.

No one can make you feel inferior without your consent.

Eleanor Roosevelt

A thermometer is a long, thin glass tube filled with mercury—a simple device designed to give a reading of the temperature of its surrounding environment. When the environment becomes warmed, the mercury rises; when it becomes cooler, the mercury descends. At a glance you can know how warm or cold the air is. Some thermometers can tell you whether your body is functioning at a normal temperature; others, if your food has been properly cooked.

Unfortunately, many people operate like a thermometer. Instead of mercury, it is their self-esteem that rises and falls according to the "temperature" of other people's opinions of them. When others think highly of them, they feel good about themselves. When they are criticized, their opinion of themselves drops to a low, cold level. Eleanor Roosevelt stated an important truth to remember, "No one can make you feel inferior without your consent." You would do well to think carefully about those words. You are not obligated to let the world decide how you are going to feel about yourself. It's up to you to judge yourself.

Most of us were raised giving others a great deal of control over our feelings. But, as we grow, it's important to learn that how we feel about ourselves, in spite of the opinions of others, is an essential ingredient of a happy life. If you give people the power to set the thermostat of your self-esteem, you will always be at the mercy of their opinions. Your happiness will depend on many conditions over which you have no healthy inner control.

How you feel about yourself determines to a large extent your experience of life. You cannot afford to surrender control of these feelings to the whim of others. If you know a person who is constantly miserable for no apparent reason, you can be certain that he or she has relinquished power over their feelings. Like a thermometer, they simply reflect the world's opinions. They have handed over to others the power to judge themselves, and this state of powerlessness creates a high level of tension and anxiety.

Unlike the thermometer, you can take your own "temperature." You can feel good about yourself and your life despite what others think. No one knows you or your capabilities as well as you do. Therefore, only you should be in charge of how you feel about yourself.

Be open enough to learn from people but never forget to stay in control of your feelings about yourself and your estimate of your worth. What works wonderfully well for a thermometer can prove to be disastrous for you. If you find that you have put someone else in charge of your self-esteem, begin making a simple statement like the following to set you free: "Today, I feel good about myself despite what others say, think, or do. I am the master of my feelings and no one will relieve me of that authority today!"

When you live from the center of your own being, you'll find life becomes infinitely more productive and joyful at the circumference.

WEEK TWENTY-ONE : LAW D

Who gossips to you will gossip of you.

Does it seem interesting to you when someone tells you something about another person? It is human to feel this way. But you might be wise to consider what the person is saying.

"Did you know Martha's grandmother is coming to live with her family?" may be a good piece of information. It might start you thinking about the way this will affect the lifestyle of your friend and her family and could open the door to asking yourself how you might be of help. This is not gossip. But what if the information-giver goes on to relate, "I heard no one else in the family would take her because she's a trouble-maker and very difficult to live with." That statement is gossip! To believe it and, even worse, to repeat it, will help make the situation more difficult for everyone involved.

But there is more to the conversation than the unfortunate and unkind gossip about Martha's grandmother. The person who gossips to you about other people will also gossip to others about you. It may be something you told the person assuming that such a personal matter would be confidential. It may be something you said which the person has added on to or changed. It might be something someone told her about you. It could be something completely made-up by the gossip spreader. Gossip can cause serious problems. It can be the basis for heartaches, worry and misunderstandings.

The word "gossip" is not an ancient word, but what it stands for, a person who habitually reveals personal or sensational information, true or untrue, has always existed. You would do well to avoid the habitual gossiper. You do not need such a person in your life.

It is vital for you to realize what a few words can do to a person's life. Saying "Joy is such a nice person, I hope you get to know her better," is the type of statement that brings good things to the one it is about. But to say, "I've never cared for Joy; I even heard that she shoplifts," can affect the way other people think about Joy regardless of any truth or untruth the statement may contain. And the really frightening thing is, the person who spreads a story like this about Joy may also be telling tales just as cruel about you.

You can help stop at least some gossip by the way you react when someone tells you something which falls into the gossip category. "Oh, I prefer to accept Joy by her actions as I know them," followed by walking away, will let the gossiping person know that you are not interested in her stories. It may also set an example some of your friends will follow. If only everyone would take this type of action, gossip would cease to exist. Unfortunately, this is not likely to happen. But you could make an important dent in the popularity of gossip in your own group of friends.

Beware of talking beyond a "hello" to someone who gossips. He or she may misinterpret anything you say.

Suppose you have a neighbor who is a salesman and on the road a great deal. A gossip may ask, "Do you know Mr. Jones?" and you might reply, "Not very well, he's away from home a great deal." The next day you may hear that the latest "gossip" involves the Jones family and how Mr. Jones hardly ever bothers to come home! That's the way it often works. Be wise. Beware the gossip.

WEEK TWENTY-ONE : LAW E

Find a need and fill it.

"I'm too young really to do anything important to help people," fifteen-year-old Beth told her mother when it was suggested that she find a way to be of help to someone in need. The mother asked Beth to look around her and, when she did, she found someone in need right next door! Her neighbor, Mrs. Mills, was caring for her elderly, bedridden mother at home. A widow, with only a small fixed income, Mrs. Mills couldn't afford to hire anyone to help her and relied on friends to stay with her mother when she went on necessary errands. "Mrs. Mills never has a chance to just do what she really wants to do," Beth told her mother. "Do you think I could learn how to help with a bedpan and things like that? That would give Mrs. Mills a little time for herself."

Beth took on this volunteer duty, and it was a joy for Mrs. Mills to have an hour or so of leisure time. A walk, a visit to the library, a bite to eat in the coffee shop—these relaxed moments revived the caretaker. And the elderly lady enjoyed the chatter and giggles of her young friend. Beth had found a need and filled it. She felt good about herself.

These are needs everywhere. Last summer Millie, age eighteen, helped with the noon meals at the Bread of Life kitchen that provides free meals for those in need. Brad, nineteen, mows the lawns in summer and shovels the snow in winter for two elderly neighbors. Billie and Mary Ann are candy stripers at the hospital.

Needs come in all varieties, large and small. An elderly shut-in may simply need someone to listen. A young mother may have spent a sleepless night with an ill baby and a volunteer sitter can give her a chance to take a much needed nap. Maybe your grandmother needs a little more of your time. Maybe you've been so busy lately you haven't spent some special time with your father. Maybe a pet hasn't received the human attention it needs. As you walk down the street you are likely to see many needs you can fill. You could carry the bag of groceries for the elderly lady. See the young mother trying to unlock the car while holding a wiggling baby in her arms? You could either help with the key or hold the baby. See that man squinting at a small piece of paper, seemingly searching for a number on the nearest building? You know the street; you could fill his need. No need is too small to fill.

Sometimes a need is so close to you, you may overlook it. Mother looks tired tonight. Couldn't you take over the dishwashing chore? Maybe if you give your dad a big smile, he'll lend a hand too. Sometimes just telling someone "I love you" fills a need. Needs are there—tiny, medium and large. Find them and fill them, and you'll feel wonderful!

WEEK TWENTY-TWO : LAW A

If you are facing in the right direction, all you need to do is keep on walking.

Buddhist saying

A long time ago, there lived a young girl who loved to walk in the deep woods surrounding the village in which she lived. She talked to the gray squirrels in the morning and rested on the cool moss in the afternoon. One day, the girl walked deeper into the woods than usual. Soon the sky began to darken, and she realized she was lost. All she could see were giant pines and the top of the highest steeple in her village.

She began to cry as she looked around her. The giant pines hovered close to comfort her. Finally, one of the taller trees spoke to her. "Walk toward the steeple," it said. "Don't take your eyes off the steeple, and soon you'll be home."

So the girl gathered her cape around her, lifted the basket of mushrooms she had picked for dinner, and was on her way. She watched the steeple with urgency, knowing if she walked toward it, she would soon be safe in her bed.

Before long she heard footsteps behind her. She took her eyes from the steeple for a moment to look. There she saw a red fox tiptoeing hungrily behind her. "Little girl," said the fox, "there is a beautiful field of wild violets just over the ridge. If you'll follow me you can take a bouquet to your mamma."

Knowing how much her mamma loved wild violets, she began to run after the fox who had visions of juicy mushrooms dancing in his head. Then, suddenly, the sun went behind a cloud on the horizon; the girl remembered the admonishment of the pine tree to watch the steeple. When she looked up from her new path, she had lost sight of it.

Panic-stricken and lost, the child began to run deeper into the woods. Before she knew it she was again in the circle of protective trees. Recognizing them, she looked up and saw that the steeple was again in her view. Concentrating as hard as she could, she fixed her gaze on the steeple and didn't look away until she was safe in bed at last.

Have you ever had a cherished goal that appeared to be out of reach? Maybe it seemed years away and the direction to travel unclear. For some of us, the path to follow might lead to a new vocation or to money for a child's education. Whatever waits for you at the end of your path, however, the only way to get there is to keep your eyes on your goal. Something may entice you to choose a diversion or an easier path, but the surest path—even if not the quickest or easiest—is the one that leads directly to your goal with the fewest distractions and false starts. Now all you must do is walk, with your eye on that distant sightline.

WEEK TWENTY-TWO : LAW B

No person was ever honored for what he received, but for what he gave.
Calvin Coolidge

In the gospel according to Luke, Jesus said, "Give, and it will be given to you; good measure, pressed down, shaken together, running over, will be put into your lap. For the measure you give will be the measure you get back" *(Lk, 6:38)*. Jesus stated a fundamental law of life that has been recognized by most great spiritual leaders as well as by most truly successful men and women.

If you love the work you do, you are going to put all of yourself into it, giving freely of energy and of your talents. On the other hand, if you're there only for the pay check, only to do what you believe you're getting paid to do and no more, chances are you'll grow to despise your job.

Bob was such a man. For eight hours a day, five days a week, year after year, he pulled down a salary while putting forth as little effort as possible. He always seemed to be tired and discontented, and he blamed his job for many of his problems.

One thing Bob loved to do, however, was watch his little girl play softball. When he was offered the chance to coach her Little League team, he eagerly grabbed it. Although coaching the girls took a great deal of time and commitment, Bob didn't mind. He said the hours he spent with the team energized him. The girls ended up taking a first-place trophy and Bob received an outpouring of praise from the parents who were amazed by his commitment.

Fortunately, the story doesn't end there. At the prompting of his concerned wife, Bob decided to seek spiritual counseling about the problem in his professional life. The counselor suggested he begin to embrace his job with the same enthusiasm that he was pouring into coaching the girls' softball team. He reluctantly agreed to give it a try.

To his surprise, Bob began noticing things at work he could do to make the day more interesting. He began to take an interest in the lives of his fellow employees. He challenged himself to improve the ways in which he was doing his job. He began to pretend he was actually the owner of the plant instead of just another cog in the machine. He began making suggestions to his superiors on how things could be run more efficiently in his department. And, to his great surprise, he found himself thinking about ways to improve his work after hours! Each day now he awoke with a sense of enthusiasm instead of dull despair.

Remember that merely putting your time into something doesn't mean you're giving yourself to it. Dedicate your attention, your interest, your love, your imagination, your creativity and you can transform an undesirable condition into something that gives back to you, in "good measure, pressed, shaken together, running over. For the measure you give will be the measure you get back." This is a law of life that will work for you in the same way it worked for Bob and for millions of other people who have discovered it. Think less about what you can get and more about what you can give and your life may take on a luster you never dreamed possible.

WEEK TWENTY-TWO : LAW C

World progress needs entrepreneurs.

If you desire to become a great person, it's important to ask yourself what it means to be great. Perhaps no single definition can encompass the meaning of greatness. But it does seem that the great person is one who has expanded the limits of human possibility. This stretching can be accomplished through a great work of industry or art or music or literature; through political or social reform; or through humanitarian or spiritual service. Greatness comes in many forms, and the great person travels beyond the normal range of human behavior to forge a new thought or act or concept or creation that ultimately serves humankind.

A great person creates something that is new in some way. What does it take to be a creator, an innovator? First, you must recognize that you have within you the power to create. We all have that power. In fact, we are always creating. With every act, every word, every thought, we create and build our lives. You create not only your own life but your environment and your world. However, to create something new, you must take responsibility for your own creations, for what you have done and what you hope to do. Otherwise you will see yourself as a victim of circumstances. Greatness will now flow from the person who once believed he was a victim.

To be great you must acknowledge your power to create—a power you are always using, for good or ill. To recognize that you create your life, hour by hour, every step of the way, is to be responsible for your life.

From this moment on, you can take charge of your own life. The past is the past; you can't change what was. But the present and the future—how you respond to the conditions and the events in your life—are yours to create. You can make choices that will begin to change them. Being responsible is acknowledging your power to respond usefully to what is. Your response to what is, ultimately determines what will be.

To be great means to choose beneficial responses that move you beyond the limitations of the past, move you beyond victimhood to the recognition of mastery. To be great means to become all that you can be and to share your talents with your world.

To be great means to move beyond the possession of wealth or fame. It means to create, to become more helpful than you imagined you could be. The price of this greatness is responsibility for your response to life, for the beauty of your thoughts every minute and every hour of every day, for knowing that your response is the very power that changes your life, perhaps greatly.

WEEK TWENTY-TWO : LAW D

Expect the best; convert problems into opportunities.
Dennis Waitley

Winter storms can be dangerous, there's no doubt about that. With freezing temperatures, snow, sleet and wind, icy conditions on the roads pose a threatening challenge to even the most experienced driver. Sometimes car batteries freeze up and it's hard to get the car started or snow has fallen that must be plowed away before cars can pass. Schools will often be closed to keep the students at home and safe from the hazardous roads. Yet it is precisely those conditions which make the schools close that can make most kids squeal with delight at the prospect of an unexpected holiday in the middle of the week. The fun-loving person can find myriad ways to play in the fluffy white stuff whether they sled, slide, or ski on it; roll it into balls for throwing; or into boulders for building. To the expectant student, who has followed the weather reports more faithfully than a meteorologist, a snowy day is no problem. An optimistic expectation has converted the problem into an opportunity for enjoyment.

What is a problem? One dictionary defines a problem as "a question proposed for a solution." A problem that occurs in your life, then, is simply a question that life asks you. It is like a jigsaw puzzle that has just been taken from its box. There are three thousand small pieces, each with the potential of joining together to complete a pattern or picture. The pieces mean nothing strewn about on the table, unconnected. It is the fun of the jigsaw puzzle to find the relationship between the pieces and fit them together. Many times you'll discover that you enjoy the search and discovery of various pieces more than the finished image, because the process is as important as the resolution of the problem the puzzle poses.

There are circumstances, however, in which a problem may cause difficulty. For example, solving a challenging engineering problem on a multimillion dollar building project can be more stressful than balancing your checkbook. You have deadlines to meet and you feel a pressure to perform well because your job, future well-being and the safety of many people depend on you. These stressers can make a problem seem like something larger than life, something you aren't sure you can tackle; you may question your ability to meet the challenge set before you. Doubt, uncertainty, and a sense of inadequacy can make a simple problem snowball into something more complex than it is. When an avalanche of negative emotions threatens, it is impossible to experience a ski slope as fun to traverse. A molehill becomes the entire mountain and an obstacle rather than a challenge to your ability and skill. Solutions elude you and your performance falters not because the problems are problems but because anxiety got the best part of your mind.

Save the best for the best by expecting the best! Your positive outlook opens the door to opportunity that fear might otherwise lock shut. Your hopeful vision asserts potential in the face of limitation. Your trusting patience perseveres when doubt would have you quit. As you look forward you see much that is worth looking forward to.

Helen Keller had a lot of problems but she never allowed negative emotions to sink her into a pit of self-pity. Imagine the optimistic expectation and hope she must have had to break out of a dark and silent prison to become self-expressive and great. She kept a high, hopeful inner eye on a light which guided her to overcome incredible physical handicaps to design a life more creative than many people with full sight and hearing.

Look for the best of what is possible in every situation and you will turn any problem you face into an opportunity to be great. Your fear will diminish and your success as a person will increase.

Give blessings.

In this life we all have many challenges to face and to overcome. It is almost as if we were going to a great training school that lasts all of our lives. As soon as one challenge is met, there seems to be another waiting in the wings. We spend a great part of our lives just trying to solve our own problems.

But let's assume that we receive everything we want in time—then what? The law of blessedness tells us there is another step to take. After we have been blessed and our problems have been solved, we will be in a position to involve ourselves more deeply in life by blessing others. When we are ready to be a blessing, we find that there are many ways in which we can bless others. We can give material goods to others and we can also give them the benefit of our experience. People who have had challenges with alcohol and drugs often involve themselves in helping others who are experiencing the same difficulties. In every area of the human experience there are those who find themselves able and willing to be a blessing to others.

Obviously, there is not one person alive who is totally problem and confusion free. Through challenges, we continue to grow and mature all our lives. However, there is a point where, with enough of our own problems solved, we are ready to become involved in helping others. Many people find that they receive more benefit from being a blessing than from being blessed. Oftentimes, being a blessing requires nothing more than a word of encouragement and hope to someone who is filled with discouragement and despair.

The law of blessedness tells us that a very real part of our life's work is to help make other people's burdens easier to bear. We open ourselves to rich blessings because we know that those blessings will go out to help other people. We want blessings of good to come to us and we want blessings of good to go to everyone else. We give thanks for being blessed and we also give thanks for the opportunity to be a blessing.

WEEK TWENTY-THREE : LAW A

The seeds of destruction are sown in anger.

The high school students lifted their heads from their books when they heard Tracy in the hall yelling at Mr. Morehead, the assistant principal. Tracy had been accused of stealing an expensive art book and she was extremely upset over the false accusation. Ms. Taylor, the art teacher, believed Tracy had stolen the book because she had been the last person seen reading it. Tracy, stung by the teacher's words, screamed at her that she'd put the book back on the shelf, but Ms. Taylor refused to believe her. The more Ms. Taylor refused to believe her, the more Tracy lost control. She began to swear at the older woman.

"I won't stand for this abuse," Ms. Taylor had said, picking up the telephone to call Mr. Morehead. "You'll stay for detention all this week after school."

Tracy had a record of getting into trouble at school. But this time she had done nothing wrong.

"You are in deep trouble, young lady," Mr. Morehead said quietly. "No one talks to me or any of the teachers this way and gets away with it."

The question to ask ourselves is: How could Tracy have avoided needless trouble? Although it is a natural reaction to be angry when unfairly treated, it only makes matters worse to act out our anger. It's better to remain as calm as possible so we can examine all the options open to us. If Tracy had remained calm, she would have remembered that a very quiet, studious boy was sitting in the back of the room who could have been a witness. By talking calmly and rationally with Ms. Taylor and Mr. Morehead, she would have stood a much better chance of convincing them that she was innocent. Also, by maintaining her calm, Tracy would have heard Ms. Taylor more clearly. The art teacher told her she was very upset because so many art books were disappearing. Although it wasn't right for Ms. Taylor to accuse Tracy, a little understanding on Tracy's part might have helped ease the situation. When we can redirect our angry feelings into positive actions that help us find new ways to deal with situations, we're no longer needlessly wasting our energy. A calm Tracy could have checked at the library to see if the book was there, or she might have asked the studious boy or other art students if they had seen the book.

Angry words and actions never serve a useful purpose because they set up a chain of negative reactions that result in a breakdown of communication. Not that it's easy to remain level headed when we're falsely accused or even when we've made a mistake. But it makes an already bad situation worse when we don't. Once anger takes over, common sense and reasonableness fly out the window. Everyone ends up hurt and seeds are planted that sprout into negative feelings and consequences that are hard to turn around.

WEEK TWENTY-THREE : LAW B

You make yourself and others suffer just as much when you take offense as when you give offense.

Ken Keyes

Have you ever walked into a room where everyone stopped talking and you were certain they were talking about you? Or you looked over at a group of people sitting together and they started whispering? You were convinced they were saying something about your clothes or your manners. How we react to these situations can either bring suffering to all involved or peace and understanding.

If we are thin-skinned, the slightest remark will hurt us to the core of our being. We'll see offenses where none were intended and become paranoid in our thinking. We will think we're justified in accusing our accusers. If we tend to be quiet and introspective, we will sulk alone and nurse our self-pity. While we're immersed in our miserable isolation, we'll fail to see that we are not the only ones suffering.

"How can the other person be suffering when I'm the one injured?" you reason. When we fail to rise above our own paranoia and self-pity, we cut ourselves off from others. When we see insults where none were intended, we are falsely accusing others, and after a while no one will want to be around us. Because of the negative energy we carry inside, we're a destructive storm waiting to happen. The friendships we could have had will never materialize.

The person who *knows* his own worth always tries to act in a way that brings harmony and peace to his relationships. He does not see insults where none were intended. He accepts criticism for what it's worth. Instead of allowing himself to be overcome with negative feelings, he will check to see if there's any truth in what was said. If there is, he'll try to change his behavior. Paranoia will not be a problem, because his self-image will be strong.

The person who knows his internal worth and value knows how to respond to the people in his life. He treats them with dignity and respect. He is kind and considerate. When faced with someone's bad behavior, he carefully weighs the situation to see what can be gained in a positive way by his response. Sometimes no response is the best response. The person who has a solid knowledge of his internal worth will generally find the appropriate words to say.

On this great journey through life, our relationships can be rewarding. We are free to choose how to react to any given situation. We can either choose to take offense, and thereby lose an opportunity to shed light on a situation, or we can respond in a way that spreads love, harmony and understanding.

WEEK TWENTY-THREE : LAW C

There is no difficulty that enough love will not conquer.

Emmett Fox

On his seventh birthday, Simon Evans adopted Sam, an eighteen-month-old gray cat, from the animal pound. Sam had been very badly treated for most of his life (his master had been a drug addict whose behavior was unpredictible and often cruel) and the effects on the cat became obvious once Simon got him home. Sam was nervous and frightened, and spent most of his time hiding behind the dishwasher.

Simon was very wise for his age and persisted with his new friend, being very gentle and loving with him. Gradually, this unconditional love began to pay dividends. Sam stayed out for longer periods of time. He was still jumpy and nervous, and would eat only with Simon guarding his back, but as the weeks progressed, the boy's love turned the little feline into a more trusting and responsive creature.

Constant, unconditional love will communicate itself to even the most badly abused. Love is the one power that eventually can cut through all obstacles. Pupils in a class taught by a friendly and warm teacher, who is understanding and patient, respond far more positively than pupils in a class taught by a tyrant. Grades are better and there is laughter, joy and a willingness to learn.

Loving, kind, nuturing behavior is our natural state. We were born with these positive social and moral gifts, but over the years we have assumed many defense mechanisms that block our true selves. Love, of the type offered by Simon to Sam, is the great healer. The pure and unconditional love of which Emmett Fox speaks is the type employed by young Simon toward Sam, his cat, and it is this love that Teilhard de Chardin had in mind when he wrote: "Someday, after we have mastered the winds, the waves, the tides and gravity, we shall harness the energies of Love. Then, for the second time in history, man will have discovered fire."

WEEK TWENTY-THREE : LAW D

The wise person looks within his heart and finds eternal peace.
Hindu proverb

Is it possible to find peace in our rapidly changing world, arrayed as it is with pleasures and pains, distractions and attractions? Can you be a part of the world, deal with its complexity which impinges upon you from every side, and still find peace in your heart? Is it only in removing yourself from the world to some remote mountaintop or desert that you could look into your unperturbed heart and find peace? Is peace possible only in a place where you never have to deal with challenging people or situations? Or where there are no conflicts, no misunderstandings, annoyances, needs, pressures or disappointments? Or does the wise person find perpetual peace even amidst the difficulties of life by simply not allowing his heart to be touched by them, by not caring or feeling?

Withdrawing from the world either physically or emotionally is not the wise person's path to eternal peace. For we are placed in this world to deal with it, not escape it; to integrate ourselves with it, not separate into a fragment apart from it; and to find a way to be of benefit and service to the world, not to shun it or harden ourselves to it. However, if you are willing to be present in the world and involved with it, it will inevitably impact your emotions in ways which will not always feel peaceful. We have both positive and negative feelings in our hearts, and our life experiences tend to stir up both. How, then, is it possible to find peace within your heart?

We tend to feel at peace when things are under control. And we do the best we can to control or manage our lives according to our ideas of order. But if inner peace depends on that control, your peace of mind will frequently be at risk. Can you control the economy or energy supplies? Another person's behavior or actions? The choices and destinies of loved ones or others upon whom you depend? When you take a good look, there is very little outside yourself that you can control. Therefore, real peace must be an inside job.

A person is truly wise who knows that the heart is the *only* place it is possible to find lasting peace. The changeability from one day to the next of your personal world or the world at large makes it an unreliable source of peace. Try going away to that mountaintop or to any place that seems serene and carefree to you, and you'll find yourself disturbed over something—a memory, a concern about a current situation, a fear about the future, or a mere gnat flying around—if you don't realize that peace dwells at your center.

This kind of peace has nothing to do with the fluctuation of life events that bring elation or grief with the passing of time. Rather, it has to do with the state of being that may be found within your heart of hearts, in the "still point of the turning world" of which the poet T.S. Eliot wrote, where you are one with the very essence of life. Webster defines essence as the "permanent as contrasted with the accidental element of being; the real, or ultimate nature of a thing, as opposed to its existence." In the changing, often confusing fortunes of time when you know and act from what is essential, you will experience the peace of this unchanging state.

Eliot wrote, "At the still point, there the dance is. . . . Except for the point, the still point,/ There would be no dance, and there is only the dance." The dance of life continually shifts its tempo, rhythm and form. As you move with it, you will find yourself facing situations you have never imagined. That is how the dance carries you beyond your limited ideas of who you are and what you are capable of dealing with. Practice looking within your heart, not for emotion but to identify yourself with the still point of your essence and, regardless of "accidental elements" existing around you, you will find peace.

WEEK TWENTY-THREE : LAW E

Be prepared.
Motto of the Boy Scouts of America

It has been said that order is Heaven's first law. Jesus acknowledged this when He said, "The earth produces of itself, first the blade, then the ear, then the full grain in the ear" *(Mk. 4:28)*. If we are to succeed in life we must bring our methods of operation into an orderly process.

The first step in the order of success is preparedness. Chance favors the prepared. Opportunity knocks at the door many more times than people may realize. If they do not seize the moment, it's because they are not prepared to seize it.

Eleven-year-old Jeremy, however, was ready and eager to seize it. In preparing for a fishing trip to Canada with his father and some of his father's friends, he insisted on buying a heavy-duty rod and reel so he could catch a big fish. Not wanting to dampen the boy's great enthusiasm and knowing he could use the equipment for a deep sea excursion he was planning, the father bought the equipment.

When the other men saw Jeremy's new fishing equipment they all joked with him. "You planning on catching a whale, Jeremy?" one of them asked.

"I'm gonna get me a big pike," he said confidently.

"Well, you could sure get a big pike with that rig," another said, laughing. Jeremy was undaunted by the men's lack of confidence in him.

Four days on the lake produced little for the men and the boy and Jeremy's fishing rig was the butt of many a friendly joke. Then suddenly one of the men shouted, "I have something!" His pole arched and strained; a moment later the pole quickly straightened and the line went limp. The line had broken! The man muttered that he should have come prepared with heavier equipment.

As the fishing party was about to return to the cabin after another day on the lake, Jeremy's line suddenly tightened. At first he thought he had hooked a log beneath the surface of the water. But then the line began to move with a force that almost frightened him. He realized he had hooked his big fish.

Forty-five minutes later he had his pike in the boat—a thirty-two pounder! The men were flabbergasted and envious. Jeremy had taught them all that if you want to catch a big fish, then you had better come prepared.

Far too often people do not prepare themselves for success. While they wish they had it, they put just enough effort into life to get by, thinking that if by chance something big falls their way they'll grab it. But if you're not prepared for success, you'll find it difficult to hold onto the opportunities that come your way. Success demands understanding, fortitude and foresight to bring the blade to the full grain in the ear.

As an exercise, ask yourself from time to time what you are doing to prepare yourself for success. Are you fully committed to it? Are you willing not only to cultivate the soil and plant the seed but also to nurture and care for the tender blade and the young ear as it appears? Are you willing to go the extra mile, willing to give all that the opportunity calls for? Are you willing to stand firm with your convictions, your principles? Are you prepared to stand alone if need be? Have you trained yourself to recognize opportunity when it knocks?

And you never know when it will knock. Opportunity may present itself in a form you aren't looking for. It may seem to require of you more than you want to give. But if your desire is to catch a big fish, you must prepare yourself as Jeremy did to handle that fish when it strikes. Otherwise it will just be the big one that got away.

WEEK TWENTY-FOUR : LAW A

You are on the road to success if you realize that failure is only a detour.

C. Ten Boom

If success were easy, then it would not be true success. Some of history's most successful people have had to cope with failure as a natural off-shoot of the experimental and creative process and they often learned much more from their failures than their successes. Only by taking the attitude that failure is merely a detour on the way to our destination, can one really hope to be a success.

How can we best define success? Does it simply mean that there was a task before us and we accomplished it? If that were true, we could call walking down the driveway and retrieving the mail a success. Thus all minor matters, no matter how trivial, could be defined as successes just so long as they were completed. Yet, success means much more than that. Success comes when we face a challenge, and struggle against odds to succeed. True success often follows a series of failures.

History has shown that many of America's greatest heroes experienced their share of failures. Abraham Lincoln suffered a staggering defeat in the first election he ever entered, and was considered a poor and bumbling speaker. Yet he went on to become one of our greatest presidents, whose speeches are still regarded today as masterpieces of political persuasion. William Faulkner suffered a number of rejections as a young writer by publishers who had no understanding of his innovative narrative style, but despite repeated failures and impoverishment, Faulkner went on to become one of the South's foremost novelists and to win the Nobel Prize for literature. Thomas Edison was another who struggled with failure. Nevertheless, through hard work, through understanding that "failure is only a detour," he invented the electric light bulb, record players and motion pictures, to name only a few of his inventions.

Because learning is a process that often requires failure, failure can be essential to success. It is important to study our failures, to learn from them, and then to make a new attempt. Eventually this process will lead to success. However, if an individual gives up at the first failure, then nothing has been learned. No skill has been gained that improves our subsequent efforts. A person is never defeated by failure so long as he understands that failure should be considered as a natural process leading to a positive conclusion. He can accept it as a mere detour and not a dead end.

Thanksgiving leads to giving and forgiving, and to spiritual growth.

Thanksgiving is the very law of gratitude. Its opposite is fear. Gratitude is the open-hearted, genuine appreciation for what is wonderful in our lives. Fear is the contracting force which takes us out of our own power and makes us the victim of lack. Thaddeus Golas writes in *The Lazy Man's Guide to Enlightenment*, "We think fear is a signal to withdraw when it is really a sign that we are already withdrawing too much."

The Course in Miracles, published by Foundation for Inner Peace, says there are two basic forces in the universe, love and fear. Another way of saying that is thanksgiving and lack. If we recognize this when it is happening, we can ride out the negative current much more easily and find our way back to the positive one through the practice of gratitude.

When was the last time you felt grateful for the simple conveniences of your life? Think about it. There is so much in our lives to be grateful for that we are often blind to it.

Eighty years ago, our forefathers (and mothers) only had outhouses instead of plumbing. Today almost everyone in America has a working bathroom. Fifty years ago it was not uncommon to have the central rooms of a house heated by a pot-bellied stove or a single fireplace, and to close off the other rooms until you had to go to bed. Do you remember when we had feathered mattresses so soft you would sink in the middle? Forget the idea of a posture-pedic bed!

How about washing machines? In most third world countries the idea of a local laundromat is a dream. A recent documentary on current life in Russia showed that the average family shared accommodations with two to three other families in an apartment the size of one of our normal houses. They hand washed clothes in the tub. And the waiting list to get one's own apartment is an average of ten years!

How about the simple aspects of eating? In 1988, a Soviet comedian did a wonderful stand-up routine about "vodka as a way of life" in Moscow using documented statistics. The average Russian man spends forty-five minutes a day standing in line for vodka. The average Russian woman spends four and one half hours a day in line for food staples, *when they are available.* The story of the man from Siberia who went into an American supermarket comes to mind. He broke down and cried at the variety of foods we have within reach of our tables every day.

The law of gratitude and thanksgiving is really an aspect of the universe that deals with energy flow. That is, as one gives out energy it returns to you. This works in almost every department of life. As one gives love, love is magnetized towards you. It may come back in a different form, but it will return when it is given without manipulation.

This law is really about combining the expectations of the mind with the power of the heart. You create a "mold" for something good in your life and with the power of gratitude, good things continue to be magnetized to you.

"Ask and it shall be given you," says Matthew 7:7,8. As you work in this state of thanksgiving you will find that money follows the same law. When one gives a little money, money seems to flow towards you. Have you ever noticed that when we hoard our resources, be it friendship, help, affection, or cash, it stops the flow of the energy circuits?

This is also true with the law of forgiveness. The lack of self-forgiveness in any single area of life brings anger, pain, and illness, festering as a poison inside. Psychologists and sociologists will tell you that the damage from childhood will set patterns into motion which may follow an adult through life, being projected outward, unless forgiveness is attained.

"Dwell not on the past," Eileen Caddy writes in *God Spoke to Me* "from this moment onward you can be an entirely different person, filled with love and understanding, ready with an outstretched hand, uplifted and positive in every thought and deed."

Let us choose our lives with love and gratitude. Let us use the law of thanksgiving to bless ourselves and to make our lives more complete.

WEEK TWENTY-FOUR : LAW C

Give credit and help to all who have helped you.

Edward is the president of a large corporation and he worked hard to reach that position. He speaks as though he has reached a final destination; he refers to himself as a success. It is unfortunate that he doesn't realize success is a journey, not a destination. There are still more steps to be taken in his life. His journey is not over. And even more unfortunate, Edward doesn't see that he is surrounded by successful people, many of whom contributed to his own success.

Millie had to leave school at age sixteen when her mother became seriously ill. But Millie attended night school when her father was home, and after earning a high school diploma continued on in night classes at a business school. After her mother died, Millie secured a position in a secretarial pool. She's taking some night classes again and hopes to become a personal secretary. She is also engaged and thinks she may give a few years to being a full-time wife and mother before she looks into new gains in her chosen field. Millie is on the journey called success.

As a high school junior and senior, Bill worked after school as a stock boy in a men's shoe store. When he graduated, Bill went to work full time, at first as a stock person, then as a salesman. He later learned how to measure for made-to-order shoes and now he's being groomed to become the manager of a second store. Bill, too, is on the success path.

But how we make a living, while most certainly an important part of existence, is not the whole of what success truly is or who we are. A successful life also involves our personal relationships, our family experiences and our spiritual involvement. Happiness is part of success, but the ability to handle the heartbreaks, the illnesses and problems that life brings to us all, and to handle them with dignity and fortitude, is also part of success. Success is a lifelong journey. We do not come to a certain destination marked "success" and then sit on it smugly, without concern for further events. People who live each day to the fullest, with the excitement and challenge those twenty-four hours can bring, are successful people. They don't have to have an important position or make a great deal of money or be famous. Success is making the journey called life as deep and profound an experience as possible. It is a giving, not a taking experience.

Each life is infinitely complex. Within each of us is the life we have chosen and the lives we might have led. Our thoughts and dreams of what we might have been or might have done are within us. The little boy wishes one day to be a fireman. Another day a policeman. For a few weeks he's certain he's going to be a doctor. As he matures, he begins to sort through his dreams and to make choices. He is on his journey. And he is a success because he has learned to choose and meditate and search; he realizes that he might change his mind, that he might make mistakes, that things will not always work out according to his plans and hopes. But this is all right because he can handle change and learn from it.

In each human being are many possibilities. Success is finding out which of these will be right for us. We select our values, our work, the person we marry, how we raise our children, the church we attend, the food we eat. Some choices change or direct our future; others are short-lived. But how we choose and what we do with our choices are the road signs of our journey and, if we follow the right road, success will be with us through good times and bad.

Success is indeed a journey. It is not a destination, for a destination means the journey is over.

Self-control leads to success.

Perhaps you've heard the expression, "the buck stops here." This saying is cousin to another one that is quite commonly used in the United States, "Passing the buck." When a person is accused of "passing the buck," he is said to be avoiding responsibility. He is passing the responsibility on to someone else. When someone says, "The buck stops here," he is saying that he will deal with the matter himself and take full responsibility for the outcome. Which one of these expressions do you find yourself in the habit of using?

Perhaps you know of someone in your life right now who is rebelling against unfairness of one sort or another. Perhaps you, yourself, are choosing to pursue this course. Many people down through history have chosen to rebel against their government or their society. Some have understood that the cost of their rebellion would be their very lives and yet they consented to paying that price. These people have been able to make great changes for the benefit of all people.

If a student chooses to rebel against his parents, for example, and as a result finds himself without a place to live or without any money for college, he must be willing to accept this as the cost of his rebellion. Likewise, it makes no sense to complain if our employer cuts our pay when we have failed to do the work we agreed to do. We have received what we have deserved and we must learn to accept it without protest.

This great law of responsibility applies in every area of our lives. For example, if we choose to abuse our bodies with excessive amounts of drugs or alcohol, it is imperative that we know the cost of this decision. We must ask ourselves if the drugs and alcohol are worth the cost in sickness and wasted time.

Whatever we choose in terms of our behavior in this life, we will be much better off if we can truly say: "The buck stops here. I am willing to pay the price for my decisions. I am willing to accept any and all of the consequences of my actions."

WEEK TWENTY-FOUR : LAW E

Your thoughts are like boomerangs.

The continent of Australia has given us many strange things. Cut off from the rest of the world by vast ocean waters for millions of years, even animal life there has developed into strange forms. For example, the kangaroo. And the platypus, the furbearing animal with the bill of a goose, which lays eggs and feeds on earthworms.

Its primitive people have their own peculiar customs and inventions. Of the latter, the boomerang is the most famous. It is a "stick which comes back." When thrown by a skilled handler, a boomerang, which comes in different shapes, may sail far away and return to the thrower's hands. Some Australian natives are so skilled in its use that they kill birds and other game for food with the boomerang. And always it returns to the thrower, the one who sent it out.

Our conduct, the way we act, is similar to the boomerang. And especially kindness. For kindness has a way of returning to those who are kind. You have probably heard of the old fable of the lion and the mouse. A hungry lion caught a tiny mouse one day who pleaded for its life, saying, "I am such a tiny mouthful for you, O great lion, and besides, some day I might be able to do you a favor." The lion laughed at the mouse and let it go.

Sometime later the lion was caught in a rope net trap. And who do you think gnawed the ropes in two and saved the lion? The tiny mouse, of course.

Often, we are reluctant, even afraid to appear kindhearted. For many of us, television and movie heroes are our role models. And because many are tough in their roles, we think we must be like these "stars." So we don't want to seem softhearted. Yet, this notion is really childish and silly.

For it is the truly brave, the truly great, the truly unafraid who are the kindest. And they are rewarded in turn with good things happening to them. They are rewarded with kindness from others. When a job opening, or an opportunity for advancement comes up, or a chance to accompany a friend on a trip or to a special event, it is usually the friend who has acted kindly towards others who gets the chance first.

When we look at the great leaders of our world, both those in past times and in the present, those who acted with intent for the good of all and kindness towards others are the ones we immediately think of and want to identify with, to be like in some way.

Kindness comes back, like a boomerang, to those who are kind. Perhaps its return takes years. Perhaps the kindness returns from a different direction than that which we sent out kindness. But it will return. It is never lost.

WEEK TWENTY-FIVE : LAW A

Often, a pat on the back works better than a kick in the pants.
William Juneau

In the days of the great cattle drives from Texas to the railhead, the cook was one of the key people on the drive. If things didn't go right and the cook couldn't do his job, everybody suffered. The cook usually had one or two well-stocked wagons that were pulled by mules. Some say mules are generally stronger than horses and require less food and water.

The story is told about an old cook who was teaching his new helper the tricks of the trade. He began with instructions on how to handle the mules. Calling the helper over to where the mules were tied, he picked up a piece of firewood and hit the first mule a terrific blow between the eyes. The young man was upset and incredulous. "Why did you do that?" he asked. The old cook answered, "The first thing you gotta do is get their attention."

That's the way some people go about dealing with their fellow humans, browbeating them into submission before they attempt to get them to accomplish something. It doesn't work with humans; it doesn't really work with mules.

In the late 1960's and early 1970's, the Texas Education Agency began a program of hiring experienced people from industry to teach vocational education. The theory was that it would be easier and faster than teaching trades to certified teachers. It has been a remarkably successful program and some of these industry people brought some innovative teaching methods with them.

One such person was an experienced homebuilder and cabinet-maker who undertook to teach a class in construction trades. His supervisor told him that his class would be made up of underachievers and slow learners and that he should not expect too much of them. The supervisor also told him he could not be friends with the students and still have their respect; they would not bother to learn from someone who let them "get too close."

That was not this man's way of doing things. He could not be distant and formal with the students. He enforced discipline when he needed to, but his years of experience had taught him that people respond to positive treatment in a positive way and to negative treatment in a negative way. He knew he would find something positive about every effort the students made; just making the effort itself was positive. He would point out the things they did right and suggest ways they could improve their skills. He got more work done by being their friend.

The last year he taught the class, nine of the twenty-seven members in the class advanced to the state finals in skills competition and four of those received first place blue ribbons. Most of those students found good jobs after graduation. Their self-confidence had been improved by their successes in the class and they remembered the teacher as a friend who cared.

In almost all cases, a pat on the back does indeed accomplish more than a kick in the pants.

WEEK TWENTY-FIVE : LAW B

A soft answer turns away wrath, but a harsh word stirs up anger.
Proverbs 15:1

We've all been involved in situations in which tempers flared out of control. Although anger is often a natural, self-protective reaction in moments of great frustration, "meeting fire with fire" only compounds the problem. Usually, a moderate approach is best. After all, water, not fire, extinguishes fire. The writer of Proverbs acknowledged this truth when he wrote, "A soft answer turns away wrath, but a harsh word stirs up anger." Learning the art of giving a "soft answer" will always give you an advantage in moments of great tension, when emotions tend to take over.

Giving in to anger robs you of your best judgment and often leaves you regretting things said or done once you've cooled down. A gentle and controlled approach to an angry situation gives you a chance to choose your words and actions rationally and almost always brings a more desirable conclusion to a potentially damaging situation. Taking charge of your emotions allows you to assess a troubled and clouding area of misunderstanding with a clear mind and then to take the wisest course toward a resolution.

People sometimes assume, mistakenly, that they have no power over their emotions. What they have done is give their power to others. "He makes me so angry," you've heard someone say. Or, "She really gets under my skin." The truth is, no one except you has the power to make you angry. If someone else assumes that power over you, you granted them that right! You may have chosen anger because you felt the other person drove you to it, but the choice—to be angry or to try a more rational approach—is yours to make.

There are two ways to approach a situation which has triggered heated, hard-to-control feelings. You can *react* to the words and actions of others, or you can *act* from attitudes of your own choosing. The word *react* is a composite of the prefix *re,* which means *again,* and the word *act,* which means to *perform an action.* In other words, to react is to *perform the actions of another.* Reacting to someone else's negativity can only raise the stakes to an explosive level. To act out of understanding, on the other hand, to give "a soft answer," allows you to remain poised and calm and creates the potential for a peaceful solution.

The next time you're faced with an angry, escalating situation, make a decision to try the "soft answer" approach. Bring your emotions under your control and proceed from a calm and peaceful state of mind. By doing so, you will remain in control of the most vital resource you possess—your mind. You will find with practice that the "soft answer" is your best defense against harsh words.

Little things mean a lot.

One morning during rush hour in a large metropolitan area, a huge moving van was stuck in the entrance of an underpass. The driver's estimate of the height of the opening was off by a few inches and the truck could neither go forward nor back out. Within minutes the police had arrived. A large crowd had gathered. Engineers were called to advise on the best way to free the truck. In the midst of all the noise and excitement, a small boy made his way to the truck driver.

"I can tell you how to get it out, mister," he said.

"Okay, Okay. Everybody's an expert around here," growled the driver impatiently.

"Just let the air out of the tires," said the boy.

Which, only minutes later, is exactly the conclusion the engineers arrived at. Those few inches made the difference and the truck moved smoothly through the underpass. The solution to the problem was such a little thing—so simple that it had been overlooked.

Sometimes the solutions to our problems are like that; just one small thing, one candle lit in the darkness, can make all the difference. Take friendship, for example. We all want to be liked, to be popular with our friends and co-workers. But often some little thing holds us back. We are stuck where we are, and we can't move forward to make friends. And very often the reason we're stuck is simple. If we could just make one small change in ourselves, we would become more interesting and more likable, and it would be easier to form strong friendships.

Maybe we appear conceited to others, too full of ourselves. Certainly a nose-in-the-air attitude won't make friends for us. It's not enjoyable spending time with an "I-I-I" sort of person. Learn to drop the "I" from your vocabulary and you'll find it easier to move through the underpass to friendship.

Could it be that we have some habits that turn friends off, perhaps a tendency to be overly critical of others, making catty remarks behind their backs, or saying things to make them feel foolish in front of others? Nobody likes to be laughed at.

Or could it be that we lack a genuine interest in others—that we're really only interested in ourselves? Do we honestly like to see our friends win honors and recognition? Are we wholeheartedly happy when good luck comes their way? And do we let them know we're interested in them and happy for them?

We have to make an effort to look at ourselves as our friends look at us. We have to face ourselves honestly and check to see if there's some quality that holds us back and keeps us from making the friendships we want and need. To have friends, we must also be willing to *be* a friend. So let's take a moment to look ourselves in the mirror honestly and do whatever it is that's necessary to become the friend we want to be. It may depend on "just a little thing."

To be upset over what you don't have is to waste what you do have.

Ken Keyes

Most commercials encourage us to believe that if we buy a certain product, we will be physically appealing, popular and successful. According to the commercial message, it's easy to make friends and influence people, if we simply do what we're told to do. It would be wonderful if that were true, but unfortunately life doesn't work that way. What is inside us is much more important and influential than what is outside.

Many people today seem to think that money and the things it will buy is the measure of success. But, in truth, things we can buy are just things we can buy—no more, no less. They don't remake the real person in any way. We can change the color of our hair, our clothes style and the car we drive, but none of these are good indicators of the kind of person we are inside.

We may fret and fuss about "the way we are" and wish we were different. We may wish we were taller, shorter, thinner, more muscular or athletic. We can wish, but nothing will happen until we are willing to do what we can to make a change.

Before making a change of any sort, think about who you are and what you have now. It's very probable that you're fine just as you are, even though you admire someone who is different from you. The difference may be in looks, in abilities, in work, or in family or love relationships, and the difference is very attractive to you. How much better to be like them than like yourself! But is it?

Each of us has things we would like to change, problems we would prefer not to have. Consider that the challenging situations in your life may be no worse than problems in the life of the person you would like to emulate. Ken Keyes says, "To be upset over what you don't have is to waste what you do have."

How important is the thing you would like to change? If it is very important, give it your all! Change what you can, being aware of what is right for you. You don't like brown hair? How about red? You want to be more muscular? Lift weights. But don't expect the change to make you into a different person. Under the red hair or muscles will still be the same you.

Before attempting a drastic change, take an inventory of your assets. You may not be an accomplished athlete or an attractive redhead with a witty tongue, but you can work at developing what is already there. Take stock of your strengths, knowing that everyone has some talents that others will appreciate.

Think about the people you really enjoy being with. Is it because of the size of their biceps or the color of their hair? Or is it because you recognize a true friend in them and are inspired to be a friend in return.

We live as we believe life should be. To change the way we see life, we must change the way we believe it should or will be. Your mind is a tool for you to use in creating your ideal life and there are many ways in which to use this tool. Belief in yourself—in what you are—is the beginning of positive change.

Honesty is the best policy.
Miguel de Cervantes

In African legend, an old chief needed to test the wisdom of the young man he had chosen to be his successor as tribal head. He asked the boy to prepare two meals for him. The first meal was to contain the very best ingredients life had to offer; the second meal would contain the very worst.

On the appointed day, the chief sat down to his first meal and it was a delicious plate of sliced cow tongue with vegetables. The chief was delighted with the food and, upon finishing, asked the boy why he had chosen tongue.

"The tongue is one of the finest parts of our being," the young man replied. "It can speak wonderful words of truth that can help our people grow and prosper. The right words can give them courage and bolster their integrity. Tongues can speak of love and harmony and hold our village together."

The chief was very impressed and waited for his second meal with eager anticipation. On the appointed day the chief sat down to eat his second meal and found it to be identical to the first. When he had finished, he asked the boy why he had prepared the same meal twice.

The young man answered, "The tongue can be the best part of us, but it can also be the worst. The tongue can speak words of anger and discouragement that tear people down and rob them of hope. It can weave deceit; it can speak untruths that cause disharmony. The tongue more than any other weapon can destroy our village life." The old chief listened closely and slowly nodded his head. He knew he had chosen the next leader wisely.

There are times when it seems that one little lie—what is called a "white lie"—would make life easier. "After all, who would know?" is a rationalization we often use when considering taking the easy way. But deceptions can become linked to further, and more damaging, deceptions, causing our thoughts and actions to become confused and impure. Nowhere is this sad state of affairs better expressed than in the saying, "Oh, what a tangled web we weave, when first we practice to deceive." Deceit takes a terrible toll on our sense of integrity and self-worth.

Even if our lies are "just white lies," the tangled web of dishonesty can choke the joy and spontaneity out of our lives. We may try to convince ourselves they weren't really lies at all, but at some level of awareness we know the truth and live with the fear of being exposed.

The ability to choose lies or truth is indeed our most powerful weapon, as the old African chief understood well in naming his successor. The young man did not sugarcoat the truth; he refused to make a "white lie" out of it. What we don't always realize is that by choosing deceit we end up hurting ourselves. There are times we may be tempted to believe that a lie will protect us, but the very best protection of all— what will assure us of a happy and successful life—is the knowledge that in every circumstance, as Cervantes said, "Honesty is the best policy."

WEEK TWENTY-SIX : LAW A

It is always darkest before the dawn.
Thomas Fuller

Those who have ever accomplished anything worthwhile have had moments when they were tempted to give up. Full of self-doubt, they have questioned their capabilities, their integrity, their motives. And yet, those who went on to achieve their goals were the ones who managed to push themselves past the dark moments. They persisted in holding to their courses when all the signs along the way told them to give up. They had taken to heart these words of Thomas Fuller's, "It is always darkest before the dawn."

As you struggle to succeed, persistence is a word to remember. It means to hold firmly to an undertaking despite obstacles. In his classic book, *Think and Grow Rich,* Napolean Hill writes: "One of the most common causes of failure is the habit of quitting when one is overtaken by temporary defeat." Hill tells the story of a young man who went out west during the gold rush to find his fortune. Having finally discovered a vein of ore, he returned to his home in Maryland. There he encouraged family and friends to invest in heavy equipment to extract the gold. Though the mine proved to be one of the richest in Colorado, the vein suddenly disappeared. Efforts to pick it up again seemed futile, and the young man and his backers decided to quit trying. They sold the equipment to a junk dealer for a few hundred dollars and went home. The junk dealer had the mine inspected by a mining engineer who told him the vein had run out because of a fault line. His calculations proved that the young man had stopped drilling just three feet short of the vein! Drilling resumed and the mine went on to produce millions of dollars worth of gold.

Persistence often pays. If you let negativity and self-doubt stand between you and your goal, you may never reach it. Resolve to hold firmly and steadfastly to your undertakings despite all obstacles. Learn to be flexible with your plans when necessary, but do not easily abandon your goal. Persistence may help you get what you want out of life.

Every undertaking is likely to have its darker moments, its challenges. Instead of allowing them to stop you, train your mind to unearth any inadequacies in your plans that may be preventing you from achieving your goal. Though "darkness" can be painful and can make it difficult to find your way, the "dawn" of a new inspiration, a new beginning may soon be upon you.

"'Shall I bring to birth and not cause to bring forth?' says the Lord; 'Shall I, who cause to bring forth, shut the womb?' says your God?" (*Isaiah 66:9*).

Learn to be persistent, for, like the young man who came so close, you may be closer to your goal than you think.

Healthy minds tend to cause healthy bodies and vice versa.

Look at any of today's newsstand magazines and chances are one of the leading articles is on stress or fitness management. Stress is one of the leading causes of illness in today's world, and more and more doctors and scientists are discovering the vital links between body, mind and spirit.

Emotional stress can weaken the immune system, making the body more susceptible to disease. Dr. Ronald Grossarth-Maticek, a Yugoslavian oncologist, recently published the results of three studies, begun in the 1960s, that have stirred international excitement. On the basis of interviews and questionnaires given to a large group of men and women, he assigned people to one of four personality types. By following their medical history for ten to thirteen years, he discovered that certain aspects of mental and emotional behavior can be linked to cancer and heart disease.

Disease-prone people usually exhibit emotional dependence, passivity and dissatisfaction with their key relationships. They all tend to be unduly influenced by the way others respond to them, and are unable to change unsatisfying relationships. They also seemed unable to take the initiative in forming or maintaining close emotional ties with others.

"There is no single cause for cancer," says psychiatrist Hans Eysenck. "It is always a combination of risk factors: smoking, drinking, genetic factors, environmental factors, psychosocial factors. We find that all these reinforce each other. But personality is one of the most important."

Louise Hay, author of *Heal Your Body* and *Heal Yourself, Heal Your Life,* says, "I find that resentment, criticism, guilt, and fear cause the most problems in ourselves and our lives. Whatever is happening 'out there' is only a mirror of our own inner thinking."

Tests have shown that people who develop heart disease appear to have problems handling anger, either by failing to control it or by overcontrolling it so that it's not adequately expressed. Frustration, fear, and helplessness are also emotions that can create disease in the body.

So, what is the answer? The fast pace of today's world makes it hard to avoid some stress. We get on the freeway and our blood pressure goes up. We work hard to make a living and achieve the life-style we want, but that means putting in fifty to sixty hours a week at our jobs. We take an evening class to improve our minds, but then we sacrifice needed rest.

Unfortunately, there are no easy answers. Some strong stress relievers, however, should be at the top of our list. First, take time to be out-of-doors. Nature is the best medicine in the world for most of us. The beauty of the earth can stimulate joy, thanksgiving and healthy thoughts.

There have been many stories in recent years of terminally ill patients who literally laughed themselves back to health. Those men and women had nothing to lose when they began a systematic program of watching funny television shows and reading humorous books. Without realizing it, they stimulated a stronger immune system and helped to conquer or at least stabilize the disease.

Meditation is a proven method of achieving a relaxed state of consciousness. Recent findings reported by Stanford University researcher Kenneth Eppley review the effects of transcendental meditation. He reports that "TM has consistently beneficial effects on anxiety." The health benefits of meditation are recognized today by physicians; it can lower blood pressure, slow the aging process, and keep the emotions in balance. One insurance company now gives a twenty percent discount to those who use transcendental meditation.

Another proven method for reducing stress is to own a pet. Long-range studies with the elderly and the ill show that having a dog or cat to stroke and love increases happiness and extends longevity. Mother Teresa of Calcutta provides animals as therapy for insane children.

Most important of all to be happy, healthy and stress-free, you need to believe in yourself and your own right to happiness and health. Louise Hay writes: "Our subconscious mind accepts whatever we choose to believe. Life is very simple. What we give out, we get back. I believe that all of us are responsible for every experience in our lives, the best and the worst. Every thought we think is creating our future. Each one of us creates our experiences by the thoughts we think and the words we speak. If you accept a limiting belief, then it will become a truth for you. The universal power never judges or criticizes us. It only accepts us at our own value."

WEEK TWENTY-SIX : LAW C

To be wronged is nothing unless you continue to remember it.

Confucius

"Codependency" and "dysfunction" are two of the most important words in today's psychological vocabulary. Support groups are everywhere for every problem—Sexaholics Anonymous, Workaholics Anonymous, Neurotics Anonymous, Victims Anonymous, Overeaters Anonymous, and Alcoholics Anonymous. It's not unusual for one person to be in three or more recovery programs at the same time.

Individually, most of these groups are indeed worthwhile. It is vital that people stop annihilating themselves with alcohol or drugs or gluttony or promiscuity. It is important to get drug addicts off the streets and into programs that might offer cures. It is also critical for people to come to terms with themselves and release the anguish of having been sexually molested or physically abused or psychologically tormented. The Unity School of Christianity offers this maxim, "If you can feel it, you can heal it."

At the same time, it is vital to address the common-sense approach expressed by Confucius, "To be wronged is nothing unless you continue to remember it." This advice may be more important than the entire recovery craze. Because if we let our past be, we are not compelled to endlessly reenact it.

It hurts to be wronged. It's maddening, it's infuriating and unfair. But repeatedly reliving it is not healing but rehearsing. It's practicing old routines rather than learning new responses or thinking in fresh channels. We are indulging instead of illuminating when we continue to pick at our emotional scars.

Sometimes it can be a healing experience to dredge up traumatic experiences and face them. Then we can see the events for what they were instead of dreading some future time when there will be revelations to hurt or embarrass us. Remembering can be healthy; continuing to remember, though, is dubious if we stroke and pet our hurts and wear them like a Purple Heart.

Secondly, we can study forgiveness. Forgiveness involves a flight of imagination—being able to understand the influences that shaped your oppressor's behavior. Here is where the self-help groups can really be a boon instead of a crutch. Once you comprehend the dynamics behind the abuse you are more ready to forgive.

Lastly, forgiving does not mean excusing. The abuse is inexcusable, but you accept it so you can go forward and grow. Dwelling on past slights or offenses contracts us rather than expands us. If we want to become fully ourselves, we must release the pain, reframe the experience, and renew our allegiance to life.

WEEK TWENTY-SIX : LAW D

What the mind can conceive, it may achieve.

It has been wisely said that each one of us is the ruler of the greatest nation on earth, our imagination. We all constantly create images in our minds. Many of us, however, don't realize that we have a choice about how we use our innate capacity to imagine. Imagination is more than a matter of wishful thinking; if we consistently use our imaginations with belief and determination, we can actually achieve what we want to achieve. If we're concerned about the future, if we're afraid of some upcoming event, that's one way of using our imaginations. We are picturing a particular outcome. We are choosing to use our imaginations in a negative and fearful manner that diminishes our possibilities for growth and productivity. However, we can just as easily choose to picture a positive outcome. From the spiritual as well as scientific disciples we now learn that using our imaginative faculty in a positive way leads to greater health and greater good in our lives. We know that what we believe in is more likely to come to pass.

The human mind is a creative tool. We are either creating negative, limiting patterns that repeat themselves with deadening regularity, or we are creating new possibilities for positive expansion in our lives. Either we are creating doom and gloom or we are creating exciting possibilities. The choice is ours.

We must begin to train our thoughts and imaginings to assist us in creating the kind of life we want and the kind of world we want to live in. We need to use our imaginative faculty in a truly useful way.

The next time you find yourself daydreaming about the future, try picturing something that you truly want. Try picturing a way you would truly like to be. Remember, you have an imagination and can choose how you will use it. If you use your imagination to create visions of negativity and self-defeating behavior, you will experience more and more of what you do not want in your life. If, on the other hand, you use your imagination in a positive, productive way, your life will begin to improve rapidly. Happy imaginings? It's up to you!

WEEK TWENTY-SIX : LAW E

Of all the things you wear, your expression is the most important.

No matter what clothes you wear, whether elegant or shabby, the most important thing that shows is your face. There are many things money can buy, or power can give, but your expression is undoubtedly one of the few things you can call your own. An expression goes beyond beauty, or wisdom or knowledge; it conveys your true feelings, your hopes, dreams, and fears. It becomes the representation of your character, the embodiment of all that is called you.

There are many examples of this truth, both in art and in life. The Mona Lisa was not known for her beauty, nor the infamy of her history, but merely for the timeless expression of her face. In Da Vinci's The Last Supper, the faces of the apostles are the tellers of the tale—John's lack of belief, Peter's anger and Judas' fear. Those we see around us every day prove the truth as well—the hurt eyes of a lover, the furrowed brow of a concerned parent, or the smile of one who cares. All of these help us to read the intentions and the feelings of those we see everyday. An expression goes beyond gifts or a touch or even words. It is a true and honest indication of who we are.

It has been said that eyes are the window to the soul, and nothing could be more true. But it goes much further than that. The expression you wear on your face not only shows emotion or pain; it is the ultimate judge of the truth in your heart. Your expression cannot truly lie; a smile without a sparkle in one's eye is dead, as the laugh that does not illumine one's whole face is imitation. The expression on your face inevitably becomes the expression of your entire being, and a lie on your face is not only a lie to others but also to yourself. Eyes. Nose. Mouth. Face. Apart, these things do little but give us the senses to unveil the world we live in. But together, they become the way in which we become unveiled.

WEEK TWENTY-SEVEN : LAW A

The pen is mightier than the sword.

E. G. Bulwer-Lytton

Some of the old sayings we hear are not true. For example, "Sticks and stones may break my bones but words will never hurt me!" may be 180 degrees off the mark. Sticks and stones *do* hurt, but so do words, and the healing process can take much longer. Blows to the body can be healed because they are in plain sight where they can be treated. Blows caused by words are often hidden inside of us and we think they don't hurt, or we pretend they don't. Words are powerful because we believe them or fear that others believe them.

Someone may call me stupid. While I know I'm an intelligent person, I may have done something that didn't turn out right and I'm feeling stupid, vulnerable. If someone calls me stupid while I'm down in the dumps, I may decide that I'm really not so very smart, after all. I may disagree with the name-caller, but inside self-doubt will begin to grow and fester. The words combined with my own doubt may not show on the outside, but the pain can hurt as intensely as a broken bone.

Luckily, there is something we can do to change the hurt. Because the hurt is inside of us, we can go inside to find the help. Words, in and of themselves, do not cause us pain. Pain comes from our belief and acceptance of what the words say to us. When I accept someone's verdict that I'm stupid, I'm allowing that person to tell me who and what I am. And yet no one knows the "real me" as well as I do. No one else knows how I think and feel.

I may give you my opinion about what you do, but stupid behavior does not make a stupid person. You may tell me you don't like the way I dress or wear my hair, but that does not mean they're wrong or that you're right, only that you don't like them. A classmate may try to pressure you to do something that doesn't feel right. But would a true friend insist you do something you don't feel right about doing?

Remember that the most powerful thing in the world is your spirit, that part of you that takes all of your words and ideas, sorts them out and tells you how to act and how to feel.

Make sure your mind is receiving lots of positive messages and loving thoughts for they are its fuel. Be aware of the words that go into your mind, both conscious and unconscious, because words and ideas are all that your mind has to use in coming to the right decisions.

Speak of others only as you would want others to speak of you, and decide for yourself if you will accept or reject whatever judgments and criticisms come your way. Your spirit and mind belong to you!

WEEK TWENTY-SEVEN : LAW B

Wisdom is born of mistakes; confront error and learn.
J. Jelinek

There is a difference between acquiring knowledge and information and possessing wisdom. You may acquire knowledge from a university, your relationships, the books you read, and all the other activities you participate in. But are you also gaining wisdom?

Webster's dictionary defines "wisdom" as "the quality of being wise . . . implies the ability to judge and deal with persons, situations, etc. rightly, based on a broad range of knowledge, experience and understanding." In other words, a wise person is one who has the ability to look for the deeper meaning of things. But in order to acquire wisdom, one must have lived enough to have developed a depth of philosophical reflection. We are then in a position to evaluate our experiences and learn from them.

Some of our mistakes—or as Maria Montesorri called them, "learning opportunities"—are clearer than others. Sometimes it seems that the world is full of people who will gladly inform us of our mistakes. The person who is willing to hear another's point of view, and admit there may be other approaches he could have taken, is the one who will grow in wisdom as he grows in acquiring knowledge.

To become wise we must be willing to suspend our own beliefs about something, to set aside our prejudices, and to think with an open mind. We must be eager to branch out and learn in many different areas, even at the risk of being embarrassed or looking foolish. We must be willing to admit we don't know everything and are willing to learn. We must see learning as a desirable process that may include making mistakes along the road to knowledge. True wisdom acknowledges that the more you learn about a subject, the more interesting it becomes and the more there is to learn!

It's not uncommon for someone to say, "I learned my lesson! I'll never do that again!" But all too rarely you may hear someone say, "That was a wonderful lesson. I'm glad it happened just the way it did, even though I was uncomfortable going through it. I now understand why I suffered, and I can change my behavior so I won't make the same mistakes in the future." This person is bravely admitting his own responsibility for creating the situation exactly the way it was. He recognizes he has choices, and that he can choose differently as long as he stays alert to each challenge, whether the challenge seems to be positive or negative.

By fearlessly confronting your own role in the experiences you judge as mistakes in your life, you can make your future experiences fruitful, and increase your wisdom.

The wise person is also a courageous person. We often think of courage in terms of outer forms of bravery—physical prowess and fearlessness in battle or in sports—yet there are many inner forms of bravery that are not recognized by anyone but ourselves as we struggle to overcome our shortcomings. This willingness to look at ourselves honestly and courageously is the first and perhaps most important step we can take on the road to wisdom and personal empowerment.

Great heroes are humble.

Humility is vastly undervalued in our modern western culture. It is a prevalent belief that humility is fine for the pious or holy, but in the "real" world it won't get you very far. Many people consider pride and aggressiveness as virtues and humility as a weakness. This is because they don't understand what humility really is. They may equate humility with self-debasement and a sense of inferiority when, in fact, this is not what true humility is.

Actually, the opposite is true. Most truly great people are quite humble. Those among the greatest who have ever lived acknowledge that their greatness came not from their personal self but from a higher power working through them. The true meaning of humility is knowing that the personal self is but a vehicle of the higher power. Jesus of Nazareth said, "It is not I but the Father within that does the works" (*John 14:10*). Every great spiritual leader has recognized this; every true genius has had a deep sense of personal humility.

Sir Isaac Newton, one of the world's greatest scientific explorers, made this statement near the end of his life, "I feel like a little child playing by the seashore while the great ocean of truth lies undiscovered before me." Another great scientist, Dr. Albert Einstein, was also known for his childlike simplicity. With all his greatness in the world he maintained a strong sense of humility. Dr. Walter Russell, a genius in many fields, echoed Jesus's teaching when he said, "Until one learns to lose oneself, he cannot find himself. The personal ego must be dissolved and replaced by the universal ego."

What is this universal ego and what's the difference between it and the personal ego? To begin with, the personal ego is what most of us identify as our "self"—it's who we believe ourself to be. The personal ego identifies with our appearance, our achievements, our possessions. It is this self that is inclined to compete with others and to feel hurt or angry if it doesn't get what it wants. It is this self that wants to feel important, to always be right and in control. Sound familiar?

Some would say, "You've just described human nature." Perhaps this is a description of the most familiar part of human nature. Yet there is another part, a "higher self," that exists in each of us as a spark of the divine. Unfortunately, most of the time this higher self remains hidden. It is hidden by the personal ego just described. We often can't see this universal self because we are blinded by our identification with the personal. It may be likened to trying to see the stars during the day; they are there but obscured by the light of the sun. Only when the sun goes down do we see these heavenly lights.

If we would truly express greatness in our lives, we must learn to be humble. For it is not our own personal greatness that we would express, but that which belongs to a power far greater than ourselves.

In being humble we will discover that humility rewards itself. When we are willing to put aside the whims and demands of our personal selves to listen to the guidance of the greater self within, we will gain access to an infinite source of power. This universal ego is as much (and perhaps more than) who we are as the personal ego. It is infinitely more loving and wise and it is always there for us. The more we put aside what we ordinarily think of as ourselves and identify with our higher selves, the more we come to recognize that this is our real, essential self. When we are humble in this new identification we are able to produce far greater results than we dreamed possible, thus securing greatness through humility.

WEEK TWENTY-SEVEN : LAW D

You create your own reality.
Jane Roberts

Do you believe that reality is something outside of you? We often hear reference made to the "real world out there." To be sure, there is a world beyond our own personal reality—an outer world that has an appearance of its own. However, there is another world, an inner one, that is also more real. This is the place where your beliefs, thoughts, and feelings reside. This inner world may be less tangible, less solid than the outer world, yet this is where you live your entire life. Your happiness, peace of mind, and enjoyment of work and friends and loved ones depends more on this inner world than on the outer one.

Some would say that the world within is simply a reflection of the outer world—that the outer world is the true reality, whereas personal perceptions, thoughts and feelings are but the effect of outer conditions. (After all, if we're unhappy don't we usually try to change the external conditions of our lives first?) Yet it's possible that our inner world is quite independent of outer circumstances.

Two people may have similar external circumstances and yet have very different internal experiences. Suppose, for example, two men were given the task of speaking before a large audience. Mr. Smith may love to speak in public and the experience is a most pleasant one for him. Mr. Jones, on the other hand, may be extremely fearful of public speaking and find the experience a harrowing test of willpower. Both men share a similar reality, but their internal realities are far removed from each other's. To cite another example, two youngsters may jump into a pool of deep water. While one enjoys a wonderful swim, the other is terrified of drowning. The pool of water is the same; how it is experienced by each individual is vastly different.

We may have lived many years believing that only by changing the outer world will we experience happiness and peace of mind. The truth is that happiness is an inside job. Outer changes alone cannot make us happy.

It helps to remember that we have far more control over our inner than our outer world. Not that changing our inner world is necessarily easy. We have developed thinking and feeling patterns, or belief systems, that are deeply ingrained. Change is not always easy but it is always possible. We begin by examining our beliefs and attitudes, by observing our thoughts and feelings. Change starts to happen when we recognize false beliefs and struggle to bring them in line with reality, when we recognize negative thoughts and choose not to listen to them, when we recognize negative feelings and choose to give them no power over us. We have the power to create our own reality by choosing thoughts and beliefs that are positive and true. So, in truth, you do create your own reality, your inner reality, the only reality in which you truly live.

WEEK TWENTY-SEVEN : LAW E

A task takes as long as there is time to do it.
Parkinson's Law

It is the week before vacation. The thought of sunny days filled with nothing to do is so sweet you can almost taste it. Another school year is finished. It's been a long time coming, but summer is almost here. Only three more finals and a term paper in social studies and you'll be done. But only is such a small word to represent a concept as large as the completion of what seems like endless study and writing in an infinitessimal amount of time. Yet this deadline, which threatens certain doom if it is not met, has the power to save you from the worst enemy you can have when it comes to accomplishing great things and seemingly impossible projects—yourself.

A deadline is to a task what a corral is to a herd of wild horses. It surrounds untamed impressions, thoughts, and feelings with a clear boundary which allows your ideas to formulate as an attainable goal. Most people cannot effectively begin a project until they can see an end to it, a point of fulfillment. A goal without a deadline is a goal never reached. Objectives never accomplished can lead to frustration and a sense of failure. A deadline lets you know when you are finished.

Without a deadline you exhaust yourself, galloping about in an open, often bleak desert of unspecific thoughts and non-productive activity. A deadline, properly developed, is actually a lifeline—like a lasso that can save you from wandering the plains of an endeavor that is without a beginning or an end. As a lifeline, a deadline draws you into alignment with your purpose and allows you to tame your time, talent and resources and apply them where they will be most useful.

A deadline concentrates time into an area of manageable interest. If you were asked to look in the flame of a candle for five minutes you could probably do this with little or no difficulty; but a request to look into a flame for an extended or unspecified length of time would be so unreasonable you would not do it at all.

A deadline also invites you to concentrate your energies on those interests which have greater value to you. Just as a spoonful of honey will sweeten a cup of tea more readily than it will a lake, our efforts must be concentrated in the direction of our priorities to be effective. If you want to avoid summer school this year, it is clear that research and writing must take precedence in the next week. To divert your attention to other interests would dilute your efforts, and blur the sharp focus the lens of your purpose must have right now. However, in a week your deadline will have passed and you'll have the satisfaction of having completed something extremely worthwhile and be free to enjoy the next project you undertake.

Time management experts say that the best deadlines are the ones you choose for yourself. You will find that setting reasonable deadlines for yourself results in a more effective use of your time. However, at times when other people impose deadlines upon you, you may waste much valuable time resisting and resenting them. When you are tempted to feel that others' deadlines are arbitrary or unfair, you can choose them for yourself anyway. As you meet the challenge of doing the best you can with what you've got, your vigorous cooperation will reward you with a sense of great vitality.

What would you like to achieve in your lifetime? How are you going to make a difference in this world? Whatever large or small ambition you have, begin today to create goals that suit your purpose, and deadlines for those goals. Remember, deadlines are lifelines that define your unlimited success.

WEEK TWENTY-EIGHT : LAW A

Procrastination is the thief of time.
Edward Young

Philadelphia is the home of the Procrastinator's Club. You can join for five dollars a year. Their publication is called, "Last Month's Newsletter." They have protested the War of 1812, attempted to get the makers of the Liberty Bell to fix the crack, and even traveled to Spain to raise money for three ships to discover America!

This may be a humorous concept, but procrastination can become a destructive habit. Learning to use time is a skill we acquire with maturity. Babies and young children live only for the moment. They have not yet learned to use the present productively to enjoy a greater good in the future. Delayed pleasure is something that takes great self-discipline.

As we grow, we learn to do our homework now so we can watch TV later; to work at a part-time job so we can buy something we want. Good use of time is a sign of maturity and leads to self-satisfaction and the achievement of important goals.

Remember the story of the ant and the grasshopper? All summer long the grasshopper played and danced and sang. His friend, the ant, was busily putting aside food for the winter. The ant kept reminding the grasshopper that winter was coming but the grasshopper procrastinated. He said, "There's plenty of time for that; I want to play now!" When the snow flurries came, the ant was snug, warm and comfortable in his anthill. The grasshopper, having nothing to eat and no place for shelter, perished in the cold.

This old fable has a lesson for us. We can choose whether to be the ant or the grasshopper. It's good to dance and sing and enjoy life but we must not ignore important duties. Time is our most precious commodity. It is the one thing we can never hoard, purchase or reclaim. Often it is carelessly spent and then regretted. Living in the future or in the past leaves us anchorless. There is no reality but the present moment and, if you waste this moment, you never regain it; you will never know the treasures it may have held for you.

So be like the ant; if you have a task to do, prepare for it. Gather your materials. Commit yourself. Often, getting started is the hardest part. Remember that a journey of a thousand miles begins with a single step.

WEEK TWENTY-EIGHT : LAW B

If any man desire to be first, the same shall be last of all, and servant of all.

Mark 9:35

A man came into a huge dining room where many were seated in preparation for a banquet. He headed for the speaker's table and sat on the right of the master of ceremonies. Soon the chairman of the affair walked hastily up to him, whispered in his ear that he was in the wrong seat, and led him to a table in the back of the room.

Another man came into the dining room, looked around and took his seat in the back of the room. The chairman hurried over to him and greeted him warmly: "You are our guest of honor. You must come sit next to me at the head table." He escorted him to his seat of prominence.

Think of a person you know who lives in self-centeredness. One who chooses to place himself first. One who has an overbearing attitude. One who is imperial, often rude, treating waiters and store clerks with disdain. One who pushes to the head of a grocery or ticket line. One who feels laws and rules are for others, not him. He passes in the no-passing lane, endangering the lives of others. He throws his litter from his car or tosses it carelessly onto the sidewalk as he strolls down the street.

Such a person is derisive of those who are thoughtful. He is disdainful of those who are attentive to others, who are considerate of the helpless or impoverished, who are respectful of children and animals. He rides roughshod over family, neighbors, and fellow employees.

The one who must be first is shouting for all the world to hear, "Me first! I am important!" While his aim is to find self-satisfaction and to express his own self-importance, he succeeds only in alienating others. There is no sweetness in the dominance the "Me-firster" maintains.

In the Old Testament, Jehoshaphat faced a one-sided battle. The three armies of the Moabites, the Ammonites, and the Meunites were lined up against him. Their numbers were overpowering. Nevertheless, he trusted not in his own resources but turned to God for guidance and protection. He placed himself last in this situation and God first.

The next day, through confusion and chaos, the three mighty armies destroyed each other and Jehoshaphat's army had merely to stand by and watch. "So the realm of Jehoshaphat was quiet, for his God gave him rest round about" *(2 Chron. 20:30)*.

Jesus was very clear about the precept that the first shall be last. He spoke of it often. One of the beatitudes addresses the idea: "Blessed are the meek for they shall inherit the earth." Among men, the meek are usually those of least note. They are not aggressive or self-important. They live quiet, self-possessed lives. Because they are not full of themselves, they are open to truth. They are teachable.

At another time Jesus says, "Become as a little child." A little child is full of wonder and curiosity. He thirsts to live life and know all there is to know. The meek and the children are considered last in importance in our society. The children and the meek inherit the kingdom. They shall be first!

Jesus was an example in his own life. Over the protests of his disciples, Jesus knelt and washed their feet. There was no inflated ego nor pride of power in him. He was the one who said it first and experience has proved it: The first shall be last. The last shall be first.

WEEK TWENTY-EIGHT : LAW C

You can build your own heaven or hell on earth.

"Where do people go when they die?" Do you remember asking that question when you were a child? It was an unsettling question, and you hoped to get a reassuring answer. But those of you who were told that people go to heaven or hell, may have been puzzled enough to ask the inevitable next question, "What's that and where is it?"

Many of us came to believe that heaven was a place up in the sky filled with harp-playing angels, where a white-bearded God sat on his throne and made judgments about who'd been good and bad, and doled out rewards and punishments accordingly. Hell, we believed, was a fiery pit, where the devil, a horrifying apparition with red skin, horns, a tail and a pitchfork, made life miserable for the bad people who got sent there. Heaven was where all the good people would go to live in eternal bliss, while the bad people would burn in hell forever.

Because to a child hell was such a frightening alternative, it seemed very important to be as good as possible so we could be assured of a place in heaven where we would be happy and have our needs met. However, as we became more independent and were challenged by the complexities of adult life, we probably began to doubt whether a reward for our behavior such as heaven or a punishment like hell existed at all. After all, we had watched astronauts travel into outer space; and, while they had brought back rocks from the moon, they did not bring back any evidence of heaven. And whereas drills had penetrated the earth, they'd found oil, not hell, in the depths. The definitive descriptions of the afterlife we received as children called for some revision in the light of the scientific discoveries of the modern age and our increased sophistication of thought. With maturity, our concepts of heaven and hell changed.

Because no one has traveled in a spaceship to the heaven or in a submarine to the hell of childhood fantasies, spiritual theorists are inclined to conceive of these as states of mind rather than geographical locations. It is proposed that everyone carries within himself the capacity to perceive life in such a way as to experience a heavenly contentment or a hellish dissatisfaction.

As children, we believed that heaven or hell was the long-term consequence of our behavior. As we grew older and assumed responsibilities, we may have believed that happiness, or heaven, depended on the accumulation of material goods. However, our experience of heaven or hell depends less on our good or bad behavior, or on our bank balance, and more on our interpretation of events as they occur each day. We are responsible for our subjective experience of life. Through our choices and attitudes we create our own heaven or hell right here on earth.

When we were younger, we believed if only we acted like a good little girl or boy, we would go to heaven. But with a more mature concept of heaven and hell, a different morality exists. No longer is it enough simply to be good. More compelling than our outer performance is our motivation for acting as we do. How we approach life from the innermost part of ourselves determines how happy we will be. We may be the most obvious do-gooder in the world and fail to enjoy happiness if our original impulse is towards self-aggrandizement rather than genuine charity. The outer action is the same, but the internal motivation is significantly different. The approval of others, or some sort of public acknowledgement, is never the real reward for what we do. The purity of the intention behind the action determines our experience of heaven or hell.

At times, despite our best and most positive intentions, the experience of heaven eludes us and the experience of hell pursues us. This often happens when we compare what we have with others and feel either superior or inferior to them. In subtle ways, we then become like yo-yo's, our emotions yanked up or down by the state of someone else's fortune, obsessed by the form rather than the content of life.

By judging only the outer appearances of anything, we can create a private hell that permeates all of life. To the extent that we look outside ourselves for heaven, it is possible that we will create a hell of discontent and dissatisfaction for ourselves. What we really want is not out there, and we will exhaust ourselves trying to find it. We may rail against the world or other people in frustration, but the only place we can find heaven is in our own hearts.

The 16th century monk, Fra Giovanni, wrote these words one Christmas time: "There is nothing I can give you which you have not. But there is much which, while I cannot give, you can take. No heaven can come to us unless our hearts find rest in it today. Take heaven."

Our innate goodness is an essential fact of our existence. It can never be taken from us. Neither can it be given to us by someone else. It already lives within us. When we perceive this truth, we will experience heaven on earth. When we experience heaven within us, we naturally are inclined to share that heaven with others through a pure, generous motive and a loving, positive attitude. When we are all that we can be, and when our actions arise spontaneously from the goodness of our being, we find peace and the presence of God within us.

WEEK TWENTY-EIGHT : LAW D

Beauty is but skin deep.
John Davies

Almost every day, in a magazine or on television, we see a handsome man and a lovely woman, often hugging, always smiling and, without exception, selling something. The message: *you can be just like us if you buy this product*. But, of course, in real life it isn't true that you can be beautiful, happy, loved and popular, just by using the right product, driving the right car, or wearing a fancy brand name.

Don't you know people who do all the "right" things and are still not liked? The beautiful, happy, loveable part of you is within; it is not created by clothes or cars. Beauty is more than skin deep; it begins at the center of your very being and is reflected in face, posture, mannerisms, speech and tone of voice—all the qualities that are recognizable as you.

Beauty is in your attitude toward other people, perhaps toward those who are not popular or can't afford the right clothes, cars or possessions. Do you see beyond the clothes or cars to the person? Have you made an effort to get to know the being within?

Many of the most influential people in history have come from humble beginnings, without the material goods and advantages others enjoy. What they had were their minds, their creativity, their respect for the worth of all persons, and their willingness to stand apart from the crowd. St. Francis of Assisi, Mahatma Gandhi and many others, who on the inside were truly beautiful and rich in spirit, lived in poverty.

Their contribution to our lives can be measured not by the size of their bank accounts but by the depth of their spirits. They were not leaders in the popularity polls or included in the *Forbes "400"* list, but their contributions have changed lives and will continue to do so as long as truth is valued.

Often the people and styles we choose for patterns in life will be no more than trivia questions in five or ten years. It's important to learn how you want to live your life, and you can start by answering these questions in preparation for the years to come: Is what you are doing now going to be appropriate and beneficial in 20 years—in 40 years?

While enjoying your present life, what are you doing now to prepare for that future time?

Love yourself by being the very best you can possibly be. Treat yourself as a close friend, one for whom you want only the best of everything—respect, honor, solid relationships, and the satisfaction of a life well lived. These things will be yours by living honorably, at the highest level of which you are capable.

WEEK TWENTY-EIGHT : LAW E

Worry is a rocking chair that gives you something to do, but never gets you anywhere.

J. Jelinek

A talented young woman thought seriously of becoming a doctor. She considered how wonderful it would be to make people feel better. She would be given the opportunity to heal the sick and help to save lives. She fantasized about the good income she would receive by following her deepest desire.

Then she began to worry. She worried about the time it would take to become a doctor. She worried about the cost. She even worried about worrying so much. Because of her rocking between desire and doubt, she never took the entrance exams for the school to which she applied. Her behavior led to her failure to achieve her principal goal in life and dramatized the truth that "worry is a rocking chair that gives you something to do, but never gets you anywhere."

Rocking can be a soothing activity. A frightened child can be comforted by a gentle, rocking motion. A physically-injured person will often rock gently to temper the sensations of pain. Rocking not only soothes the body, it also can be as comforting to the spirit as watching the ocean rise and fall in the rhythm of its waves. However, rocking leaves us in the place we are. It doesn't move us forward.

In some ways worrying is the same as rocking. Worrying can become a familiar behavior, and in this sense a comfortable one, that tricks us into believing we're doing something to solve a problem. Once worrying becomes a habit, we are no longer conscious of choosing to do it. It's automatic.

Although comforting and familiar, worry, like rocking, never moves us forward. It achieves nothing and wastes valuable time that could be spent in finding ways to approach a challenge creatively. Worry occupies a place better given to rest and relaxation, activities that sitting relaxed in a real rocking chair can provide. Rest and relaxation allow us to approach a challenge with refreshed and revitalized energies.

If the young woman who wanted to become a doctor had used the time she spent worrying to study for her entrance exams and concentrate on a positive attitude, she would surely have taken a significant step out of the worry rut. She probably would have been admitted to the medical school of her choice.

The way to promote change is to quit rocking in the worry chair and to use that energy to make a decision or to take an action, no matter how minor. It's certainly justified to sit and rest for a while if you need to. Then, get up and move forward by placing one foot in front of the other, one step at a time.

WEEK TWENTY-NINE : LAW A

Defeat isn't bitter if you don't swallow it.
Ted Engstrom

At one time or another in our lives, we have all experienced failure. In fact, the more often we are willing to risk trying a new approach, a fresh concept, the more likely we are to experience failure, at least in the short run. It is not easy to succeed when we first try something new and ambitious, and if we're afraid to fail we will be afraid to take risks. If we never risk anything new, we will stagnate. Growth requires a willingness to risk failure and defeat. If, as toddlers, we were afraid of failure, few of us would have learned to walk and talk! To learn to walk we had to be willing to fall down at times, scrape our knees and bruise our shins. To be successful—to become victorious—we must be willing to risk failure. But the important lesson to learn is this: *failure is not defeat unless you let it be.*

In the process of inventing the electric light bulb, Thomas Edison tried and failed over a thousand times! It's been reported that someone asked Edison if he didn't grow discouraged by all his failures and consider giving up. He replied: "Those were steps on the way. In each attempt I was successful in finding a way *not* to create a light bulb. I was always eager to learn, even from my mistakes."

In other words, while Edison did not always succeed, he refused to swallow defeat. Edison tasted defeat many times, but he did not swallow it. To swallow defeat is to believe that because you failed at something, you *are* a failure There is a crucial difference between saying, "I failed" and "I am a failure." When a project doesn't turn out right, we might say to ourselves, "I failed at what I attempted." We might even say, "I could have handled it much better than I did." But to swallow defeat is to say, "I failed, therefore *I* am a failure" or "Because I did not do well, *I* am no good." To swallow defeat is to believe that what we do or fail to do makes us the person we are.

When we swallow defeat, our ability to function effectively is impaired from that moment on. Every great leader, every great athlete, every great explorer, thinker, inventor, businessman, has made mistakes, has experienced failure. They became great, however, because they did not blame themselves for their failures, but, rather, they used their mistakes as lessons on how to improve their performance. They knew that failure was only momentary and did not have to mean defeat. They refused to swallow the bitterness of failure and were willing to struggle on to the sweetness of success.

A defeat can be one of the best things that ever happens to us if we choose to learn from it. A defeat may be bitter, but after all, bitter is not bad, and our food would not taste nearly as good were it not for the touch of "bitter." Likewise bitter experiences can help us to spice up our lives if we choose to learn from them rather than to be afraid of them or become embittered by them.

Where there is no vision the people perish.
Proverbs 29:18

An ancient proverb states, "Where there is no vision, the people perish." It's a way of saying that everyone needs dreams and a goal in order to live life satisfactorily. If we don't have a specific goal in mind, if we don't know where we want to go, we're more likely to end up in places not of our choosing. Having goals, and milestones toward our goals, keeps us focused and energized, and makes our lives more interesting and useful.

Florence Chadwick provides us a clear illustration of the importance of keeping our goals in sight. She swam the Catalina Channel in southern California and set many national and international records. She then attempted to break the record for swimming the English Channel. On the day set for the Channel swim, Chadwick encountered heavy seas. But because she had trained in the Atlantic Ocean, she was in peak physical condition, prepared to do battle with the large waves. Along with the rough weather, she encountered chilling cold. That was a problem but, again, her training made a difference. She was used to cold water and her trainers had greased her body to help insulate her from the elements. In addition, Chadwick's trainers, rowing alongside her, were able to give her hot soup from a thermos and words of encouragement as she fought the cold and rough sea.

Yet, with all the planning and all the superior training, the one thing Chadwick and her trainers hadn't anticipated was fog. As a fog bank descended, visibility closed in to just a few feet, obscuring the horizon and distant shore. Although her trainers continued to shout words of encouragement, Chadwick started to flounder. With the loss of visibility, the ice-cold, heavy seas seemed to grow to towering proportions. Chadwick began to suffer cramps in her arms, legs, feet and hands from the effects of the severe cold. Her muscles screamed in pain as she battled the huge waves. Finally she asked her trainers to bring her on board the boat and to take her ashore.

Later, when she was warm and dry, newspaper reporters asked her if she knew that she'd been only a very short distance from the shore when she gave up her valiant effort for the record. She responded that, even though her trainers had told her the same thing, it simply hadn't made a difference to her. "You see," she said, "I lost sight of my goal. I'm not sure I ever had it firmly in mind."

When we have no goal, or when our vision of the goal is obscured, we lose our sense of purpose. Even when we've prepared ourselves well and have an aptitude for a given activity, poorly-directed efforts can rob us of vital energy. We may spend a great deal of our time, money and other resources running around in circles. Unless we create specific goals that match our purpose in life and unless we keep a clear vision of those goals, we may eventually falter and fail.

Classic advice for golfers has always been, "Keep your eye on the ball." The professional knows it is virtually impossible to hit a ball you aren't looking at. If you want to be "on the ball," it's important to decide how you want to make a difference in the world. Once you have your purpose clearly in mind, explore the various ways you can make it happen, and visualize the process you believe will work best. Set goals, do what it takes to accomplish them, and enjoy your success.

WEEK TWENTY-NINE : LAW C

The greatness is not in me; I am in the greatness.

Sunlight travels ninety-three million miles in a little over eight minutes to reach our earth. It is tasteless, odorless and, unless a rainbow occurs, invisible. Prismatic droplets of mist make what was there all along suddenly visible. The rainbow is a powerful symbol reminding us that the unseen world holds many treasures for those with eyes to see.

As we live each day, our senses are bombarded with stimuli. As a result of coming in constant contact with objects, we attach special significance to them. We begin to believe that a slice of cake, for instance, can cheer us faster than a good word. We count on sweets to sweeten our disposition because our senses tell us the taste and sugar-high are reality.

In fact, many material goods are designed to distract us from feeling sad when we should grieve a loss. They disguise our errors when we should admit a mistake. They stimulate happiness when our health and environment should warn us of disease. The moment our status quo is threatened, we rush to our nearest commodity center for a "fix," expecting money to buy for us what it cannot buy—spiritual happiness.

When we achieve success, we are no longer the possessors of wealth, we are the possessed. Eventually, though, stabilizing forces can bring us back into balance—just as gravity acts on a pendulum's swing. These forces may come in the form of an economic recession, a job transfer, or a health crisis. These setbacks can become opportunities to grow spiritually.

Not that one cannot be materially wealthy and spiritually enriched at the same time. It is not gold or silver in themselves that are dangerous, but our attachments to them. We need to ask ourselves: "With what consciousness and purpose do I dispatch them in the world? Am I the slave of materialism, or a good trustee, acting selflessly and ethically in my handling of my worldly assets?"

Apart from its ability to serve the legitimate needs of humanity, money is meaningless. And spiritual belief, divorced from the tangible world, is naive. True happiness comes from bringing a wonderfully creative idea from the world of spirit into the world of matter, enjoying the benefit it brings others, and then reclaiming it through gratitude. Furthermore, spiritual affluence operates under the same universal principles as material wealth. The physical objects in our everyday world are merely the manifestations of their spiritual essence. Everything was envisioned in the creative mind as a vital idea before it was crafted in the material world. The adage "As above, so below," affirms that ideas in the spiritual world also can have partners in the physical. Unlimited imagination corresponds to finite action; spiritual wisdom to worldly knowledge; unconditional love to actual service; and the dreaming self to the conscious self. There is a flow between the spiritual and the material worlds that needs to be honored if we are to live fully and with purpose.

Ultimately, money is a convenience for organizing and harmonizing human enterprise. Material wealth needs to be redeemed for this higher purpose. In fact, much of our fretting over what is and isn't adequate can be let go, if we remember, "The greatness is not in me; I am in the greatness." What a freeing notion this is! We are not the source of generosity and fruitful acts. We are vessels through which these virtues are poured out to humanity. We are not the owners of earthly resources, but rather the overseers.

When we begin to act out of this knowledge of the heart, the masks that conceal truth will fall away. When all is said and done, human beings are attracted to the lessons they learn on a spiritual level. Desiring a new car is often an awareness that the old car is no longer functioning satisfactorily. When this is recognized, the "newness" of the car becomes secondary. Moving from a larger home to a smaller place may be a need for simplification. Far more than a setback, it is a reordering of priorities. Glutting ourselves with the sights and sounds, taste and feel of the material world may be our unconscious way of seeking out the sacred in the profane—of convincing ourselves that we are alive and of forcing the rainbow into visibility.

If we happen to be spellbound by materialism ourselves, all is not lost. Isn't the breaking of the spell the turning-point of all great tales? We can think of our days of enchantment as the world initiating us in the lessons of abundance and the secrets of the rainbow.

WEEK TWENTY-NINE : LAW D

Laugh and the world laughs with you; weep and you weep alone.

Ella Wheeler Wilcox

"Wipe that smile off of your face!" Have you ever had these stern words spoken to you while you were being scolded for something? Whether you deserved the reprimand or not, the person who spoke knew a great deal about the human response to the law of life, "a smile breeds a smile." Like a bonfire on a crisp autumn evening, a smile has a way of sparking a light that may joyously ignite into happiness. Those with excessively serious minds and heavy hearts must exercise caution around it; for a smile is likely to consume all that is somber in its gentle flame, leaving in its glowing embers a sense of warm well-being. That is why, when you're supposed to be feeling remorseful, many people won't understand if you have a smile on your face and they may demand that you get rid of it.

While it is true that there may be times when it is not appropriate to giggle or laugh aloud, your genuine smile is never out of place. Can you think of a time or place when the world could not use a little more light and love? Every person has the capacity to bring these vital qualities to life with their smile. While not all of us will smile in the same situations or in the same way, you will bring a little more warmth into a sometimes cold world with a smile that brings forth the best part of you. The smile you bring to a difficult life challenge infuses it with the light of understanding, and with love, which attracts harmonious solutions. It also inspires those around you to respond in a similar manner. Your smile makes a difference wherever you are!

Studies have shown that it takes far fewer facial muscles to create a smile than it does to make a frown. The choice to smile in a trying time is a decision to take life in a way that is light on you and loving to everyone around you. A smile is the expression of a lighthearted person; when you smile it shows your willingness to relax, enjoy the moment, and share in a good feeling no matter what stressful circumstance may be testing you. And when you take life more easily, life will be easier on you, for the energy you might have spent on a frown is freed for more useful purposes.

Have you had the experience of being around someone who was so bored or tired that they began to yawn, and whether or not you were tired or bored, you also began to yawn? Soon many in the room where you were joined in a quiet chorus of yawns. Or perhaps you were feeling pretty good one afternoon until you discovered your kids engaged in a quarrel. Each one pulled you to take their side and soon you felt as angry as any of them. Like an ape in the zoo who mimics whatever he sees, we often take on someone else's behavior or emotion without any conscious thought.

Fortunately, we do not have to respond mindlessly if we will be conscious about our choices. When you choose to smile, even when the situation does not seem to warrant it, you will find yourself reliving in an unconscious way all the times your smile did come easily and feel good—and soon you will rediscover ease and good feeling in this present circumstance. As you touch once again the light and love within you and begin to share this with the world, you set off an almost irresistible chain of cause and effect that restores understanding and harmony to the situation.

Your smile can breed many more smiles because of the good feeling that is generated just in being around you. Your smile, aimed in the direction of any hostile emotions, could be the smile *felt* around the world today by people everywhere. Say "Cheeeeese" now. The world needs your smile.

WEEK TWENTY-NINE : LAW E

If nothing is ventured, nothing is gained.
Sir John Heywood

Have you ever thought what the world was like at the birth of the human race? The first people, we are told, occupied a very small portion of the earth's surface. To them, the rest of the world must have seemed like a vast and frightening place. Great creatures wandered the earth; there were volcanic eruptions, exposure to the natural elements and a constant search for food and shelter. It would come as no surprise that the earth's earliest inhabitants found life fragile indeed. We can be grateful to those intrepid ancestors who had the courage to venture forth, risking their lives to explore the unknown. What would have happened if they hadn't gone forth to explore the world's awesome riches and possibilities? We might not be here at all! Fortunately, a strong urge impelled those early pioneers not only to make the best of their struggle to survive but also to improve their circumstances by going beyond familiar bounds.

Today we think nothing of flipping a switch to heat our house, of turning a knob to light the flame under the teapot. When we barbeque, we soak the charcoal with lighter fluid and strike a match to start the flame. The innovation of fire is something we take for granted. Try to think back to prehistory when people encountered fire for the first time. It must have piqued their curiosity and, at the same time, terrified them. And, like a small child who puts his hand on the flame and gets burned, fire may have revealed its more ominous side to our ancestors and discouraged them from further investigation. It took an adventurer who risked getting burned to discover the beneficent possibilities of fire, and further risk to learn how to contain and use it.

The spirit of adventure is a deeply human trait and one that has helped us develop over thousands of years of recorded history. It is the potential you have within you to leave the world a better place than you found it. Not that you have to; few are likely to notice if you do nothing with your life. You can be one of those who plays it safe, who ventures nothing. But, "nothing ventured, nothing gained" applies to you as well as everyone. However, when you choose to leave what is safe and familiar and voyage into uncharted waters of intellect and creativity, you become like that first person who set out to conquer fire—an adventurer who dares to go forward into the unknown, a pioneer. You become one who makes a difference.

Today's frontiers are no longer the uncharted lands that challenged our ancestors; yet the territories of the human mind and heart are no less awesome in thier mystery. The exploration of the power of love may be humanity's next great challenge. Father Pierre Teilhard de Chardin, the priest-scientist, wrote that when we have learned how to harness the energies of love for mankind we will have discovered fire for the second time in history. Will you be the one to meet the task?

Self-control wins the race.

Can you imagine what it was like to live in the world when it took a month or more to cross the Atlantic Ocean? When you might have had to wait months in San Francisco for a letter to arrive by Pony Express from New York? When you had to travel long distances over bumpy roads to the nearest town to buy a new pair of shoes? The slow pace of life at the turn of the century is difficult to comprehend today when the Concorde travels between New York and Paris in three hours, when fax machines transmit letters in seconds, and the local mall is only minutes away by car and super highway. Cutting-edge technology allows us to do just about anything instantly. As accustomed as we are to the high speed of life today, we sometimes fail to realize that, as a wise person once said, "The faster we go, the behinder we get."

The ancient fable about the hare and tortoise illustrates this peculiar phenomenon. The hare was a long-legged creature capable of leaping and bounding over long distances in a short amount of time. He enjoyed teasing the tortoise who was, after all, just a sluggish old turtle with short legs, who moved only a little faster than a snail. One day the tortoise had had enough of the hare's boasting about how speedy he was and challenged him to a race. The hare was delighted to oblige.

When a forest animal gave a starting whistle and the race began, the hare literally ran circles around the tortoise, laughing and bragging, totally confident that he was going to win the race. The tortoise simply ignored him as he plodded along the race course that ran several miles down a country lane. When the hare couldn't get a rise out of the tortoise, he sped on down the road to see what kind of fun he could have. He chased a squirrel off into a field and then explored several rabbit holes. Having grown tired from all his chasing around and confident the tortoise would never catch up, the hare decided to take a nap in a soft bed of grass. Meanwhile, the tortoise continued to put one foot in front of the other. He moved slowly, one step at a time, along the race course. Eventually he reached the place where the hare was sleeping soundly by the side of the road. Quietly the tortoise passed him and moved on to the finish line. The sound of the other animals cheering for the victorious tortoise awakened the hare, who skulked off into the woods, embarassed that in his hurry to be the fastest and the best he had neglected to stay in the race. Although he had been the faster of the two, he failed to finish. The steady tortoise had put him in his place.

The ability to do something quickly is a useful quality, but, as the tortoise taught the hare, speed isn't everything. In fact, the hare was so beguiled by his natural ability to outrun most other creatures that he made the mistake of thinking no effort was required of him. Because he was so sure he would win, the hare allowed himself to be distracted by other interests and eventually tired himself out. The tortoise, on the other hand, made up for his lack of speed with an abundance of determination and discipline. He realized that natural gifts can take you only so far. In the long run, using what you have to the fullest degree is the way to attain lasting success.

Do you sometimes envy people who seem to have it made without even trying? They've got the money, looks, talent, connections, they're on the fast track to success, while you plod along, making progress a small step at a time. But it's important to remember that it's not *what* you have, but what you *do* with what you have that counts. Like the hare, the best and brightest often resemble fireworks. They dazzle on-lookers with their spectacular displays but lack the staying power. However, if, like the tortoise, you keep an eye on the goal and your feet on the ground, you will be able to go the distance in any endeavor. You may be tempted by instant success, but history has proven that "slow and steady" translates into lasting progress over the long term. If you want to back a winner in today's rapid-paced world, study the wise and steady tortoise. He embodies the law that perseverance and self-control win the race.

Love thy neighbor as thyself.
Matthew 19:19

The actor-humorist, Groucho Marx, once joked that he would never belong to any club that would accept him as a member. For people, though, the inability to appreciate themselves is no laughing matter. People who suffer from low self-esteem often resign themselves to a life of painful alienation.

The belief that you are less worthy, less attractive, less intelligent, or less good than another in any way, sets you apart from those who would love you and would accept your love in return. Feelings of inadequacy, shame and self-pity can consume your energies in an emotional tornado that drives destructively through all your relationships. The devastation that often occurs as you live out your self-doubts serves only to reinforce the beliefs you hold. A vicious cycle is perpetuated— a self-fulfilling prophecy. It works this way: You say to yourself, "If I let others close to me, they'll see through me and I'll end up friendless. So I don't let people get close to me, and it's just as I suspected. I'm friendless."

The human mind often breaks reality down into simple forms: Black or white, good or bad, me or you—And this either/or way of thinking may confuse some into believing that it's not possible to treat another with care, while at the same time giving care to themselves. With our cultural traditions that value love and thoughtfulness to other people, many are convinced it's selfish to be considerate of their own feelings and needs. While you may have been taught that you should "love thy neighbor as thyself," in truth, the only way you will be able to love others is also to love yourself.

The scales of loving human relations must be balanced; this can happen only when each individual is honored as being of equal value. If you're in the habit of putting yourself down, you make it difficult for anyone to accept you as an equal. True love grows usually between those who, despite their differences of appearance, talents, opinions or any other external measure, know themselves to be equals. When you know yourself to be as valuable and as deserving of love as anyone else in the world, you'll find a world of people who want to love and support you.

Holding yourself in healthy self-esteem is different from being narcissistic. Narcissus, the figure in Greek mythology who spent his days pining after his own reflection in a pool, neglected everyone else in his life, preoccupied as he was with himself. He was like those who spend hours trying to get their hair perfect or their makeup flawless so that others will think them beautiful. The underlying assumption is that they're not good enough as they are, that they must alter and improve themselves in order to be acceptable in other's eyes.

True self-esteem belongs to the one who looks in the mirror not to criticize or admire but to see past physical appearance into the essential being reflected there. The one who moves past fear and discomfort to look deeply and lovingly into his or her own eyes will be able to share that look of love fully with another.

We are invisibly tied to one another by a loving force much greater than we can conceive of with our either/or mind. It's a force that speaks the language of both you and your neighbor. You both receive the love that lives inside of you. Next time you want to increase your ability to love someone else, look first into your own eyes and see your own goodness. Enjoy the person you are, risk sharing yourself with another, and then watch how you grow in honest and healthy self-love.

WEEK THIRTY : LAW C

Freedom is a fact of life.

Are you free? Do you feel in charge of your life. Can you pursue your chosen aims without restriction? Or do you feel someone is hampering you—that your life is not really yours to do with as you please? Do you sometimes think you could be free if your family or your boss would only give you a break?

In *Man's Search For Meaning,* Viktor Frankl tells of his own experiences in a Nazi concentration camp. He reflects on the irony that he never felt so free as he did during that dreadful period. How could that be true? Even though all obvious freedoms had been taken from him and he was living in constant threat of sickness, torture and death, he discovered a depth of freedom inside of himself he had never before experienced.

If we come to understand that freedom is inescapable, it will serve us greatly in living a happy and productive life. In the middle of the most restrictive environment imaginable, Viktor Frankl discovered this truth about freedom. He learned that no matter where life might take him, no matter how terrible the external conditions might be, he still had the freedom of his own thoughts and attitudes.

No one can ever control our thoughts and our attitudes. We can choose to give this inalienable freedom away by saying that our parents or our teachers or our employers make us feel a certain way. However, when we truly understand that no one can make us think or feel anything unless we give them our permission, we begin to understand just how free we really are. No people or circumstance can ever change that truth. Our thoughts and attitudes toward life are ours to choose. Viktor Frankl has shown us, eloquently and movingly, that even in the midst of a horrible experience valuable lessons can be learned. He could have given up. He could have said to himself that the Nazis made him give up. Instead he realized that even the Nazis could not control his thoughts and his attitudes, and that he could choose to make his experience whatever he wanted it to be.

Do you believe your negative attitude toward life is the result of some external force? Do you sometimes hear yourself saying that you have no future because someone is coercing you into staying in the same rut? Do you often feel you could be happy if only others would change? Or are you choosing to look for the meaning and the good in every situation?

We cannot escape the truth that we are free to think whatever thoughts we want to think. We are responsible for our own thoughts and attitudes. We can change them and thereby change our experience of life. That is a freedom that, so long as we cherish it, can never be taken from us.

WEEK THIRTY : LAW D

Honesty is the first chapter in the book of wisdom.
Thomas Jefferson

"To be, or not to be: that is the question." So speaks Hamlet in his famous soliloquy of self-doubt and reason. If you remember, he is trying to decide whether to follow his own conscience or to pretend that he does not know the truth of his father's murder. He is torn by the desire to be honest with himself and therefore, the world, or to turn his back on that which he believes.

Sometimes in our own lives we find ourselves in variations of his peculiar predicament. Hopefully, not as melodramatic, yet just as real for us.

"Honesty is the first chapter in the book of wisdom," Thomas Jefferson wrote. This has been true for all people everywhere, in every period of the world. The fight to honor truth within and without, has never been an easy one. But we must begin simply if we are to know how to do it.

"Know thyself" is the inscription at the early Delphic Oracle of ancient Greece. "Hold faithfulness and sincerity as first principles," Confucius wrote, "When you know a thing, to hold that you know it; and when you do not, to allow that you do not know it—this is knowledge."

Lao-tzu wrote over 2500 years ago, "He who knows others is wise; He who knows himself is enlightened."

All of these great philosophers and sages began with one truth—be honest and "all things will be added unto you." They knew that all men share the same basic drives: a need for love, for freedom and respect, and the desire to feel as if their life has mattered. By looking within, the keys to understanding all human behavior are slowly revealed *if* you are courageous enough to search your innermost heart.

But how many of us know where that heart is? How many of us have fallen into the habit of being out of touch with what we intuitively know? Often this seems to be most true when we apply it to knowing our own feelings. The noisy hustle and bustle of the outer world distracts us so much, that we have a hard time listening to that small, still voice within that usually knows the truth of any situation.

In *Hamlet,* Shakespeare says: "This above all: to thine own self be true, and it must follow, as the night the day, thou canst not then be false to any man."

Yet, not listening to the voice within on a daily basis, we fall out of practice. It becomes easy to be false to ourselves—and then to other people without even meaning to.

Perhaps your wife said to you this morning, "Honey, why were you late for dinner last night?" Trying to avoid a long explanation or a scene, you tell a little white lie. Your boss asks if you'd mind working overtime for another weekend. You're afraid to say no, even though it means you'll miss your daughter's birthday party. A friend asks if you're not drinking too much. Too embarrassed to admit it, you fling out an answer of denial—another white lie in the wall we build between ourselves and truth.

Happens to everyone, doesn't it? When we begin to lie to ourselves, we become increasingly disconnected from our true feelings.

Thomas Jefferson wrote in a letter to one of his contemporaries: "He who permits himself to tell a lie once, finds it much easier to do it a second and third time, til at length it becomes habitual. He tells lies without attending to it, and truths without the world's believing him. This falsehood of the tongue leads to that of the heart, and in time depraves all its good dispositions."

Jefferson tried to be as far-sighted as possible so that a nation of honest men would endure. "Sometimes it is said," he wrote, "that a man cannot be trusted with the government of himself. Can he, then, be trusted with the government of others?"

A compelling thought, when we extend it beyond our small personal world. But what is any nation made up of, except the entwining of many people's small, private worlds? How often have we all read in the newspapers of injustices in our own cities and towns, and shrugged? What can we do? How can we make a difference? Truth isn't our jurisdiction. Or is it?

The first thing you can do is to get in the practice of being honest with yourself and others at all times. When we disconnect from our feelings to avoid a scene or to appear "cool," we silence the voice within. We silence truth. After awhile we can no longer hear its voice. That is one reason there are so many busy psychologists and psychiatrists in today's world. We are paying to learn how to reconnect to our own inner promptings. The old adage, "practice makes perfect," still applies to truth perhaps more than any other reality of our existence.

Begin today. Get out a sheet of paper and divide it into two columns. On one side write down the things you like about human nature—the things you honor. Don't be afraid to write down qualities like tenderness, strength, humor, diplomacy, love or hard work. Then, in the other column, write down those qualities that most offend you—the ones that push your buttons or drive you crazy. Perhaps you'll write down anger, laziness, deception, cowardice, brutality, or jealousy.

Then take a look at both columns. In total truth claim them both. Name the aspects of honorable character as you see them in yourself. Find where they resonate with you. And recognize which, if any, may need to be strengthened and worked on. Take the undesirable column and address them. Recognize that you probably have them in some small measure, even if they are hidden from sight of most people. Acknowledge them for the times when they arise. Do not deny them utterly, or they will creep up on you as the disowned enemy in yourself—sometimes coming only in the guise of the people that you draw to you, because they are denied within.

Be honest. Be true. Love all parts of yourself. You are human and, like the rest of us, the godhood within you—the goodness within you—is in a state of becoming perfect. With honesty and free will you can claim those aspects of yourself you choose to live out in the world.

"Know thyself," said the oracle. In so doing, you claim your heritage and your greatness.

WEEK THIRTY : LAW E

Thanksgiving, not complaining, attracts people to you.

It was the four-year-old's birthday. Around the room were strewn heaps of wrapping papers and tangles of ribbon. Everyone smiled expectantly when the mother said, "Dear, what do you say now?"

The child answered, "Where are the rest of my presents?"

That may be typical behavior for a four year old, but how many of us still ask similar questions—"Is this all I get?" There always seems to be an expectation of more—of something better, newer, faster, hotter, colder, bigger, gaudier.

We can be grateful for the things we have or we can focus on things we don't have and make ourselves and others miserable. Our mind has the power to determine if we'll be satisfied or left wanting more. What is it we want so badly? What is this emptiness we're trying to fill?

Just as an obese person continues to eat long after the hunger pangs have been suppressed, so do we look for things outside ourselves to satisfy our deepest hungers. We might hope for fame to fill our desire for belonging. We might count on money to bring us all the things we believe will satisfy our cravings. We might turn to drugs to alter our senses so that we don't have to be conscious of failure and hopelessness. All of these things we do because we believe we don't have what we need to be happy and productive.

"I can work better when I'm making more money," we tell ourselves. In truth, better work brings greater rewards and the best work is done for the joy of working. There is no greater reward than a sense of having been of service to others and having done the job well.

"When I'm famous, everyone will love me," we tell ourselves. But fame doesn't bring true love. One is loved for who one is and everyone on the face of the globe is worthy of being loved. This sense of being loved and loveable is the thing that attracts people to us—people who love us without demands, without any strings attached. When we know we're loveable, we can be alone without being lonely.

Knowing our true worth is the best defense against the empty feelings that often lead one to mind-altering substances. Being grateful for who

we are and what we have puts a smile on our face and gives us a radiance that attracts even greater things to us than we could have ever imagined.

Worry and concern cause the face to wrinkle and restrict the blood flow throughout the body. Tension within the body can be a factor in various ailments such as headache, arthritis, heart trouble, digestive upsets and even the spread of cancer.

You might try the following quick test: Wrinkle your brow and purse your lips, just as you do when you're worried or angry. Do you notice how every part of your body feels? Now, relax your face and take a deep breath. Think of something pleasant or make your mind as blank as you can. Now do you notice the difference in how all parts of your body feel?

Instead of saying, "That's not nearly enough; I want more!" try to say, "Thank you very much." Doesn't that response feel better throughout your entire body? Isn't that the feeling you want to experience? Let gratitude be your attitude every day.

Ask not what you can expect of life; ask what life expects of you.
Viktor Frankl

What are we going to get out of life? is, understandably, a question of fundamental importance to all of us. We begin with certain basic needs and desires. We want to have enough to eat and we want to have companionship and joy and a meaningful and well-paying job. However, many of us have never learned that, for our receiving to take place, we must often give something first.

President John F. Kennedy, advised Americans to "ask not what your country can do for you, ask what you can do for your country." This is an expression of the law of giving and receiving, and it applies to everyone in our world. For example, if we seek a certain type of employment and there are no jobs available, we might see if there is some volunteer position to be found in our area of interest. Rather than

demanding of life that we receive the job we want, we ask if there is anything we can give. Through volunteering, we gain experience and contacts and, oftentimes, the job we've been seeking eventually becomes ours.

Many of us want love and companionship, but it is a law of life that we must first be loving and friendly if we would attract to us the love and companionship we all require. We give and then we receive. It is often true that we must first give up negative attitudes and judgments about other people for our love to be given.

The law of giving and receiving also asks us to be good receivers. As we are giving of ourselves, our time and resources, our positive attitudes and loving thoughts and actions, it is also important to be able to receive the gifts of others in a graceful way. Everyone truly loves to give, and there are times when we are being of service when we graciously receive what another would give us—when we find a way to say, "Thank you; I accept that."

The law of giving and receiving is basic to a life of successful and graceful living. If we are feeling a lack in some area, our first thought must increasingly be: "What can I give? What do I have to give?" The more we give, the more we receive.

WEEK THIRTY-ONE : LAW B

A man can fail many times but he isn't a failure until he begins to blame others.

Ted Engstrom

Have you ever heard the statement, "If you are going to learn anything you will make mistakes?" It's true. Sometimes people refuse to try new things because they're afraid of failing and, consequently, of being considered a failure.

There is distinction between failing and being a failure. Few things are learned in life without failing at least once. Did you learn to rollerskate without falling a few times? Did you learn to ride a bike without losing your balance? Chances are you didn't. You wanted to be able to

do those things so badly, you quickly put your unsuccessful attempts behind you and kept trying. Soon you acquired the skill to do the thing you wanted. Even though in the process of learning you failed many times, you were not a failure.

Do you remember that sometimes in your frustration with the process of learning, you blamed your interim failure on the person trying to teach you? If it was bike riding, maybe someone was running along beside you holding you up. Soon you wanted them to let go so you could ride on your own. If you then fell, perhaps you blamed them for letting go too early or too late.

As you gained confidence and skill, you may have been riding along the sidewalk and someone was walking there. You weren't sure you could guide the bike through the small space available and going off the walk seemed too scary to try. If you fell, did you think or say something like: "You made me fall! If you hadn't been in my way I would not have gone over!" The reality was that if you'd had more skill and practice, you could have easily handled the situation, as you surely did many times in your subsequent biking experience.

In life, it sometimes seems as if there is someone or something that makes us fail. It is not unusual to feel that another person or circumstance keeps us from achieving our goals. What is unusual is for us to admit that maybe we haven't done our best, and then to analyze our own preparation and effort. Ask yourself whether you did the best you possibly could have and be fearless in admitting mistakes and oversights. If you realize you're at fault, simply resolve not to repeat the error, forgive yourself for the mistake and move on. Remember, as you learned to ride the bike, as you kept trying, and persisted, you got better and better until bike riding was almost as natural as walking.

There is no one to blame, not even ourselves. The person who gets stuck in self-blame or in blaming others or circumstances, only slows his or her own recovery and risks becoming a failure instead of simply having a temporary setback. Rather than feeling sorry for yourself or being angry at others, ask: "What now? What else can I do to accomplish my goals?"

If we waste time and energy blaming others, we will never see what we need to see about ourselves to learn and grow and get better results from our efforts. We can fail many times, but it is never final. Those who fail are not failures, unless they let blame and self-pity prevent them from reaching their goals.

WEEK THIRTY-ONE : LAW C

A soul without a high aim
is like a ship without a rudder.

Eileen Caddy

A ship with properly trimmed sails can travel in any direction in relation to the wind except directly into it. While the set of the sails determines the most efficient use of the available wind, the rudder enables the ship to travel in a specific heading. Without a rudder, the ship can do little more than blow helplessly downwind.

What is true of the wind-powered ship is also true of people. There are many things you can do to contribute to your success. You can cultivate a charming personality, develop a dynamic appearance, receive the finest education. Making these preparations is like setting your sails. Without a proper steering device, however, without a rudder, you still may fail to get anywhere in life. You need a goal, a purpose, an ideal that will steer you in the direction of your choice. "A soul without a high aim," said Eileen Caddy, co-founder of the Findhorn community, "is like a ship without a rudder."

There are many people who work hard all their lives with a minimum of personal and professional satisfaction. They engage in aimless thought and activity rather than steer themselves in a direction they have charted. Like a rudderless ship, they blow helplessly on the winds of circumstance, wasting their precious mind energy. Feeling ineffective, they live in a chronic state of unhappiness. A high aim and a clear purpose, however, acts as a rudder for the unlimited potential of your mind and helps you move in a direction that will fulfill your thoughts and actions. As your effectiveness and productivity increase, feelings of uselessness, of drifting, diminish.

If you choose carefully and navigate your course with care, you can move in any direction you care to go. Chances are you will set your sights on many things before you find the one direction you really want to pursue heart and soul. That is perfectly natural. We gradually evolve into the field that best suits our deepest interests and needs. Each time you set and attain a specific goal, you will learn that much more about the dynamics involved in taking command of your life. Then, when you find the thing you most want to do, you will not automatically pass it off as a dream beyond your capacities. You will be prepared to reach out and attain it. Success will no longer be a mystery that only comes to others. You will be well acquainted with it and ready to seize the moment.

Don't make the mistake of allowing yourself to be blown aimlessly through life. You have it within your power to set any course you wish. Do not hesitate to follow the highest dictates of your heart. Aim high, set your sails for success, grasp the rudder and start moving. When you do, you'll find the challenge, the adventure, the usefulness and the happiness the amazing seas of life have in store for you.

WEEK THIRTY-ONE : LAW D

Beautiful thoughts build a beautiful soul.

There are ideas that help us repair our refrigerators or automobiles; there is another set of ideas that help us solve a knotty problem that's giving us trouble. But we often fail to realize there's still another way that ideas can serve us and help us. We seldom hear about the "law of good ideas."

The law of good ideas states that there are certain powerfully good ideas that we need to learn and practice and cooperate with to lead a happy and successful life. These ideas, when believed in and aided by, begin to work a kind of magical transformation in our lives. For example, if we look at ourselves and find that we could be more loving individuals, we entertain in our minds the idea of love. We give our minds and hearts to the idea. We state our belief in the idea and our willingness to learn from the idea. We let it have its way with us as if it were some kind of living entity. We give ourselves to the good idea of love.

It is a law of life that whatever we give our attention to, and believe in, becomes our experience. The law of good ideas instructs us to begin to practice the art of giving our attention and belief to good ideas. As we practice abiding by the ideas of abundance, wisdom, strength, love, faith, imagination, life and health, we will begin to see positive and distinct changes for the better transforming our lives.

Try making friends with the most powerfully good ideas that are available to you as human beings. Try giving them your attention and belief. Instead of filling your minds with aimless chatter or with fears and negativity, work at filling your minds with the presence and instruction of positive ideas. As you do, you will not only be blessed but you will become blessed representatives in our world of the life-transforming "law of good ideas." You will slowly and surely grow from negativity and limitation to an abundance of usefulness and happiness.

WEEK THIRTY-ONE : LAW E

A happy person is not a person in a certain set of circumstances but rather a person with a certain set of attitudes.

"Which do you see, the donut or the hole?" "Is your glass half full or half empty?" Your answers to these often-asked questions will tell you whether you're an optimist or a pessimist, as the following scenario illustrates.

Two women work in the same office and receive the same pay. Anne complains that she is underpaid. She feels she's asked to handle too many things for someone on her salary level. She arrives dreading the day ahead and leaves tired and discouraged. Mary, on the other hand, is happy to have a secure job and enough money to pay her bills, with some left for extras and for savings. She looks at each task as a challenge and does her best to accomplish whatever is demanded of her. She arrives looking forward to the day and leaves happy to be heading home to her family, feeling good about what she's accomplished. Not surprisingly, after an employee review, Mary receives both a promotion and a salary increase. Anne is let go.

The simple things in life can bring much joy if you look at them with a positive attitude. Flying a kite with a child can be fun or it can be time wasted if you wish you were doing something else. Receiving a compliment from your employer, a teacher or a family member for something you did especially well can make you feel wonderful. Facing each task with the determination to do the job to the very best of your ability will bring something positive to the actual doing and a solid feeling of accomplishment after the job is completed. You can get out of bed ready to make the day an adventure. Or you can drag yourself out of bed dreading the hours ahead. You can get up early enough to have the time to relax with a healthful breakfast. Or you can stay under the covers as long as possible and rush to work, mind and body already weary and your thoughts all scrambled from hurrying. Your attitudes help create your circumstances; they make you either a happy or an unhappy person. Of course, life inevitably brings problems, troubles and sadness to us all, but if your glass is half full, your attitudes will help you triumph over those times.

WEEK THIRTY-TWO : LAW A

Seeking entertainment prevents greatness.

Do you ever find yourself held hostage by the television set, unable to switch it off when you want to? Do you sometimes feel more committed to your favorite TV show than to your marriage or work? Have you ever felt you knew a character in a soap opera better than your next door neighbor?

If you've answered yes to any of these questions, you may be suffering from couch potato syndrome. A euphemism derived from the inert, vegetative posture of the television viewer on the sofa, "couch potato" aptly characterizes the TV addict. Because couch potato syndrome is far easier to see in others than in yourself, self-diagnosis is often difficult. Many times, however, those close to you will help you discover the disorder. When your friends or family start complaining that they can't find time to talk to you except during the re-run season, you might begin to suspect you've fallen prey to the disease. When they stop trying to talk to you at all, move out, or file for divorce, you can be sure you've caught the disease.

TV's been called the "boob tube." We don't have to look far to discover why television has earned this derisive nickname. Just look around the living rooms of most modern households and it's likely you'll see countless children, teenagers and adults reduced to mindlessness by the flickering images on the TV screen. Mesmerized by sitcoms, football games, musical videos, soap operas, movies, talk shows, cartoons, news programs and the myriad other forms that abound on television, the brain power of the world is held captive until the next commercial break.

As benign as watching a few hours of television might seem on the surface, the mass hypnotism of this kind of entertainment is the symptom of a serious malady of modern civilization. Couch potatoes, glued as they are to the "tube," tend to become passive. Despite their innate potential for establishing meaningful relationships and a creative environment outside of their daily work, they while away precious hours of the day being distracted from life. Along with providing short-term relief from stress, television entertainment actually creates changes in the viewer that can prevent him from expressing his greatness.

Individuals who watch television regularly become passive witnesses of what is projected onto the screen. As a result, they tend to become reactive rather than proactive in their approach to life. They may come to feel that anything beyond watching the screen is just too much work. Educators today are aware of television's impact on students. Some educators predict that textbook learning will be almost obsolete in the future because reading has become too much of an effort for students. This may not be pure laziness, either, for scientists have begun to see actual changes in the brain structure of those who have been exposed to long-term television viewing. These changes make it difficult for the student to concentrate long enough to read a book.

The visual media often induce a kind of trance, and, in it, viewers are highly suggestible. Through extended periods of viewing, people tend to grow less discerning; they simply accept what they are shown without regard for the value of its message or aesthetic quality. The blitzkrieg of information in the rapid succession of visual images can overload the circuits and may make the processing of information at the conscious level next to impossible. The conscious mind becomes lazy because it is not given time to think, while the unconscious mind becomes clogged with undifferentiated data. Today, this includes graphic images of crime, disaster and violence which frequently induce anxiety and fear in the viewer.

Despite some of television's drawbacks, however, a run through the channels confirms that it is indeed fascinating. Television creates imaginary worlds that are larger than life while it reduces actual world events into media displays. It manipulates reality and invites us to be entertained by these distortions. Because they are so intriguing, we tend to be drawn in by them. If television did not do all of these things effectively, it could not so readily capture the attention of so many people for so many hours each day. However, we need to be aware that this fascination may also detract from our lives. The escape into passive entertainment of any kind may ultimately sentence us to the mediocre expression of those talents which could be best and most creative in ourselves.

Occasionally it is good to take a break from the routine of everyday life. It is frequently helpful to withdraw from the pressures of daily work and decision-making, for the old adage is true, "All work and no play makes Jack a dull boy!" To be more effective in life we need some balance of work with recreational activities. But we should keep in mind that entertainment is significantly different from recreation. Recreation is often entertaining and enjoyable, but recreation is never merely entertaining. Entertainment diverts us from life, while recreation can take us more deeply into it.

In recreation, we re-energize ourselves in ways that can lead to new creativity. Recreation can take many forms but, at its most effective, it provides some contrast to usual activities. For example, someone who spends most of his day behind a desk working with a computer will probably find a great deal of refreshment in taking a long walk. When the environment expands beyond the rectangular video display, the walker's world-view is likely to expand; the intellect engages and processes new information. And, while strolling along, there may come a moment of sudden insight, "Aha!" The solution to a stubborn problem that weeks of concentrated labor had not unraveled comes clear in an instant. The one who takes time out for some recreation may return to work, eager and enthusiastic to tackle problems from a fresh viewpoint.

Some days it certainly seems easier to simply kick back, pop a top, turn on the boob tube and be a couch potato. Going for a walk, or reading a book, or finding something to do that is truly creative may seem to be too much trouble. Sometimes we get so stuck in our habitual ways of escaping the routines of life that we even forget there is an option besides entertainment. But every time we seek simply to be entertained, let us be aware that there is a price to be paid. Mediocrity or greatness? Which do you choose?

What you resist, you draw to yourself.
Dick Sutphen

There is a legend about a small boy who was afraid of ghosts. He feared that one day a ghost would come and carry him away from his home and family. In order to prevent this from happening, the boy began to study everything he could learn about magic and ghosts. Each night before going to sleep, he would put charms around his bed to protect himself from every type of ghost he could conjure up in his vivid imagination.

According to the legend, none of the ghosts cared about the boy at first. Yet, once they noticed all the charms with which the boy surrounded himself, they grew very curious about him. Why was he using so many charms against them? One ghost, whom no one liked, took the charms to be a challenge. The ghost spent years finding a way to circumvent the charms. Eventually he got through them and spirited the boy away.

In another legend, a poor king stumbled across a vast treasure of rubies and other gems. The king, knowing nothing of such stones, proudly displayed them throughout his domain. Then, one day a visitor came to his castle. He lectured the king, telling him he was extremely careless with his valuable stones. For the first time, the king, realizing what vast wealth he had, locked the rubies and gems in a vault and hired a large garrison to guard them.

Before long, the ruling monarch of the neighboring kingdom noticed the large garrison the king had hired and wondered what enormous treasure the king must be guarding, surely one of immense value. The neighboring king, deciding that no garrison was a match for his own, attacked the king's castle, robbing him of his precious stones.

It's not only true in legend that what we resist is drawn to us. For example, when someone is learning to water ski, the one such thing that can keep the novice from staying above the water is the fear she will fall. If she doesn't worry about falling, she can easily stand up on the skis. However, if she's constantly worried about falling, then she'll fall almost every time before she's managed to stand up on the skis.

Whether we resist something real—a robber, for instance—or something in our thoughts, such as anxiety or fear, the energy we invest in the fight becomes irresistibly attractive to the object of our interest. Often, if we fight against such things, we draw them closer to us. If we leave the things we fear alone, they are more likely to leave us alone. Never forget that "what you resist, you draw to yourself."

WEEK THIRTY-TWO : LAW C

All sunshine makes a desert.
Oriental Proverb

What would life be like on earth if we had no clouds, no rain, nothing but sunshine? Sometimes we may think we would like to have only sunshine but without the rain we would be left with a dry, barren planet, incapable of supporting life as we know it.

Our lives are filled with sunny days and stormy days, good times and frightening times, pleasure and pain. Often we try to create only experiences of pleasure and happiness. However, by attempting to control our experiences, we often set ourselves up for an existence full of fear.

Have you ever known someone who lived in fear? There was once an escaped convict, a man who had run from the law enforcement officials of his country for many years. He was plagued by confusion and doubt and, over time, began to use drugs in an attempt to feel happier. His need to escape his doubts and confusion was so great that he did whatever was necessary to buy the drugs. The drugs numbed his inner pain and blurred his mind, blotting out the things that bothered him. This desperate attempt at control worked for awhile, but soon he required even more drugs to push away the pain and fear. He began to steal from others to buy his drugs and eventually he was caught and imprisoned. The man's desire to feel happier by avoiding pain ended in a long prison term, in an environment that he later said was designed to support the dying, not the living.

We all need balance in our lives. Very few of us would survive an existence that is totally filled with fear, doubts and negativity. Just as rain nurtures beautiful green grass and sunlight can kindle a sense of warmth and inner peace, so confusion and doubt can compel us to seek for a greater understanding—engendering new beliefs and ideas about life. Happy times provide for pleasant memories to relive during difficult experiences and, like old friends, fill the void when we feel like everything good has abandoned us.

Remember the Chinese proverb when the road ahead looks rocky: "All sunshine makes a desert." Remember that a desert will not support life without some rain. Look for the balance in your life. If it is not there, then it's time to create it!

WEEK THIRTY-TWO : LAW D

Comparisons give us cancer of the soul.
G. Jampolsky

Jill sat down and looked to see who was in her new class. Her heart sank as Katy, laughing with the football captain, floated to a seat and eased into place, arranging her expensive skirt and crossing her legs so that her stylish leather boots blocked the aisle.

Katy was beautiful and so sophisticated. She wore a different outfit each day or so it seemed to Jill and her friends. With her wealthy parents, she traveled to famous cities and exotic places Jill had never even heard of before.

Jill was a good student and a talented actress and singer, but when she was around Katy, she felt awkward and gauche. She lived with her mother who worked hard to pay the rent and buy groceries and keep their old car running, and there was little to spend on clothes. Jill was very creative and sewed her clothes and was often complimented on her outfits, but whenever Katy was around, the difference between Katy's expensively-made outfits and Jill's own homemade clothes seemed obvious to Jill. So she avoided Katy.

The teacher was assigning study pairs, and, to her dismay, Jill heard him assign Katy as her study partner. Katy turned and smiled. Jill dutifully pulled her chair toward her, tripping over an extended foot. Her classmates' laughter burned her cheeks as she sat down next to Katy. "Well, let's get to work," Jill said, exasperated. She chose words from the text and asked Katy to define them, correcting Katy's mistakes with grim satisfaction.

After several tries, Katy seemed more confused than ever and finally said, "Look, I know you would rather have a smarter study partner, so if you want to trade, it's all right with me." Startled, Jill looked into Katy's eyes for the first time and saw how miserable she was. Jill looked away, confused and embarrassed. "I've always felt so unsure around you anyway," Katy continued, "I don't know if I could get anything right."

Jill looked at Katy in astonishment. "You feel unsure around me?" she asked.

Katy looked surprised. "Why yes! I could never get up in front of people and do what you do! You're so confident, as if you know you can do anything. You never get nervous when you read out loud or speak in class, and the way you sing! I'd give *any*thing to do that."

Jill realized she had been comparing the way she felt on the inside, with the way Katy looked on the outside, and Katy had been doing the same thing. All those times when Jill felt inadequate and insecure around Katy, Katy felt the same way around her. It had nothing to do with the clothes they wore or the way they acted. Each felt the other was better, because of their perceived appearance.

At times, all of us feel inadequate, but our outsides seldom reveal our true feelings, and when we compare ourselves to others, it only eats away like a cancer at our sense of well being. It's natural that others do some things better than we do. Each of us has unique talents and abilities, and developing our own talents is the true path to happiness.

Whether you think you can or not, you are right.

Henry Ford

Would it surprise you to learn that everything in your life right now is pretty much the way you made it? That from hundreds of options you chose your responses to whatever situations presented themselves? Would you agree that you have exercised the capacity to choose what you have received? If so, doesn't it stand to reason that if you made the choice in the first place, you can change it?

What a powerful notion! Whatever happens to you, you can say, "I am the master of my life."

But just as the good that comes to you is a demonstration of your mastery, so is the negative. Consider how hopping fleas are trained. The fleas are put into a glass jar. As they try to jump in the jar, they bump their heads on the lid. Over time, they forget they can jump and, for fear of bumping their heads, never go beyond the limits of the jar, even though the lids have been removed. Through continued failure they have become conditioned to confinement. So it is with us, if we let it be. Our self-made limitations sometimes cause us to forget that we can fly. We often needlessly confine ourselves to glass jars. We may yearn to use our lives creatively, but our invisible prisons remind us: "You can't do that. It isn't practical. You're not smart enough. It will cost too much. People will laugh at you. You're too young. You're too old. Your health won't allow it. Your parents won't allow it. It will take too long. You don't have the education."

But suppose we could remember that we were made to achieve? Suppose we really believed that we are children and heirs of this magnificent universe? Would we then still allow our jars to limit us to hopping just so far and no further? Suppose we became aware that resentments, hurts, hates, grudges, illness, greed and the like are glass jars that have been, or can be, removed, that, indeed, we may be hampered by the illusion of our own self-imposed limitations? We attract to ourselves whatever our minds are focused upon.

Once aware, we can change and then we will no longer be confined to that glass jar. We will be ready and able to achieve!

Use wisely your power of choice.
Og Mandino

Of all powers that you possess as a human being what do you believe is the greatest power of all? Your greatest power is the power *to choose*. What you are, right now, is the sum total of all the choices that you have made in your life. The power to choose is the power to create— the power to create *who you are*.

Every choice that you make is a building block of your life. Every act, every word, every decision becomes a part of you. The way that you see and respond to the world you live in is the result of the choices you have made. So, in a sense, not only do your choices make who *you* are, but they, in effect, make *your world* because the world that you *see* is the world that *you* live in.

Some choices are obvious. We choose what clothes we wear; what we eat for lunch; the friends we wish to be with. Some decisions are easy; some are difficult; but *you* always make the choice. Some things may appear to be forced upon us, yet they are still our choices. For example, we may say that we *have to* go to school or work. True, we may be encouraged or even pressured to make certain decisions yet ultimately it is *we* who make the choice.

Rarely are there times when you have absolutely no choice as to what you will do; and, even if there were, you still have the choice as to how you will respond to what you "must" or "can't" do. Whenever we believe that we have no choice and that we are powerless over our life experiences, we are denying the most important power that we have— the power to choose. Be aware of the times when you say, "I can't. . . ," "I must. . . ," "I've got to . . . ." You probably have many more choices than you realize.

What if "I can't help the way I feel"? You have a choice as to how you respond to what you feel. For example, maybe you're angry because you have to get up and go to school when you would much rather stay in bed. What can you do with your anger? You have many choices. You can (mis)direct it at someone else; you can suppress it into a sullen resentment; you can work it off by running or hitting a punching bag; you can talk about it with a friend; you can "listen" to the anger to hear what it has to teach you, etc. etc.

If you have to do something you don't like you can ask yourself: "Is there another way to do this that might work better for me? How much longer must I do this? What alternatives do I have now or in the future?" When you really become conscious of your power of choice it may amaze you as to how many choices you really *do* have. You have much more power over your life than you may realize. You have the power to change your life and indeed even to change who you are through your power of choice. Use it wisely!

By choosing bad thoughts you can build a hell on earth but by choosing good thoughts you can build your own heaven on earth here and now.

WEEK THIRTY-THREE : LAW B

Work is love made visible.
Kahlil Gibran

The transition from adolescence to adulthood is often filled with stress and fueled with both anger and confusion. Suddenly you are more independent than you've ever been before and, while the freedom can feel great, there comes with it a responsibility you may not be ready to shoulder. It has probably grown increasingly clear that your parents aren't going to take care of you forever and that you'll have to find something worthwhile to do with your life.

Suddenly you are asked to make choices about college and a career that will affect the course of your entire life. There's a lot of pressure on you to choose wisely. Maybe you think you need to go to a prestigious school that will put you on the fast track to riches and success.

Or maybe you feel you should let your parents decide for you. But in the end, abdicating decision-making to others will cause you more stress than the temporary discomfort of reaching toward a decision on your own.

On one level, a career can be described as a job that sustains your interest while you make enough money to support yourself in a comfortable life style. But a career can be more than that—it can be a vocation. The word vocation is from the Latin root "to call." Your vocation, then, is a calling, and in a very deep sense finding your vocation is finding yourself. When you have found your calling, you can give love through your work. In fact, love is the key to your success in mastering your vocation. It directs you to those special talents you can give to the world and shows you how to share them with others.

Kahlil Gibran wrote in *The Prophet* that "work is love made visible." Every invention and work of art begins with love. The Wright Brothers' love of the idea of flight—their vocation—produced the first airplane. Your own careful choice of a career can be a contribution to others as well as to your own sense of fulfillment—it can be an expression of love. It can be a life's work with rewards far greater than the accumulation of wealth.

You shouldn't expect to find your life's work—your true vocation—in a college catalog, nor should you expect that the company you join will have a ready-made position waiting for you. A vocation cannot be given out by order of a personnel department; it grows, as an original, not a copy, within each one of us. A vocation is not putting in hours to earn a pay check; rather, it is your most valuable asset and the greatest gift of yourself and your talent that you can give to the world. Every useful work is a ministry.

The Wright Brothers dreamed a magnificent dream and worked to make it come true. If you follow your vocation faithfully, if you're not afraid to dream and to use your talents to the maximum, you, too, may reach the pinnacle of accomplishment.

WEEK THIRTY-THREE : LAW C

No man is free who is not master of himself.

Epictetus

"No man is free who is not master of himself." The Greek philosopher and slave, Epictetus, declared this truth in the first century A.D. Of course if you were a slave, then as now, freedom to control your own destiny would very likely be the foremost thought in your mind. But while it is true that the owner, the slavemaster, stands between the slave and his freedom, Epictetus understood that true freedom results not merely from escaping the slave master but also from becoming master of yourself.

There are many paths—and a wide diversity of philosophies and practices—that lead to self-mastery, as countless books written on this subject can attest. Yet a common theme runs through each of them. In Christian teaching it is stated this way: "The kingdom of God is within you" [Luke 17:21]. Freedom, happiness, peace of mind, all that we seek—and more—lies within us.

Self-mastery begins the moment you realize that you make your own prison and that you're the only person who can set you free. Sometimes we blame another for keeping us in bondage, but we are free or not free only to the extent that we can master ourselves.

What is freedom? Is it the right to do anything we want without restriction? Not really, for even in the freest of all societies, laws are needed to insure freedom for everyone. Perhaps true freedom is not the freedom to *do,* but rather the freedom to *become* all that we can be.

How do you earn the right to play a musical instrument or to create a work of art? It's not a right given to you by someone else but comes only once you master the skills necessary to create music or art. How do you attain the freedom to live a happy, creative life? Can anyone else grant you that freedom? No, that freedom also results from mastering the attitudes and skills needed to create a happy life.

When you conquer those twins enemies—your own fear and ignorance—you will be on your way to true freedom. Fear and ignorance are indeed slavemasters and we will remain enslaved as long as we give them house room in our hearts and minds. Only by overcoming our fear and by knowing the truth can we become truly free.

The best way to overcome fear is to face squarely whatever makes us fearful. Avoiding fear-provoking situations does not resolve them. Like the mouse that roared, often the things that cause us the greatest anxiety are much less threatening than we imagined. Whenever life challenges you with something unknown and you find yourself afraid, face and analyze your fear and watch it diminish.

Freedom can be ours only when we recognize that we create our own prisons and that we can set ourselves free at any time. By facing our fears we can learn to relinquish them and begin to take full responsibility for the usefulness of our lives. That is true self-mastery and true freedom.

WEEK THIRTY-THREE : LAW D

By choosing your thoughts, you can create either hell or heaven on earth.

There is an ancient legend about three men, each of whom carried two sacks that were tied around their necks, one in front and one in back. When the first man was asked what was in his sacks he said, "All my friends' kind deeds are in the sack on my back where they're hidden from sight and soon forgotten. The sack in front carries all the unkind things that have happened to me and as I walk along, I often stop, take those things out and look at them from every angle. I concentrate on them and study them. I direct all my thoughts and feelings toward them."

Consequently, because the first man was always stopping to mull over unfortunate things that had happened to him in the past, he made little progress.

When the second man was asked what he was carrying in his two sacks, he replied, "In the front sack are all my good deeds. I keep these before me and continually take them out and flash them around for everyone to see. The sack in the rear holds all my mistakes. I carry them with me wherever I go. They're heavy and they slow me down, but for some reason I just can't put them aside."

The third man, when asked about his two sacks, replied, "The front sack is full of wonderful thoughts about people, the kind deeds they've done and all the good I've had in my life. It's a big sack and very full, but it isn't heavy. The weight is like the sails on a ship—far from being a burden, it helps me onward. The sack on my back is empty because I have cut a big hole in the bottom of it. In that sack I put all the evil I hear of others and all the bad I sometimes think about myself. Those things fall through the hole and are lost forever, so I have no weight to make my journey more difficult."

From time to time, as each of us journeys down the path of life, we should examine what we are carrying with us. Are we weighted down by negative thoughts about ourselves? Are we weighted down by lumps of fear that tell us we don't measure up to some artificial standard? Are we weighted down by protective shields and psychological armor that prevents us from relating to others in a free and wholehearted manner? Do we carry with us all those misdeeds of friends and family that have caused us distress in the past? Do we carry with us all those false lessons that teach us to look for undesirable characteristics in others and then run the other way when we detect one of those characteristics?

Each of us is born with the freedom to choose the thoughts that will direct our lives. We choose the path we want to walk down. We have the power to choose what we wish to carry along the way. With that in mind, it would seem to make good sense to choose thoughts that will form positive attitudes and that stress our unlimited potential. Negative thoughts and attitudes weigh us down; they make our journey through life so much more difficult. Every thought we allow into our mind affects the thoughts, feelings and actions we express. If we hold negative thoughts, our actions are going to be negative and, in turn, negative results will be returned to us. However, positive thoughts return positive results and life becomes a happy, motivating adventure in which we see ourselves and all others in the true light of what we really are. We suddenly see that each of us is a wonderful, magical, mysterious expression of life. As long as our thoughts remain positive and are grounded in accomplishing the goal in front of us, the progress we make on the path of life will be steady and rewarding.

WEEK THIRTY-THREE : LAW E

The greatest charity is to help a person change from being a receiver to being a giver.

Edward was fifty-two years old when he finally admitted that he was an alcoholic. Like many before him, he knew that Alcoholics Anonymous was his only remaining option. It was a move he was reluctant to make, however. No one wants to admit defeat, but he was thoroughly beaten, not only physically but also emotionally. He was embarrassed that others would know he was an alcoholic, though in fact everyone who knew him at all well was aware of his condition.

After a few weeks of attending AA meetings, the fog began to clear from his mind. He kept hearing the strange phrase, "You've got to give it away to keep it." The "it" was sobriety and AA told him that once he attained it he would have to share it with others to maintain his own good. But unfortunately Edward was a self-centered and selfish individual. He thought to himself: "No way. Whatever it is, as soon as I get it I'm going to hold onto it and keep it just for me."

When we hoard things instead of passing them on, they become valueless. It's much better to follow St. Francis's edict, "It is by forgetting self that one finds." When we choose to get beyond the self and act with a loving, generous spirit, then we receive what we're giving away.

But how do we help someone become something they don't want to be, even if they'll ultimately benefit from it? Perhaps the best way is to lead by example. Those of us who have learned some of these "giver" lessons can become role models to the takers in life. If we are willing to perform a task for another, others are more likely to follow. And now a paradox comes into play. Someone who is incapable of receiving love will not be able to give love. We have to be able to receive God's love in order to give it away, for we cannot give what we do not have.

In order to be a true giver, our motives for giving must be pure. Give because you genuinely want to. Give because you believe in life. Give willingly and joyfully and joy will be your reward.

Let us return to Edward, who truly changed through the gift that others shared with him. He became an avid sharer of experience, strength, hope, time and love. He has learned to give to others that which is given to him with an open hand and heart. Sometimes what he gives is not accepted, but the good he is trying to give away returns to him.

And so the ripples from the stone thrown in the pond move out and those of us privileged to watch and experience this movement have a vital role in passing on the good we receive in order that others may benefit. And when others benefit, so do we. The ripples of love and giving move out, and farther out, and all of us are blessed.

WEEK THIRTY-FOUR : LAW A

Leave no stone unturned.
Euripides

What Euripides intended to express was the idea of going to whatever lengths necessary to achieve a worthwhile goal. He was advocating the virtue of diligence. Mother Teresa of India goes so far as to declare that "diligence is the beginning of sanctity," sanctity in simple terms being a closer walk with God in the path that that higher power has lovingly designed for each person. In working with steady, trusting effort, a person can arrive at the place prepared by divine order, even though obstacles may be present. The person possessing diligence does not allow stones or any other obstacles to remain in his way.

While turning over the stones along one's search for direction and progress toward one's goal, it is also important not to let the process itself cause us to lose sight of what we're striving for. Frantically wasting energy in trying to move enormous obstacles blocking our way can be an exercise in futility. Calmly allowing guidance to suggest an alternate method of action shows greater wisdom.

Explorers, inventors, scientists, and artists all have at one time or another transcended the limits of the known in their journeys of discovery. Applying diligence, such individuals found the strength to struggle onward toward illusive goals.

Leaving no stone unturned, Noah Webster spent twenty years compiling the first dictionary of the English language. Robert E. Peary tried for twenty-three years to reach the North Pole before succeeding on April 6, 1900. Songwriter Irving Berlin received only thirty-three cents for his first song, yet remained undaunted until he ultimately received international recognition for his music.

Diligence can often produce startling success that at first may be unimaginable. Before he was able to set sail, Christopher Columbus left no stone unturned in acquiring financial backing for his expedition. His diligent pursuit of a new trade route to the Indies resulted in the discovery of entirely new lands—the Americas.

Mme. Curie spent her entire adult life conducting scientific research. Her diligence in the laboratory resulted in the discovery of the elements radium and polonium and laid the groundwork for nuclear physics and theories of radioactivity. In her case, one stone overturned became a stepping stone to the next discovery. Mme. Curie was the first person to be awarded the Nobel prize twice.

Removing obstacles requires stamina. When strength is severely tested, discouragement may result, at least temporarily. At such times repeating the edict of Euripides and continuing to exert more energy may be fruitless. Words found in The New Testament may help us to continue our efforts: "God did not give us a spirit of timidity, but a spirit of power and love and self-control" (2 Timothy 1:7). Renewed and refreshed, keeping in mind the power within, a person will have greater strength to follow the counsel of Euripides and continue to "leave no stone unturned."

WEEK THIRTY-FOUR : LAW B

What we focus on expands.
Arnold Patent

When we focus on a particular thought, our mind immediately responds by calling up similar thoughts. Positive and loving thoughts and feelings spark a whole range of thoughts and feelings that lift our spirits. If, on the other hand, we concentrate on negative thoughts and fearful emotions, we conjure up an ever greater negativity. Our success in performing a task often depends on whether we focus on positive or negative thoughts. Remember that if we're preoccupied with what we *don't* have (the negative side of our thinking), we are unable to see what we *do* have (the positive side).

Stop for a minute and focus on the word "blue." Images probably come to mind of the sky or the ocean. We can observe the same effect with words of a more intangible nature. Consider the word "happy." Focusing on this word might expand our image to such things as a wonderful vacation we once took, a smiling child at play, or to an entertaining movie we once saw. Whatever we choose to focus on, our minds automatically expand that image for us.

Given this truth, wouldn't you rather focus on positive images than negative ones? Assume you are faced with a complicated task and your mind focuses on the word "failure." Suddenly an image is evoked in which you fail at your task. The image expands to the point where you fail at other tasks and, possibly, to the point where people ridicule you for your failure. Now, assume you are faced with the same task and decide to focus on the word "success." Positive images of accomplishing the task fill your mind. You see images of others appreciating your success, shaking your hand, smiling with admiration. This success image snowballs and you see yourself succeeding at other, more difficult, tasks.

But do these thoughts affect your actual performance? When you focus on a particular image, you tend to talk about what's on your mind. Thus, if you're focused on positive images, you're likely to mention these to the people you're in communication with. A good listener, who focuses on what is being said, will absorb your positive words and many positive images might come to him. Like the spark that ignites the flame, he may share these good ideas with others and they in turn will share them with still others. Thoughts expand not only within our own minds, but expand through others as well.

Focusing on positive thoughts often produces more positive thoughts and these can help improve our success when performing tasks. What we focus on, we talk about and can cause others to focus on. Thus our thoughts expand to those around us. Always try to keep this law of life in mind: What we focus on does indeed expand. By developing a happy, positive acceptance of the good you have right now, you can be sure that in the future you will know how to enjoy the surprises that come your way. It takes practice to do anything well. Instead of dwelling on your dissatisfactions, focus on your happiness and watch it expand.

By developing a happy, positive acceptance of the good you have right now, you can be sure that in the future you will know how to enjoy the surprises that come your way. It takes practice to do anything well. Instead of dwelling on your dissatisfactions, focus on your happiness and watch it expand.

WEEK THIRTY-FOUR : LAW C

By free will each of us is a co-creator in life.

"As above, so below" has in more recent years been translated to "As within, so without." As you think, so you are. Indeed, it is not only "new thought" practitioners who are proclaiming this but even modern day physicians are coming to understand that our thoughts create our reality and our state of health.

Each of us has a choice about how we react in any given situation. We can be positive or negative; we can choose to trust or to fear. We were not originally created with the spirit of fear; rather, as spiritual beings, we were designed to be filled with love and trust but, over the years of human existence, negativity has become incorporated into mankind's collective consciousness.

Even so, more and more people are becoming aware of their responsibility to each other. Physicists and scientists are now conducting experiments to prove that we all are one, that each living soul is interlinked with all others; that we are indeed part of the whole; and that what each of us does, affects all others. In the last two decades there has been an enormous upsurge of people choosing to believe this and act accordingly and, as a result, our world is changing for the better. More and more people are coming to believe that a power greater than themselves is in charge.

Sophie is a recent convert to a belief in spiritual progress. She had experienced a dysfunctional childhood and much of her thinking was very negative. As long as she continued to hold on to her old ideas, her journey to spiritual maturity was difficult and slow. One day, she was moaning, as was her habit, about a headache. She was rehearsing the headache's progress, how it would develop into a migraine by the evening and how she would miss work the next day, which she couldn't afford to do. A friend overheard her and suggested that she was enjoying her misery. "Why don't you take an aspirin and a hot drink and lie down? Stop holding on to what you don't want. Start believing the headache will go away and look forward to a wonderful day at work—or do you *prefer* being miserable?"

The truth of her friend's words struck Sophie and her headache was gone when she awoke from her nap. It was then that she started doing some serious self-examination; she saw how she used sickness as a way of getting attention and vowed to begin reprogramming her thinking.

Like Sophie, we can begin to work to become masters of our world instead of its victims. Instead of allowing ourselves to be consumed by our egos, we need to remember that each of us is a co-creator in life. When we do that, we can rise above negativity and allow the indwelling divinity in each of us to guide us to best solutions.

When we rule our minds in a positive way, not driven by our egos, we truly do become masters of our world and our destiny, and we can create for ourselves a life that is happy, joyous and free.

WEEK THIRTY-FOUR : LAW D

Thoughts of doubt and fear are pathways to failure.
Brian Adams

One summer evening a man sat alone in his backyard; it bordered a peaceful forest. His goal was to relax and enjoy the quiet pleasures of an evening close to nature. As darkness fell, the man began to notice the wind becoming stronger in the trees. Soon he began to doubt the fine weather would last. Next, he began to listen to the sounds stirring from the depths of the forest. He imagined menacing animals stalking close by. Before much longer, his mind was completely taken up with negative thoughts and he grew more and more tense. The more the man allowed thoughts of doubt and fear to enter his mind, the farther he moved from his goal of enjoying the peaceful summer evening. His experience illustrates the law of life expressed by Brian Adams, "Thoughts of doubt and fear are pathways to failure."

Definitions of failure will vary from person to person, from situation to situation, but whatever the definition, failure involves the inability to achieve some predetermined goal or objective.

The twin monsters, doubt and fear, frequently play a leading role when a goal is not achieved. Doubt and fear are experts at infiltrating the camp where success plans its strategies. When allowed to remain in mind, these two negative forces multiply rapidly and can overrun a person's ability to enjoy a situation or to see positive strategies that can help overcome temporary difficulties.

For example, a student who is mentally or physically fatigued, poorly nourished or emotionally upset may provide the twin monsters with a resting place. Once this happens, watch out! One worry will bring on another doubt and that doubt will have for its companion another fear. Soon the student will become tense and anxious and begin to question his ability to remember material he studied for the exam. A student who seriously doubts his ability to perform on a test will, in fact, frequently perform poorly. Tension created by a growing sense of insecurity will mentally erase the facts a person needs to remember.

"Thoughts of doubt and fear are pathways to failure" holds true in the animal kingdom as well. A horse about to take a hurdle will sometimes balk short of the jump if it senses doubt or fear in its rider. The situation that the rider fears most, failure to complete the jump, is the end result.

To avoid failure in any situation, thoughts must be focused in positive directions. Successful athletes illustrate such positive thinking when they perform. Concentrating on successfully completing the play at hand leaves no room to consider any outcome other than success. A supportive audience will aid the player's performance by concentrating on the action along with the athlete. In professional golf, the audience surrounding the player often joins him in deep, silent concentration. The audience collectively holds his breath until the golfer takes the shot. After the shot is completed, onlookers let out their emotions in the form of shouts, handclapping, cheers. Even the disappointed "oh's," should the shot fall short, show that the audience believed the shot would be successfully completed.

Thoughts are pathways, and positive thoughts are clear pathways. When clogged by the monsters, doubt and fear, our thoughts are often of failure and defeat. When the pathways are well-guarded and fortified with positive thoughts and expectations, the monsters are usually defeated. In a positive mind, doubt and fear are not present to sabotage ultimate success.

If you can't say something good, then don't say anything.

When David's parents were divorced, the settlement provided that he would live with his mother. Because tightened financial circumstances forced them to move, David had to attend a new school and make new friends. The changes were traumatic for him. He resented the children whose parents were still married; he often got into fights, with little or no provocation. In his bitterness, he developed the habit of being overly critical of others. He rarely had a kind word to say about anyone.

One day a classmate, who was aware of David's situation, approached him. "My parents are divorced too," he said. "I know what you're going through. But you have to let go of your anger and bitterness. You're really hard on people," he continued, "and it only hurts you. If you can't say something good, it's better not to say anything at all."

In his pain, David found it difficult to appreciate the boy's advice. But since things only seemed to be getting worse, he became more cautious about what he said to others. He refrained from speaking where before he would have said something sarcastic and cutting. He began to see how insensitive he had been to those around him. Many of the other children had also been through family break-ups, and he soon found ways to encourage them and help them deal with their own pain and confusion. By the end of the school term, David made a complete turnaround in his attitude and gained the respect of many he had alienated in his anger.

We all experience stressful times at home, at school, or in our work. When things are not going well it is often tempting to criticize others. Perhaps it is because we think finding fault with someone else will help us feel better about ourselves or our condition. Or maybe it is simply that misery loves company.

In those down moments that all of us have experienced, it is best to remain silent if we cannot say things that are helpful and kind. Destructive language tends to produce destructive results. Besides causing unnecessary suffering for those around us, our negative words frequently compound our own problems.

We may feel justified in using harsh and cutting words if we are having difficulty dealing with life's challenges. The young man whose parents were divorced was torn by many unresolved emotions, many feelings he did not understand. He eventually found, though, that belittling and hurting others was not the way to resolve his problems. Through kind and understanding words, or simply by listening with compassion, he learned to give support to others and, in turn, to receive support from those around him and to find it within himself.

"If you can't say something good, then don't say anything at all." You would be wise to use this time-honored adage as a benchmark for the words you speak throughout the day. If you feel down about something, talk to a friend, or a counselor if necessary. Everyone has dark moments. But be careful not to lash out and hurt others when you're not feeling good about yourself, for they too may need words of understanding and support. Always be sensitive in what you say to others. Try to remember that the bad moments will pass and, when they do, you will have no unnecessary wounds to heal.

WEEK THIRTY-FIVE : LAW A

Give the extra ounce.

John worked for six years as an orderly in a large city hospital. Because he was crippled in one foot, he was initially hired on a trial basis. John went through that trial period with flying colors. Because he was handicapped from birth, John had learned how to move quickly and adjust to his disability. The result was that he not only performed his duties well but he actually moved as quickly as most of the other orderlies.

John did much more than his duties. He found time to hold the hands of frightened or worried patients before moving them to the operating room. Often John ran an errand for a patient, losing all or part of a break period. Sometimes, after duty, he would stay on to write a letter for someone too sick to do it for herself, or to talk to a lonely patient who never received visitors, or to sit for a while with the parents of a child in surgery.

Giving that extra ounce came naturally to John, perhaps because his parents had given him and his sister that extra ounce. During his childhood and youth, his doctor had given him that extra ounce. When he started school and other children stared at him, his kindergarten teacher gave the extra ounce. John was fortunate; he grew up believing that giving the extra ounce was the right way to live. It simply never occurred to him not to give the extra ounce himself.

He was a happy young man who fell in love and married during his sixth year as an orderly. Occasionally, John wished he could do more with his life professionally but then he'd thank God for allowing him all that he had. His lovely bride never thought about his crippled foot. She saw an attractive young man who worked hard and conscientiously and made others' lives happier with his extra giving. If her groom came home later than usual she only asked who had needed him. John decided that his life couldn't be better or richer or fuller.

But his life was to become richer and fuller. One of the facts connected with giving the extra ounce is that the giver nearly always receives the extra ounce in return. The giver's attitude and willingness to give of himself freely and gladly serves as an inspiration to those around him. And this is what happened in John's case.

He was called to the office of the president of the hospital. Not surprisingly, John was concerned. He enjoyed his work and the opportunities to help others; he suddenly realized that if for any reason his position was taken away from him he would feel crushed. But when John entered the president's office, the man shook his hand warmly. John was motioned to a chair.

"Would you like the opportunity to train to be an emergency technician?" the hospital president asked the young orderly. "To ride in the ambulance with the paramedics?" John couldn't answer: he was too choked up. Tears ran down his cheeks. The hospital president needed no response. It was a dream come true for John.

When he could speak, his first words were, "Sir, may I telephone my wife?" Two weeks later, he started his training. He had some classes in the hospital and some in a university connected with the medical facility. John finished the course with top grades. Next came a period of on-the-job training, going out on ambulance calls under the watchful and helpful eye and guidance of an experienced medical technician. But John accomplished more than learning how to be a good medical technician. He automatically went the extra mile and gave that extra ounce as before. While studying in class, in the field and at home with his young wife helping, he always found time to give a hand to other students, to make his own learning process pleasant and satisfying for his instructors and, once in the field, he did what he was supposed to do quickly and correctly—and with passion, comfort and kindness.

Today John is a full paramedic. He teaches classes in first aid and life-saving techniques to residents of his city. He is also the proud father of a four-year-old girl and a one-year-old boy. John's story illustrates that when we go the extra mile, when we give the extra ounce, we get many extra ounces back from others. And our lives are full of love and inner peace.

WEEK THIRTY-FIVE : LAW B

Success feeds on itself and creates more success.

Sometimes as we start out in adult life it may be difficult to feel like much of a success. Our society frequently defines success as the material goods and lifestyle secured by large amounts of money earned over a long period of time. We tend to think success is something that occurs only later in life. However, this belief may impede us from achieving success even then. Success takes practice and successful people start practicing when they're young.

Think about it for a moment. A musician must practice diligently to become a virtuoso. An athlete trains long hours before becoming a star. Likewise, it takes practice to experience success in life. If you want to feel like a success, it's important for you to begin to acknowledge your successes right now.

Many times the things at which we're naturally gifted are the hardest for us to claim as a success. "If I can do it so easily, why can't everyone else? If I can do it, it can't be that hard." It is important to listen to the acknowledgement we receive from parents, teachers, employers and friends. Don't brush it off as if they're just being nice. They are telling you, "You are a success, right now!" Answer with a sincere "Thank you." There is no need to say anything else. Making disparaging remarks about yourself or your performance is false modesty and negates the compliment that was given to you.

Maybe, when a compliment is delivered with some criticism, you're tempted to give up. You may feel that since nothing you do is good enough, why bother to try. Don't give in to those feelings. Many people, especially in your family, may have a difficult time making it clear that they appreciate your talent and are behind you. Although they want you to develop your skill to the best of your ability, it may be hard for them to express this in words. And if they take time to point out your mistakes, they may be really saying, "I know you can do better than this. I care and I want to help you."

We are often our own harshest critics and we have a tendency to hear only criticism from others and not their praise. It is important to practice hearing both compliments and constructive remarks from those who have good advice to offer. As you begin to recognize and build on the success you're experiencing now, you will discover that this is a feeling you can create again and again in all aspects of your living.

Whenever anyone says to you, "Good work!" think to yourself, "Yes, it *is* good work. I am successful with this." A swelled head is never helpful, of course, but to acknowledge your gifts is not necessarily self-indulgent, especially if you recognize you couldn't have achieved success without the support and guidance of parents, teachers, friends, and co-workers. If others say, "Okay, but you might do better," realize you may have more to give, and receive this advice with an open mind and heart. Determine to do your best. You are the one who will benefit.

Knowing right now—feeling inside right now—that you're successful whether you're a singer in the church choir, a waitress in a restaurant, the coach of the softball team, or the budding mechanic spending every spare moment in the garage rebuilding the engine of that antique car, will prepare you for greater and greater success. Success is not a one-time event. It is an accumulated series of wins that creates a successful life.

WEEK THIRTY-FIVE : LAW C

Never put off until tomorrow what you can do today.
Lord Chesterfield

Did you ever have a problem so difficult and so complex that you didn't know how to begin to solve it? Did you ever have an examination that involved so much material you didn't know where to begin to study for it? Most people have found themselves in such situations and have felt overwhelmed.

In the mid-1770's, Philip Dormer Stanhope—known to the world as Lord Chesterfield—decided to write his son a series of letters that would pass along sensible advice for living what he considered to be a positive life. Among the counsel offered was the now famous, "Never put off until tomorrow what you can do today."

There are many reasons why one should not delay action. Problems can grow more serious when they're not addressed promptly, as they arise. Minor difficulties treated in a positive, active manner generally do not become major ones. For example, a minor cut properly treated will heal quickly. But if left untreated and exposed to additional adverse conditions, the same cut can become infected and require serious medical attention. A minor inconvenience thus becomes a major problem.

In the same way, loans of money that are not repaid on a timely basis can become major debts when interest on such loans accumulates. Doing what is possible today to make life better translates into a more orderly and productive tomorrow. The key is careful assessment of what needs to be done immediately, and then how much of what needs to be done can be sensibly accomplished without damage to other areas of one's life.

If you are one of those who feels overwhelmed by an approaching examination or job test, take heart. By steadily reviewing notes and asking questions about confusing material when confusion first surfaces, you can lessen your ordeal considerably. When studying is approached sensibly, there is no need to lose sleep or to forego healthy exercise and relaxation. Good study habits practiced today prevent the need for ineffective panic-cramming tomorrow.

Steady effort is more productive than sudden, frenzied activity. Orderly progression toward a goal prevents the tangle of problems that so often occurs when too many small areas needing attention suddenly come together. Doing the best you can do on a daily basis frees more energy for further steady progress in the future. Steady effort moves a person comfortably toward a goal, with energy left to handle unforseen difficulties.

If a person were to ship a fragile vase in a carefully packed, sturdy box directly to a friend, most likely the vase would arrive in good condition. If instead the vase were poorly packed in a thin-walled box and delayed at many stations along the way, the vase would most likely arrive in damaged condition. The same is true of any problem or difficulty. The longer you ignore it and the more poorly it is handled, the bigger the problem will become.

Each of us moves toward major goals by steps. Usually these steps are small ones. Whenever we put off taking the necessary steps, progress comes to a standstill or recedes even farther into the future. By following Lord Chesterfield's advice and not putting off until tomorrow what can be done sensibly today, we can achieve an orderly, harmonious, steady movement toward whatever goal we have set for ourselves.

WEEK THIRTY-FIVE : LAW D

The things that are seen are temporal; but the things that are not seen are eternal.

2 Corinthians 4:18

When you listen to a lecture, does it sometimes seem as if the words go in one ear and out the other? Or when you read a book, do you ever see the page as just so many lines of squiggly black marks? On a purely physical level, your experience is almost accurate, for a spoken word is only a transient vibration of a sound wave upon your ear drum, and a written one is simply the momentary reflection of light waves upon the retina of your eye. In an instant, the vibration dissipates and the speech is complete; or your eye blinks and the text on the page disappears.

The significant aspect of the lecture is found far beyond the sensual perception of sound waves in the idea the speaker seeks to convey. Pleasant words that do not say anything, like the pink fluff of cotton candy, melt in the mouth and are soon forgotten. But plain and simple words, spoken from a strong realization of an important idea, carry with them a power to transform and create.

Words exist merely as physical symbols of a greater and more enduring reality. The words we use will always be, like any material thing, to some degree inadequate to the task of expressing ideas, although with practice we can increase our ability to communicate clearly. The important thing to remember is that the idea, not the word or thing that describes it, is what is real and enduring. In selecting values to live by, it makes sense to build a value system that is based on ideas which will be lasting and strong.

The singer, Madonna, once had a hit song that described her vision of a person happily living in modern culture. She sang, "I am a material girl, and I live in a material world." On the surface, this song may express the false ideal of a life filled with fun and pleasure, an existence teeming with all the bodily things a person could ever want. Yet what it fails to convey is the temporal nature of the material world. What we wanted yesterday and got today will rust or fall apart tomorrow and we will be left wanting again.

In the Buddhist tradition, it is taught that the root of all suffering is in desire and this seems most clearly true when it comes to the desire for material things. We often suffer the loss of things and, as most material objects always are lost eventually, the desire to possess something material is an automatic invitation to a certain amount of grief. And, as desire often triggers a compulsion to replace or improve upon the lost object, the materialist may soon find himself to be living, in Thoreau's words, a life of quiet desperation, trying to grasp and maintain a material lifestyle that will never satisfy.

The story is told of old King Midas who loved the sight and sound and feel of gold. The king was convinced that enough gold would bring meaning to his life and was delighted when he was granted his wish that everything he touched would be changed into gold. Yet his golden world came to have a hollow ring to it. He discovered he couldn't eat because his food would turn to gold as it touched his lips. He couldn't embrace his young daughter because that would turn her to gold. As long as he had the Midas touch, the king could not have life or love. He soon realized the boon of materiality was in fact a curse of death, and begged to have it removed so he could once again enjoy more genuine blessings.

The good you want will never come from a material thing. Material goods are nothing but physical expressions of ideas of good things. But the *real* good things never break or go out of style because they are invisible and eternal. Enjoy a good, loving or creative idea today—it will last forever!

What is done is done.
William Shakespeare

Two Zen monks were on their way to the market one day when they came to a large mud puddle that prevented them from continuing on without getting dirty. By the puddle was a fair young maiden who wished to continue on but also didn't wish to get dirty. To solve the problem, one of the monks offered to carry her across the puddle, even though this kind gesture violated the vows he had taken never to speak or have contact with a woman.

Once safely across, the woman thanked the monk and went on her way. The two monks also continued on to the market, but did not exchange a single word for the remainder of the day. That evening, when they returned to the monastery, the monk who had watched the other carry the woman across the puddle accused his friend of being unfaithful and sacrilegious. Over and over, he asked the other monk how he could have taken his vows so lightly. The angry tirade continued for well over an hour. Finally the monk who had done the good deed turned to his fellow monk and said, "I'm the one who violated my vows by carrying her across the mud puddle, but whereas I set the woman down on the path many hours ago, you continue to carry her."

In examining our own lives, we might be able to spot the heavy weight of yesterday's deeds that we persist in carrying with us. We might be carrying bitterness and resentment because we felt betrayed by a friend. We might be carrying anger and a feeling of injustice because we lost out on something we really wanted while someone else got it. We might be carrying hurt feelings because someone we liked criticized us. But continuing to carry harsh and negative feelings from the past is like picking up a pebble in your shoe while you are out walking. You can stop and remove the pebble or you can continue to walk and let the pebble irritate your foot and cause pain. The choice is yours. You can release your anger and hurt feelings, just as you can remove the pebble.

When you try to continue living a normal life while carrying harsh feelings about someone else, everything in your life is affected. There is always that small dark cloud hanging overhead that warns of foul weather. The next time you feel angry or hurt, give the situation time to settle down, then go directly to the source of your anger and settle it. This oftentimes means swallowing your pride and forgetting about who is right or wrong so that you can continue along the path of life without the extra weight of negative feelings. As Shakespeare said, "What is done is done!" Nothing you or anyone else can do will erase the events of the past. Forgive but also forget.

WEEK THIRTY-SIX : LAW A

It is not so much ours to set the world right, rather it is ours to see it rightly.
Eric Butterworth

We have all heard the phrase "What you see is what you get." This saying calls to mind a law of life that has nothing to do with *what* is being seen and everything to do with *who* is doing the seeing. Two people can wake up in the same neighborhood on the same day to the same conditions and yet have a vastly different day depending on who is doing the seeing. So, what *you* see is what *you* get and what *I* see is what *I* get!

The renowned Christian author, Eric Butterworth, puts the idea this way: "It is not so much ours to set the world right . . . rather it is ours to see it rightly." What can we do to see the world rightly?

The concept of choice is of utmost importance whenever we talk about perception. We must first understand that we are making a choice to see the glass as half full or as half empty. We must understand that in reality there is no outside influence of any kind that is making us see this day either as a day to be endured in a negative, limiting way, or as a day filled with infinite possibilities for good. Once we understand that we're a very short step to a conscious commitment to see the world in a way that is productive and inspiring.

Belief is another important concept to reflect on as part of seeing rightly. What is our belief about life? Do we believe that life is forward-moving? Do we believe that the very nature of the universe is progressive? Do we believe that we are all endowed with a limitless potential for creating good in our lives? Obviously, if we have this belief in ourselves and in life, we are seeing the world rightly.

What we are choosing to see is what we are choosing to get. To follow this law of life is to accept responsibility for ourselves and for our world, and this can only lead to greater and greater progress. We can choose to look beyond outer appearances to a better humanity and a better world. It is up to us.

WEEK THIRTY-SIX : LAW B

We can become bitter or better as a result of our experiences.
Eric Butterworth

Two brothers, identical twins, attended their twentieth high school class reunion. One had become a successful writer. The other had failed miserably at everything he'd tried. The successful brother was asked what he thought was the critical factor that had helped him achieve success and he quickly answered, "My parents." The other brother, when asked what major factor had contributed to his career and personal failures, answered, "My parents."

This story illustrates how two people can come from the same background and yet interpret its effect on them in entirely different ways. The story doesn't tell us how the parents treated each of the brothers as they grew up. It's possible that they favored the successful one; they may have seen a potential in him and therefore given him advantages the other did not have. It's also possible that they favored the one who failed; they may have absorbed the consequences of his mistakes instead of letting him learn from them himself. Whichever was the case, as a result of their childhood experiences, one brother was prepared to move ahead and explore his potential, while the other brother held back and wallowed in negativity—a truth expressed most eloquently by minister Eric Butterworth who said, "We can become bitter or better as a result of our experiences."

What happens to us in life is not nearly as important as how we handle what happens. Life sometimes takes unexpected twists and turns that can throw us off course for a time. We may have had an unhappy childhood in a broken family or with parents who were alcoholics. We may have been considered the black sheep, the one who just never fit in with the others. Almost anyone can find reasons for not doing as well as they think they should have. The key to successful living, however, is to learn from our experiences, good and bad, and go on from there— on to forge the kind of life we desire to live, in spite of some of the falls we've taken. Nothing can hold us back but ourselves.

Imagine, for a moment, that you have reached the end of your life and you are looking back over it all. Wouldn't you want to look back with pride, knowing you had made the best of every situation, regardless of how difficult it was? Isn't that better than looking back and wishing you had handled things differently? To guard against this, it's important to handle every experience to the best of your ability now. You may have to practice more patience, strive that much harder, reach inside yourself for a little more strength, muster a little more faith in God and yourself. You may need to make a commitment to push yourself harder and farther than at any time in the past. If, after you have given everything you have to give, you still come up short, you will have nothing to be ashamed of. You can experience the inner peace of those who know they gave their all. You will be a success regardless of the outcome. You will be better, not bitter, knowing that you did your best.

It is this kind of commitment that is able to find value in and lend value to every experience. Take what is given you to do today and make the most out of it. If you do the best with the resources you have within you, you'll never have any regrets. When you do look back over your life, it will be with satisfaction and peace of mind.

WEEK THIRTY-SIX : LAW C

We carry within us the wonders we seek without us.

Eric Butterworth

When you were a baby, you were aware of your own needs and desires and nothing beyond them. If you needed food or a dry diaper, you didn't care whether your parents were asleep, or needed time to finish their own meal, you simply demanded what you wanted. As you grew, confident your survival needs would be met, you moved on to other aspects of the world around you. Have you ever seen a baby playing with its toes and fingers? You did that, too, and, as you gained mastery over each little bit of your physical world, you went on with your exploration.

During your childhood years, you were mostly concerned with your parents' expectations. When you started school, you also became concerned with your teachers' expectations. During your adolescent years, you became preoccupied with what your peers thought about you. As an adult you have had many opportunities to experiment with creating a satisfying life. Each of these stages has prepared you for the time when you can discover the real truth: That what really makes the difference in the way we experience life is what we believe about ourselves and what we believe is possible for ourselves.

The love and approval we first seek from our parents and family, then from other authorities, such as teachers, then finally from our friends, can be felt and experienced only if we love and approve of ourselves. Do you remember an incident from your childhood when you worked very hard to accomplish something? You felt proud, good about yourself, and if your parents or someone else told you how well you did, you knew they were right. You felt affirmed. Do you also remember a time when you thought you got away with something? Maybe someone talked about you when you hadn't done your work or hadn't done the best you could. Can you now recognize your feelings at the time as confusing, embarrassing, or deceitful?

Can you now see that in the first incident, what happened was that someone merely affirmed what was true about you? Your feeling of value did not come *from* them, but was merely confirmed *by* them.

If you're fortunate, you have a teacher or a mentor you admire and want to learn from. Sometimes you feel you could never be like that admired person, but you can. The fact that you're attracted to that person is proof you have the capacity to express the same qualities you so admire in them. It works the other way too. Sometimes we feel repelled by or hateful toward another. Those feelings are warnings that we, too, are capable of behaving in that same unattractive way. At such times, it's important to recognize that you can choose to always express the loving, kind, caring, qualities you possess.

Because, as children, our needs are basic and are met by people other than ourselves, it's easy to believe others always have the answers for us. As we grow and our needs change, we can come to recognize we have within us everything we need to create lives of joy, usefulness, wonder and value. Whatever you seek as desirable in this world, you carry within you the qualities to express that in your life.

Misfortunes can be blessings.

There is an old story that the missionary Robert Livingston lived among the natives in a small, primitive African tribe. He suffered from a rare blood disease that required him to drink fresh goat's milk daily. On a visit the tribal king made to the village during the period when the missionary lived there, he became enchanted with Livingston's goat. Now it was the local custom that everything belonging to the villagers was automatically considered to be the king's property if he desired it. Having no choice but to honor the village custom, the missionary offered his goat to the king, knowing he had just given away the very thing his life might depend on.

The king appreciated Dr. Livingston's gesture and, in return, handed him what appeared to be a long walking stick he had been carrying. As Livingston turned away to go home, he sadly lamented to his house servant that he was afraid he wouldn't be able to live without his daily supply of goat's milk. The servant quickly turned to Livingston and said with a gasp of surprise: "Master, don't you realize what the king has given you? That's his scepter, and anything you desire in the entire kingdom is yours!"

How many times have we faced a disappointment or misunderstanding in our relationship with a colleague, family member, or friend? Whatever the difficulty, it's important for us to realize that a positive outlook can make a difference, can turn a "stick" into a "scepter." A poor evaluation at work can actually lead to a promotion if you accept it positively, as a challenge to do better.

Throughout history there are countless examples of famous scientists and explorers who set out to prove one thing and failed, but who went on to discover something more significant. For example, Christopher Columbus was trying to find a new trade route to China and Japan. Imagine his disappointment when, instead of landing in the Orient, he found himself thousands of miles away from his original destination on some strange, unknown land mass, later called America. This failure, however, would eventually earn him a permanent place in history as one of the world's greatest discoverers.

By turning our thoughts around, we can turn our own lives around. If we let negative ideas and fears invade our minds when our plans fail, our entire world will be filled with self-doubt and insecurity. Once we become aware of how we limit ourselves through negative attitudes, we can begin to concentrate on positive thoughts. A consistent, positive attitude—making a stick into a sceptre—allows us to turn an impossible situation into a positive opportunity to find happiness and success.

WEEK THIRTY-SIX : LAW E

Happiness pursued, eludes; happiness given, returns.

There once was a man determined to find happiness for himself. He created a business that made him very wealthy but he worked much too hard and found no happiness in that. He gathered people around him who were also wealthy, who were interesting and led fascinating lives. But something was missing and their companionship did not bring him happiness. He married a woman whom he thought had all the qualities of wit and grace that would make any man happy. But she too was looking for someone to give her happiness and neither of them could live up to the other's expectations. When a child was born the man was convinced that at last this would give him happiness, but children require time, patience and nurturing; and he was too busy with his career and his many friends. Instead of happiness he found that his children became just another responsibility. One day he decided happiness might be found in having no responsibilities at all. He left his business, his friends, his wife and family and ran away where he could live an idyllic, carefree life of leisure.

There is no end to this story. It is doubtful that life of leisure brought this man any happiness either. He is probably still looking. He might even try a new career, new friends, new family, thinking that it was these things in his life that were the problem. He may never realize that it is within himself that happiness will be found. In truth, he has always carried it with him. His own uniqueness as an individual is like a deep well of happiness. But it needs the pump started so the good can flow forth, circulating to others and back into his own life. It is a choice that must be made. If only he had learned that "happiness adds and multiplies as it is divided with others."

If his work had been about sharing his special talents and giving and serving others instead of accumulating money he might have found happiness there. If he had learned to give of himself to his friends and family, to consider their happiness instead of just own, then the love he gave would have been returned to him.

This man is every one of us. We all have believed that the outer things in life bring contentment. We all pursue happiness and it eludes us. But if happiness is already within us, a product of our own individuality, how do we give it away?

We initiate the flow of good by first appreciating our own uniqueness. Then we must feel secure enough in it that we can look for and appreciate uniqueness and diversity in others.

Be aware of the power of words. Sometimes they are the greatest gifts we can give. Look with sincerity for the special talents of others and express to them what you see. Give encouragement when it is needed. Be a reminder of past accomplishments, joys, and triumphs. Be appreciative and accepting. Be willing to say, "I love you" to those close to you.

Forgive generously. And perhaps, most important of all, learn to say "I'm sorry" when it needs to be said. No matter who is right or wrong these words can be a gift that reverberates happiness to all involved.

Be kind. Happiness given is a smile towards a stranger on the street or someone at home. It is a phone call to a friend who may be lonely or ill or facing a difficult time. It is listening, without giving advice, to someone who needs to talk. Helping with a chore, running an errand or anticipating a need.

Can money and possessions be gifts from our own well of happiness? Yes, they can when given with a joyful heart. Sharing what we have with those who are in need can multiply our happiness if done with the right motive. We must give with the idea of sharing, of easing another's pain or hardship, and not to glorify a false sense of benevolence—not to get our name in the paper or a good tax write-off.

True giving is done with no other motive than to share the happiness we find within ourselves. It is not manipulation of others. When we are blind to our reservoir of happiness and believe we are empty inside, we give out of our own sense of lack or unworthiness. We try to fill the void by buying or earning happiness. It defeats our purpose. We must not be fooled in our giving. To sacrifice self and always put others' needs before our own can become destructive just like not giving at all. We can always measure our giving by the barometer of our own feelings of well-being. If we have given in love from our own store of happiness it is like the ripples on a pond that move outward but also ripple inward to their source.

Like the man who hungered after happiness, it is easy to mistake getting with being. Adding anything to our lives in a material or outer sense only gives a very fleeting, and often false sense of contentment. The paradox of achieving personal peace and happiness is that what we are looking for is already within us, but in giving it away we experience it most powerfully for ourselves.

WEEK THIRTY-SEVEN : LAW A

No one's education is ever complete.

There is a children's story about a young man who went in search of the stupidest person he could find. As he walked down a country lane early one morning, he heard strange noises coming from a small house near the road. There was a thump-thump-thumping, followed by a crash and the sounds of groaning. He stopped and listened for several minutes; the sounds were repeated several times. Finally, the young man was unable to contain his curiosity. He walked up on the porch and peered through the curtains. To his astonishment, he saw a middle-aged man in his underwear run across the room—thump-thump-thump—leap into the air, and crash into the back of a chair where a pair of trousers were hanging. The old fellow fell to the floor and lay there a moment, groaning from the pain. Then he pulled himself up, picked up the chair, hung the trousers on it, and backed across the room. Thump-thump-thump. Leap into the air. Crash. "Ooooohhh."

The young man knocked on the door and the old man let him in, "Tell me, sir," said the young man, "Why are you doing that?"

"This is the way I put my trousers on. I hang them on the chair and run and jump into them," the old man replied. "My daddy did it that way and his daddy did it that way before him, and what was good enough for them is good enough for me."

"But that's a slow and painful way to do it. Most men put their trousers on one leg at a time. It's much easier and faster, too," the young man said. "Here, sit on the chair and I'll show you."

It was the old man's turn to be astonished. "It was a lucky day for me when you came by. I guess you're never too old to learn."

Anyone who believes that he has learned all he needs to know or all there is to learn makes a critical error. Albert Einstein, one of the great geniuses of our age, once said: "A day without learning is a day wasted. There is so much to learn and so little time to learn it." He followed his own precept by continuing to work and study diligently until his death. We are inspired by many examples of great people who never stopped learning.

Grandma Moses, who painted in a primitive style, took up art late in life. We might never have had the opportunity to enjoy her work if she had lacked the courage to continue her education late in life and to never stop growing as a creator. Colonel Sanders, of Kentucky Fried Chicken fame, learned the fast food business and franchising in his sixties.

"Live and learn" is a wise motto to live by if you agree that no one's education is ever complete. It reminds us that we can always learn something that will enrich our lives and the lives of others. We may need to let go of some outmoded ways of thinking and acting in order to try a new way. But when we do, we'll find that life is more exciting and fulfilling than we'd ever dreamed possible.

Edison said, "If you are doing anything the way you did twenty years ago, there is a better way." You can become successful and sought after if you can gain more knowledge about some division of any subject than anyone else on earth.

WEEK THIRTY-SEVEN : LAW B

Failing to plan is planning to fail.
Ben Franklin

If you decide to drive from Maine to California, one of the first things you will probably do is study a road map. You will see there's a choice of routes to your destination. If you're in a hurry, you will choose the route that will get you there the fastest. You can then estimate how long the trip will take and plan an accurate arrival time.

What holds true for a trip holds true equally for the accomplishment of any goal. Without a "road map," your mind wanders aimlessly and is ineffective in reaching out for solutions. By putting together a plan in much the same way as you would use a road map—by being systematic and studying the various alternatives—you focus the direction of your thoughts and find yourself capable of reaching almost any goal you please.

Many people know what they want out of life, but few turn their dreams into a carefully planned success map. They often depend on lucky breaks or the help of others. When they fail, they will often say of those more successful, "They just happen to know the right people" or "They get all the lucky breaks." But planning for success has no more to do with luck or knowing the right people than does planning carefully for a cross-country trip. It's true that when you start moving toward your goal you'll meet people who can help you advance. You'll also get certain "breaks" that a person without a plan will never get. But you'll know that you earned those breaks because you had a goal and a plan in place to help you get there.

To develop a plan of action, mentally visualize the thing you want to accomplish, jot it down across the top of a sheet of paper, then list the steps needed to accomplish it. Long-term objectives, of course, involve more steps and more elaborate planning, but the principle remains the same: When you know what you want to achieve, create a plan for getting there. Once you have a plan, devote some time each day to changing it as you gather new information. Then stick with it until you achieve your objective.

Stephen Covey, author of *The Seven Habits of Highly Effective People*, recommends that you "begin [planning] with the end in mind." The best planning encompasses what you want to accomplish and where you want to end up. Whether it is a special project or a simple daily routine, begin by setting a goal that takes into account the steps needed to reach it. If your goal is composed of many levels, you might want to prioritize them. Make a list, giving them a rating of A, B or C. Then tackle the A's first. Professional planners have shown that tasks written down are much more likely to be completed.

The following five rules may help you to achieve your goal:

1. Think of your goal not as something vague but in specific terms.
2. Write about your goal in detail.
3. Keep your mind on your goal by reviewing it every day.
4. Learn everything you can relating to your goal.
5. Be willing to work as hard as you can when the opportunity comes along.

Remember, "failing to plan is planning to fail." Just as a road map is an indispensable tool for travel, a plan is an indispensable tool when

you travel toward your life goals. Follow *your* plan to a more successful life!

WEEK THIRTY-SEVEN : LAW C

By their fruits you shall know them.

In the course of his spiritual instruction Jesus said, "By their fruits you
shall know them." He went on to say, "Are grapes gathered from
thorns, or figs from thistles? So, every sound tree bears good fruit, but
the bad tree bears evil fruit" *(Matt 7:15–17)*. He was warning the
people of false prophets who might lead them astray, people who were
saying one thing while demonstrating something quite different.
Wolves in sheep's clothing, he called them. But beyond that he was
revealing a very important law of life—a law that, when you understand
it, can help you to demonstrate success in virtually every area of your
life.

The unique conditions you find in your life are the fruit Jesus spoke
of. The condition of your health, your finances, your relationships, your
livelihood; all of these are the fruit of certain attitudes. If you don't
like the fruit you're harvesting—if you're always in poor health, if you're
struggling financially, if you're having difficulty maintaining meaningful
relationships, if you don't like the kind of work you're doing—it's
essential that you harvest fruit from another tree.

The writer of Proverbs said, "As a man thinketh in his heart, so is
he." He understood that it's what we think in our heart that expresses
itself in our lives. What you believe about yourself, what you believe
about life, will work itself into and through everything you do. Successful living begins by believing yourself worthy of success.

Marianne believed she was inferior and her life bore the fruit of the
belief. She had grown up on the wrong side of the tracks. All her life
she was warned not to expect too much because life was hard and it
was unfair. For years her life bore the fruit of that belief. She became
a prostitute and a drug addict. She was in and out of jail regularly. One
day, while walking through a mall, Marianne stole the wallet from
another woman's purse. The wallet contained a few dollars, some credit
cards, and, among other things, a small pamphlet. Intending to take

only what was of immediate value and get rid of the rest, a sentence from the pamphlet caught her attention: "As a child of God, you are worthy of the best life has to offer."

In the moments that followed, something strange began to happen to Marianne. All her cold, bitter attitudes toward life and people began to melt. Somehow those words struck a familiar note that had long been lost but not quite forgotten. She was further surprised when she found herself desperately feeling the need to return the wallet to the woman. Getting the phone number from a blank check in the wallet, Marianne phoned her that day. She explained what she had done and said she wanted to bring the wallet over to her home immediately.

To Marianne's surprise there was no bitterness in the woman's attitude. Instead, there was compassion and understanding. Marianne told the woman of her hard life and her story was received with tender sympathy. The woman offered Marianne a job in one of the many dress shops she owned in the city. She went out of her way to help Marianne release the harsh training of her past and begin to believe in herself. In time, the young woman's life began to bear a whole different kind of fruit. She gradually gained confidence in herself and was able to begin to trust others and see the good in them.

Pay close attention to what your heart tells you. If you are working toward prosperity and harmony in life, be certain you truly believe you are worthy of having them. This inner conviction, coupled with action, may produce the fruit in life you so deeply desire.

WEEK THIRTY-SEVEN : LAW D

Instead of cynicism, try optimism.

It is an oddity of human society that the people who are the most distrustful, who raise the most objections to what is happening or what might happen, who can point out the most faults in a system or proposed idea, and who can see other's lowest possible motives, are considered by some to be wise! These cynical views are actually considered insightful, realistic and helpful to the common good because they see everything that might threaten it.

Cynicism has its roots in an ancient Greek school of philosophers who believed that virtue is the only good and is found in self-control and independence. Good in life comes about by conforming to a rigid standard of moral behavior, segregating right from wrong by a strict exercise of restraint over one's impulses and feelings, and by neither relying on others nor being influenced by them. In our own times, we have come to learn the great importance of freedom of thought, of self-knowledge and trust of feelings, of cultivating our creative and intuitive abilities, of the joy and wonder of spontaneity, and of the vital richness of being open and trusting of each other in relationships. All of life is interconnected and interdependent.

In both the ancient and modern forms of cynicism, there is lack of awareness of the universe's natural order, harmony and infinite goodness. The cynic sits in a dark room on a sunny day and says, "I see no light; there is only darkness." Unaware of the good, the cynic naturally fears misfortune and therefore attracts it. From that standpoint it makes sense to be on the lookout for everything wrong before you become a victim. Misguided fear, not wisdom, is the guiding force here; illusion, not reality. And anxiety, not security, is the result.

Optimism, on the other hand, has its roots in the abiding reality of life's basic goodness. The optimist interprets life in the most favorable way possible and confidently trusts that whatever is best will happen. Have you noticed that things often work out well for the people who expect good things to happen? As Ralph Waldo Emerson wisely said, they know that their "welfare is dear to the heart of being" and that the universe is a hospitable place. Instead of yearning for some little shred of good fortune to come one's way, Emerson said the healthy attitude of human nature should be an easy freedom from concerns. We should be like children who are sure of their dinner, knowing that their needs will be provided for.

Not that optimism means nothing bad will ever happen to you and that you will get everything you want. We all face challenges, but optimists know that any situation has the potential of being made better and therefore contains the potential of good. Their intent is to discover that good. When confronted by difficulty, the healthy optimist doesn't pretend there is no confusion, fear or pain. He is honest about his feelings and still believes in a good outcome, even if he doesn't yet see how it will manifest itself.

No one writes more fervently or eloquently about optimism than Emerson, and he did so in the years following the ill health and deaths of his first wife, two brothers, and his adored six-year-old son. Such tragedies would cause some to become bitter and cynical. But though he experienced deep grief, Emerson's love of life's goodness would not allow any warping of that high belief.

You too can carry what Emerson called that "infallible trust and . . . the vision to see that the best is the true. In that attitude, one may dismiss all uncertainties and fears, and trust that time will reveal the answers to any private puzzlement."

WEEK THIRTY-SEVEN : LAW E

Tithing often brings prosperity and honor.

Nearly all civilizations have practiced some form of philanthropy. Many ancient civilizations levied a tithe, or tax, for the poor. The Egyptians and Grecians gave money to establish libraries and universities. By encouraging members to tithe, medieval churches supported hospitals and orphanages.

Tithe is from the Anglo-Saxon word, *teotha,* which means a tenth part. To tithe means to tax one-tenth of a person's possessions or the yearly increase thereof. In the Bible, to tithe was to support the religious order as in *Numbers 18:26–27:* "When you receive from the Israelites the tithe I give you as your inheritance, you must present a tenth of that tithe as the Lord's offering. Your offering will be reckoned to you as grain from the threshing floor or the winepress."

Many people believe that by tithing they appease their God and secure their place in heaven. Inside of King's College chapel in Cambridge, England are these words of William Wordsworth: "Give all thou canst; high Heaven rejects the lore of nicely calculated less or more." The underlying belief is that if we give our bountiful share of this life's bounty, then we will receive all we are due on earth and in heaven.

Benjamin Franklin is remembered not only for his statesmanship but for his tithing. George Washington wrote to Franklin in 1789: "If to be venerated for benevolence, if to be admired for talents, if to be esteemed for patriotism, if to be beloved for philanthropy, can gratify the human mind, you must have the pleasing consolation to know that you have not lived in vain."

In Franklin's will, he left five thousand dollars each in trust to Boston and Philadelphia for philanthropic purposes, a sizable amount of money at that time. Franklin also established America's first city hospital, the Pennsylvania Hospital for the Unfortunate.

Andrew Carnegie used a large share of his fortune to establish many cultural, educational and scientific institutions. He believed that "surplus wealth is a sacred trust which its possessor is bound to administer in his lifetime for the good of the community." In 1901, Carnegie's fortune was estimated to be an outstanding $500 million of which he donated $350 million to a variety of causes. His generosity established 2,500 public libraries throughout the world, provided construction for the famed Carnegie Hall in New York City, and created the Carnegie-Mellon University in Pittsburgh and the Carnegie Institution of Washington to encourage research in biological and physical sciences.

Carnegie said, "Individualism will continue, but the millionaire will be but a trustee of the poor; entrusted for a season with a great part of the increased wealth of the community, but administering it for the community far better than it would have done for itself."

In my lifetime of observing many hundreds of families, almost without exception, the family which tithes for more than ten years becomes both prosperous and happy. This is the one investment suitable for all persons.

WEEK THIRTY-EIGHT : LAW A

The shadow of ignorance is fear.

Fear is one of the greatest challenges we face today, as individuals and as a society. Fear holds us back from the fullest expression of ourselves; it prevents us from loving ourselves and others. Unreasoning, irrational fear locks us in an invisible prison.

And yet fear has uses that can serve us. Some fear is necessary for self-preservation. An instinctive awareness of danger alerts us to potential harm and thus helps us mobilize the resources we need to keep ourselves from injury. Without fear of consequences in risky situations, we would rush in "where angels fear to tread."

Yet many times we fear things that cannot hurt us. We may accelerate a natural anxiety we feel in an uncomfortable emotional situation into a state of fear and panic; when that happens, we are unable to live fully. Then we cower in the face of possible humiliation and forgo making a creative contribution. For fear of rejection, we avoid asking for the things we really need. We refuse to commit ourselves because of the risk of failure. Fearing nonconformity, we may relinquish our individuality. It is important to distinguish between fears that help us and those that hurt us.

Because of our fears many of us compromise and settle for less. Why? Because of ignorance—not necessarily an intellectual ignorance but rather an emotional or spiritual ignorance. Many of us were frightened in childhood by what we thought was a ghost or a dragon and later discovered was a shadow or a curtain blowing in the wind. Our fears came not from what *was* but from what we believed *might* be. Irrational fear takes root in anticipation of the worst that can possibly happen. Like the child who discovers that the "ghost" was not real, and not worthy of his fear, we can come to see that most of our fears are also phantoms.

Often an intellectual awareness of reality is not enough. The individual who's afraid to swim may consciously understand that the water will support his body, that there's really nothing to fear. But even watching others swim effortlessly and with obvious enjoyment seldom allays his fears. He must *experience* the truth for himself—nothing else will work.

Consider the ultimate fear—the fear of death. There have been many reports of "near death" experiences in which the subjects claim they no longer fear death because they have actually experienced dying. Our fear of death is largely a fear of the unknown—the shadow of our ignorance.

Behind every irrational fear lies an illusion. Much of our fear stems from an incomplete sense of identity. We may fear disapproval or rejection by others because we tend to see our self-worth as being dependent on their good opinion. But once we know our talents and our purpose, we will never again experience that particular fear.

Perhaps you've heard the old saying, "What you don't know won't hurt you." Nothing could be further from the truth. Ignorance is never bliss. Instead, it produces fear and confusion. However, once you know the multitude of your blessings and how you can help others, the shadow of false fear will no longer have power over you.

WEEK THIRTY-EIGHT : LAW B

Imitate that person in history whom you admire most, after you list the reasons why you admire that person.

The I Ching; or, Book of Changes is an ancient Chinese wisdom text honored as one of the five classics of Confucianism. In over three thousands years of use, many have found its oracular advice to be helpful in the development of character and ethical values. "The superior [one] acquaints himself with many sayings of antiquity and many deeds of the past, in order to strengthen his character thereby—In the words and deeds of the past there lies hidden a treasure that [one] may use to strengthen and elevate their own characters."

For assistance in developing greatness in our own characters, we are told to unlock the treasure chest of the past, examine the lives of history's heroes and heroines, and accept the keys to the future these great persons offer us in their words and deeds. But who is truly great? What makes a person a hero worth emulating?

Is it simply someone who is an easily recognized historical figure? Everyone knows who Hitler was, yet few would designate him a hero. And surely there are many people who have lived great lives but remain unsung heroes, people who have been anonymous in their deeds, yet whose impact has been monumental. Movie and music personalities are frequently highly visible, yet how many demonstrate a heroic quality?

Greatness is something far beyond the outer fame or fortune society may heap upon an individual. It is an inner quality of being which is expressed in such a way because of that person's contribution. It may or may not ever be recognized or acclaimed. It needs no spokesman, for when it is fundamental and enduring, it speaks for itself.

A heroic person serves love by lighting a torch for us, illuminating a principle or attitude that will make life work better, not only for us, but for everyone in our lives. The light of a great person's life can also be a beacon by which we may be guided to make the wisest and best contributions we may offer.

The I Ching advises, "The way to study the past is not to confine oneself to mere knowledge of history but, through application of this knowledge, to give actuality to the past." When we choose to study the lives of great men or women we can learn from them the treasured secrets of a truly worthwhile life and let their lives give life to our own. The process of selecting certain heroes or heroines to emulate will allow us to fully enjoy the treasures they bear.

Who do you consider to have qualities of greatness? What person has won your admiration for his or her accomplishments? Can you list what it is about that person that makes them deserve your high esteem? Are these qualities you also would wish to embody in your life? If not, choose again; but, if so, let the deeds and words of these great persons live on in you!

Every day of your life you will touch the life of someone else. Will you touch it with greatness? Every time you do, your light will shine as a star that guides many.

As Henry Wadsworth Longfellow wrote in "A Psalm of Life," "Lives of great men oft remind us that we can make our lives sublime, and, departing, leave behind us footprints on the sands of time."

WEEK THIRTY-EIGHT : LAW C

You can be either part of the problem or part of the solution.

There are two kinds of people in the world. There are those who see a problem, define and describe the problem, complain about the problem, and finally become part of the problem. And there are those who look at a problem and immediately begin searching for a solution. For the problem person, life is an uphill battle. But if you are among the solution seekers, life will present you with many exciting opportunities for growth. The choice is entirely up to you: "You can either be part of the problem or part of the solution."

It's all too easy to become a part of the problem. Anyone focusing on a number of conflicting facts and possible scenarios can come up with a dozen reasons why something cannot be. It's much harder to set your mind to work on ways in which the problems can be solved. What proves to be an insurmountable obstacle for problem people, becomes an opportunity for growth for the solution seekers.

There is an old story about two men who were walking along a forest path at night. Suddenly, both fell into a large pit; escape seemed impossible without outside help. Lamenting their terrible misfortune, one man sat and did nothing. The other man immediately began to search for an escape. While groping in the dark, his hand touched a long tree root hanging from the side of the wall. He quickly pulled himself out of the pit, helping his complaining friend out as well.

The challenge you face may not be as extreme as falling into a pit, but the decision you make about handling it will be crucial in terms of success or failure now and in the future. You may be given the opportunity to engage in gossip. Perhaps you'll join others in complaining about a co-worker. You may be tempted to disobey a company policy just because everyone else is doing it. In each case, you can either be a part of the problem or part of the solution. Whichever role you choose will have an enormous impact on your future.

When you're part of the problem, you contribute to making the problem larger and more difficult to solve. For example, while there is a growing awareness of the need to conserve the earth's natural resources, some people still neglect to recycle. The result is a larger volume of garbage which strains the increasingly limited capacity of waste disposal sites. On the other hand, a little effort made to deal with waste products in an ecologically sound manner results in less trash to deal with. Recycling may be only one step toward the solution of the complex environmental issue we face today, but by doing your own small part, you become part of the solution.

Try to make a conscious effort always to be a solution seeker. Remember, it doesn't take any courage, genius, or effort to be a problem person. Becoming a solution seeker makes you feel good about yourself and confident of your capabilities. It also evokes feelings of admiration in those around you: They will see that you are a person who knows how to get things done. Through your positive, goal-driven approach, you may even inspire them on to greater levels of achievement. When two or more solution seekers get together, there is no limit to what they can do!

A wise boss can help his colleagues to become problem solvers by keeping on his desk a sign saying: "What do you suggest?" He can encourage each assistant to begin with the words, "Wouldn't it be better if. . .?"

Learn mind control.

Do you believe it's always possible for the mind to tell the difference between a real event and something imagined in great detail? Take a moment to relax your body and to calm your thoughts. When you feel quiet, imagine that you have a lemon in your hand. Feel its waxy, dimpled exterior. Feel the weight of the lemon pressing down in your hand. Now, imagine yourself taking a sharp knife and cutting the lemon in half. You can smell its tartness. Running your finger over its sliced surface you can feel the slippery juice. Now imagine yourself taking one of the lemon halves, putting it in your mouth, and taking a bite from it. Can you taste a pungent sourness? Do you realize that your mouth is filling with saliva? What happened demonstrates that your mind was so convinced you were eating a real lemon that it activated physical mechanisms to offset the citric acid found in the fruit.

The fact that the mind cannot always tell the difference between something real and something fully imagined, offers us the key to creating an effective life. As we imagine ourselves expressing confidence, intelligence, and caring, the mind accepts these qualities as part of us and directs our actions in confident, intelligent and caring ways. Through the faculty of imagination, we are exerting positive thought control. When we're in charge of our thoughts, we have the power to shape our life experiences.

Consider that your mind is like a ship that's about to sail to a foreign land. In order to reach its destination safely and swiftly, it must be piloted by a qualified captain, who, supported by an able crew and the proper maps, charts, and navigational instruments, knows exactly how to reach the desired port. A ship managed efficiently is likely to reach its destination directly and on time, just as a well-managed mind is more likely to reach its goal.

In contrast, consider starting the engines, disarming the automatic pilot, and turning the same ship out to sea without a captain or crew. Under these circumstances the ship cannot control its destination and is at the mercy of winds, waves and currents. A ship so poorly managed will probably end up on some desolate beach far from its destination.

If we don't use the power, wisdom and understanding available to us to build our thoughts and direct our mind where we want it to go, we can be like a ship adrift on the high seas. We, too, may become lost—subject to the direction of the strongest wave of influence to come our way.

Your mind is your ship and you are the captain. The thoughts you focus on will determine where you go in life. Your potential is unlimited. Usually you can go wherever you want to go; you can do whatever you want to do; you can become whatever you want to become, as long as you control your mind positively and generate thoughts that will guide you to your desired destination.

WEEK THIRTY-EIGHT : LAW E

Use it or lose it.

Is this just another of life's seeming threats, another demanding edict from the "do-it-right-or-else" mentality beyond which we can see humanity evolving? Such threats do not fit the growing vision of humankind endowed with confidence, power and freedom to create in wholeness and joy. No, like the other laws of life, this statement simply tells how things work; and the *it* to be used or lost is that very endowment of our natural gifts as human beings.

We can look at various physical gifts and see how the law works. The natural state of the human body is that of health, strength and flexibility. But what becomes of it if it is not used? If we spend most of our time inactive, muscular atrophy, stiffness and weakness set in, along with the devitalization of our internal systems. This, in turn, affects the mind and can lead to lethargy and depression. Our natural state of health is lost. Time is lost in the same way. Twenty-four hours a day are available to everyone but, if they are not used for some constructive purpose, they are irretrievably gone. Talents unused likewise become rusty.

Money is another physical, material consideration of human existence, one that we think of as providing some degree of security, opportunity, ease, enjoyment and freedom. One man spent many years laboring hard to earn money, which he saved diligently. Over the years, it gradually accumulated to quite a sum. Whenever this wife, who also worked, wanted to spend some money, such as on necessary improvements for their home, a trip for the two of them or to assist someone in need, he would either veto the idea or permit it grudgingly. He lost in various ways. He lost his wife's respect, and opportunities for companionship with her. Their home became dilapidated. He lost any feeling of enjoyment because he was so driven to guard and increase his savings, watching every penny. The fear of somehow losing any of it undermined whatever sense of ease and security it might have offered. He lost the feeling of abundance and heart-reward that comes from generosity in sharing. His penury cost him his joy, and almost predictably, his health became very poor. Eventually, large medical bills and nursing care eroded the bulk of the savings.

The gifts of the inner being are just as clearly seen to be used or lost. Confidence is a good example. Think of the confidence you feel when an idea comes to you that you know holds real potential for success and satisfaction. Develop it and act on it, and there will be fruition of some sort, whether or not it is exactly what you had in mind. Allow fear, doubt and hesitation to hold you back, and everything is lost; the possibilities the idea held disappear increasingly and your confidence dissolves.

The human endowment of love provides the most fundamental illustration of this law, since love is the basis of all other forms of good that we experience. Loving life, self and others generates confidence, empowerment, joy, wholesome relationships, generosity, service, goodwill, humor and health. They are used, shared and expressed in their myriad possible forms. However, love that is withheld, stifled, suppressed and guarded appears to wither out of sight. Having no outlet, no expressed use, it has no life to sustain it and is therefore lost.

It is usually fear that prevents the use and expression of that which is valued, whether it is love, money, confidence or opportunity. Ironically, the very fear of losing *it* is what keeps us from using it, and therefore we lose it. The key to freedom from this fear of loss is in the realization that life's true gifts are limitless in nature. We need have no fear of "using it up," for the free and constructive use of any such good is self-generating and only opens the way for more. It is thus that we become part of humanity's creating wholeness and joy.

WEEK THIRTY-NINE : LAW A

It's nice to be important, but it's more important to be nice.

Television's J. R. Ewing, the character in "Dallas," is the epitome of someone who places great value on being important and absolutely no value on being nice. In the game of life, getting what he wants is the all-important rule. No act is too devious or mean; he'll lie, cheat or steal to achieve his goals. J. R. is a firm believer in the theory that "nice guys finish last." Because he is "important," he usually gets his way. J. R. Ewing is the classic playground bully—everyone does things his way because they're afraid to challenge him. In the process of gaining importance, however, he gains many enemies. They're always lurking around applauding when someone gets even with him.

Our lives are woven from the patterns of our thoughts and beliefs. If we believe that nice guys finish last, we will live according to that belief. If we believe we have to lie, cheat and steal to get ahead, we will have as many enemies as J. R. Ewing. If we place more value on being important than on being nice, no act will be too devious for us. Like J. R., we will claw and scratch to get what we want. The fabric of our lives will be woven with flimsy thread that will break when we least expect it.

If we are successful in becoming the playground bully, others will give in to our wishes, not because they believe in us or our cause, but because they are afraid to challenge us. To live this way is to build our lives on shaky ground. There will always be someone ready and eager for us to make a mistake. Playground bullies last only until other, bigger bullies come along to take their place, or until they learn that by being nice they can achieve all they want.

What a different story "Dallas" would be if the writers of the show had created a kind, generous and loving J. R. who had learned at an early age how important it is to be nice. What a difference it makes in our lives when we learn the importance of being nice to others. Not the "pretend" nice that everyone can see through, but genuine niceness that comes from the heart. This kind of person acts on the golden rule. He has taken the theory, "Do it to them before they do it to you," and changed it to, "Do unto others what you would have done unto you, only do it first." This person believes in the value of being kind, considerate, loving, honest and open to others without regard to return. To lie, cheat or steal to gain importance would be foreign to him. This person knows the code of life is that what you sow you also reap. He knows that making an effort to be kind to others is making an effort to be kind to yourself.

It's nice to be important, but it's more important to be nice. When the pattern of our life is woven from this philosophy, we set in motion a circular effect that creates for us all we could ever hope for. What we do for others certainly comes back to us. If we are kind, generous, loving, honest and open, others will react the same way toward us. Our importance to others will depend not on our bullying tactics but on showing through our actions that we truly care about them. We can weave our life with the golden thread of caring concern for others; the by-product will produce for us a life that is truly important.

With my experience over more than half a century of studying corporations, it is clear to me that the higher up the corporate executive ladder you interview, the greater proportion of executives are nicer. I also have noted that they are more active in religious work. Maybe this is partly why they were promoted to their high posts and why they learned to be more effective executives.

WEEK THIRTY-NINE : LAW B

Those who seldom make mistakes seldom make discoveries.

In the Gospel According to Matthew (25:14–30), Jesus tells the story of a man who left money with three of his servants before setting out on a journey. To one servant he gave five talents (approximately five thousand dollars today), to another two talents; to the third man he gave only one talent. On returning, he called in each of the three for an account of how they had used their portion of the money. The servant who had been given five talents had doubled that amount through investments, as had the man who had been given two talents. But the servant who had been given one talent, afraid of making a poor investment, had buried his portion in the ground. The two servants who doubled the man's money were rewarded handsomely, while the third servant was condemned and penalized.

How many times have you missed out on an opportunity because, like the fearful servant, you were afraid of making a mistake? How many times have you limited yourself because you were afraid you might appear foolish in the eyes of your peers? Self-imposed limitations based on fear can be very difficult to break. The sooner you learn to cope constructively with such fears, the better off you'll be, for "those who seldom make mistakes, seldom make discoveries."

Life is as interesting and stimulating as the discoveries we allow ourselves to make. Staying within known parameters of thought and action may prevent mistakes, but they will also prevent your life from becoming rich and exciting. Exploring frontiers of thought, feeling and action means you have to put yourself in places you have never been before. In such places it is easy to make mistakes. But mistakes are negative only when they inhibit further growth. If you become fearful of testing out a new thought or trying a new approach to a stubborn problem because you're afraid of making a mistake, you are probably making the biggest mistake of all. While it's foolish to plunge into situations you haven't planned for, it's equally foolish and futile to be afraid to venture into unknown territory. If you're committed to growth, you can learn that each new situation finds you better able to cope. Your guidance may come either intuitively or through someone else, but it will come.

While mistakes can cause stress and pain, they can also provide you with an excellent resource for learning what not to do next time. Often you learn more from your mistakes than from formal instruction on the correct way to proceed. Trial and error, which allows you to measure the impact of your misguided actions, is a great teacher.

Whether you fully realize it or not, you are like the men in the parable. You have been given many "talents" that can take you as far as you want to go in life. Don't make the mistake of fearfully burying them for fear of making a mistake. You don't want to look back over your life one day with regret that you did not pursue an opportunity because you were afraid of making a blunder. Instead, invest your talents wisely, confidently, to the best of your understanding and with self-trust, and you are likely to enjoy a profitable and exciting life!

The measure of a man's real character is what he would do if he would never be found out.

Thomas MacCaullay

Thomas MacCaullay says that "the measure of a man's real character is what he would do if he would never be found out." Would he be totally honest and aboveboard with others? Would he cheat or steal? If what is done in secret stays a secret what would *you* do, how would *you* live? If you found a wallet stuffed with money, would you return it to the owner? Our conscience should be our friend and our guide. It nudges us when we contemplate doing something wrong. It warns us of the danger that could be done to us or to others. The person who learns to ignore his conscience forsakes his best friend and lifetime guide.

If the measure of a man's real character is determined by what he would do if he weren't found out, the only person capable of judging his actions is the man himself and his God. If he can look at himself in the mirror each day and know he's living as honestly as he can, he will see that reflected there. The essence of his character is written on his face, and he can read the lines.

We've been building our character since we were little children, and part of the building process is learning to listen to our conscience and following its guidance. We know there are times we can do something wrong and not be found out. We also know that if we get away with doing something wrong, *we* will know what we did, and we have to live with ourselves twenty-four hours a day. Every time we put a chink in our character we are diminished. Our pride and self-esteem suffer.

Our real character can be measured by us. If we do an inventory and find we are lacking, only we can fix it. We can determine to live honestly with ourselves and others. We can determine to be as honest in secret as we are when others are present. We can determine that our character will be of value to *us*. The choice is ours to make.

Life will sometimes push us to violate the moral and ethical standards we try to live by. Desperation may tempt us to abandon our highest standards for the sake of short-term gain or a quick solution. When we do such things, we walk a path that leads to further deception, pain, and the erosion of self respect.

You alone live with your motives and secret actions, and only you can set the standard of your personal integrity. Eventually the temptation to abandon your high standards will arise. It may be encouraged through circumstances, a friend, a co-worker, a mate, or even an employer. It will come unexpectedly and it may even seem the logical thing to do. Certainly it will appear to be the easiest answer to a complicated situation. At such times you would do well to ask yourself if you will be able to look back later, satisfied that you did your best. Will you be able to review your conduct and feel successful deep within you? Perhaps no one will ever find out how you performed—whether you cut corners or, instead, went the extra yard to do the right thing. But *you* know. Will you be proud of your performance or will there always be the gnawing feeling that you should have been more honest?

Your life will openly display what you do in secret. If you always remain true to your ethical principles, your personal integrity will become an attractive beacon for success on every level.

WEEK THIRTY-NINE : LAW D

Change your mind to change your life.

What does your mind have to do with your life? Everything! To illustrate, if you believe you're unworthy of love and happiness, you will attract to yourself situations that disappoint, frustrate, and hurt. Conversely, healthy self-esteem will give you healthy and positive results.

It's all up to you! Your mind is the projector, your attitudes are the film, and your experience is the movie projected on the screen. If you see a pattern of sincere good feelings and satisfying relationships, it shows that you have a healthy respect for yourself and others. If you see frequent hurt and frustration, there must be negative thinking and a belief inside you that says you don't deserve better.

Listen to this negative thinker: "I know I'm kind of pessimistic, and lots of things frighten me. I'm told I'm hard to get along with and too negative about things, but it's no wonder! It seems there are always people out to get you and take advantage of you. It's not safe to trust anybody; they'll hurt you. People are so uncaring, just out for themselves. Besides, I know I'm unattractive, so why should anybody really care about me?"

You can guess the nature of this person's experiences. Her relationships are difficult or fleeting. She can walk into a restaurant with her negative force field and, sure enough, people treat her rudely, or eye her disapprovingly. The prices are too high, the food's no good. Everything seems to work against her, others get all the breaks. But does she think the way she does because of the bad things that happen to her or do bad things happen because of the way she thinks?

Both are true, and it's hard to get to the source of the problem without knowing the person's entire history. But even if you can point to unfortunate circumstances and say, "There's the origin; that's why she thinks the way she does," what good does it do? Can blaming the past do anything to lessen its negative influence? And if we say a person can't be expected to think well of herself or others because of something that happened in childhood, is she burdened that way for the rest of her life?

Not at all. It's within anyone's power, regardless of the circumstances, to change a thinking process. Thought by thought, moment by moment, it can be done. Indeed, it's important to do it if a person wants the quality of life to improve. You can think in a new way and start finding the good that exists in you and in others by deciding to change. You only need to be willing to try. Nothing is more powerfully creative than your own mind and it's capable of higher levels of thinking than you've yet called on it for. And no one controls the attitudes your mind will hold, express and project except you. It's your projector and your film. You have the freedom and authority to create the best life and attitude you can possibly make.

Making the change does require being continually alert and aware of your thoughts so the negatives don't slip in. It takes the courage of facing your negative thoughts with mindful, compassionate honesty. It also requires a firm belief in the equal value of yourself and all others. Inferiority and superiority work equally well to hold life's goodness away from you. If you tell yourself, "Life is good and people are good," but you don't think you're much good, then the good in life and people will elude you. If you regard yourself highly but hold critical thoughts about others, people will not please you. Your judgmental attitude will keep you from appreciating others' good qualities.

Change your mind and you will find life's unlimited good in all directions, awaiting your recognition and acceptance. It will change your life and all the world around you!

WEEK THIRTY-NINE : LAW E

You get back what you give out.

A gentleman we'll call Mr. Smith was the richest man in the small town in Tennessee where he had lived all of his life. He was not rich in money. He and his wife lived comfortably but carefully on social security and a small pension check. The wealth Mr. Smith enjoyed was quite different from the financial kind.

The days were not long enough for him. He started each day by filling the feeders and water container for the birds. A neighbor once asked him why he bought so much birdseed on a fixed income. He was well paid for the birdseed, however. The birds sat on the white picket fence, the porch rail, tree limbs and bushes, and they chirped, giving the Smiths a world filled with music. Mr. Smith got back much more than he gave out.

Each weekday morning Mr. Smith walked two blocks to the handsome old Victorian house that housed SARC—the Seaton Association for Retarded Citizens. Mr. Smith worked with the children. They were unable to attend regular school but at the center each was helped to reach his potential. Although Mr. Smith was not a trained teacher, there was much he could do. With endless patience he helped little ones learn to tie a shoe or eat with a fork and spoon. Friends tried to tell the retired man that with his talent for this work he could certainly find a part-time paying position. But Mr. Smith was paid a huge salary for his work with these youngsters—a tearful "thank you" from a mother and father, a bear hug from a tot overjoyed at successfully doing something on his very own, a "God bless you" from one of the paid workers. Mr. Smith gave much to the children, but he got back much, much more in return.

While Mr. Smith was at the center, Mrs. Smith worked in the Chamber of Commerce office, which helped the business and professional people in town. Money was not plentiful and the office had only two regular people, the director and the office manager/secretary. Mrs. Smith gladly helped with mailings, copying, telephoning, filling the counter rack with town maps and postcards and other free leaflets. She even watered the plants. Mrs. Smith loved the office. She was right in the middle of what was going on. She gave a lot of herself in that office but she received so much back that it literally filled her heart with joy.

The couple also gave time to their children, and to their three grand-children, and the Smiths' lifestyle was so inspirational it was reflected in their children. Their son was an accountant who spent every Saturday morning at a senior center in his city helping seniors handle money problems. No charge! His wife was a volunteer at the grade school their son attended. And the little boy was raising a puppy for the seeing eye dog group. Their daughter helped out five mornings a week at the town's small hospital. Her husband, an insurance executive, was a member of the finance board at his church and worked many hours in this role. Their children were members of a youth group that visited a nursing home Saturday mornings, listening, writing letters, combing hair, taking someone for a ride outside in a wheelchair. They gave and they gave. And received and received!

We always get back what we give!

WEEK FORTY : LAW A

Minds are like parachutes—they only function when they are open.

Dick Sutphen

At one time people were certain that earth was flat and those who thought otherwise were ridiculed and scorned. People once laughed at the Wright Brothers for building a machine they believed could fly through the air. These are obvious examples of closed minds on a global scale, but a closed mind can also affect our everyday lives in subtle ways.

For example, Alice believed her classmate Amy was rich because her father owned a factory that made small metal springs. When Alice and her mother saw Amy and her mother shopping for groceries, Alice said, "Why are they comparing prices and picking up the least expensive items when they can buy whatever they want?"

Two weeks later, the factory was placed in bankruptcy! Many kinds of electronic equipment that had once used the springs Amy's father manufactured now operated with batteries and microchips; the lack of demand for his product caused the business to fail. But Alice had already made up her mind about Amy's circumstances. Even though some of the other students at Alice's school had talked about the problems

Amy's family was facing, Alice had not heard them. She had tailored those conversations to fit her own sense of reality. She believed that owning a business meant financial security and her mind was closed to other possible interpretations.

A closed mind can have an important effect on your future. Two high school seniors, Bill and John, were invited to an open house at a college they were both interested in attending. They joined a group of students who were discussing physics. Bill broke in, talking confidently as though he had a good grasp of the subject, although he had never studied physics and his knowledge was superficial. John was as ignorant of physics as Bill was, but he listened carefully to the discussion, which had to do with atomic structure and the origin of the universe. Before long he realized the ideas he had concerning the subject were different from those being discussed by the college students—different and not very informed. Bill, who had acted as if he knew it all and had had his ignorance exposed, went home and told his parents he didn't want to attend "that stupid college." John, on the other hand, got out his encyclopedia and read as much as he could understand on the subject of physics. Even though physics was not his major subject of interest, he realized he didn't fully understand the principles involved, so he made the effort to learn. He followed this up by reading a book recommended by his high school librarian. He ended up attending the college and graduated in the top quarter of his class.

While you should not turn away from values and ideas you have good reason to believe are true, it is important to continue learning and growing mentally. A narrow mind is the straightest avenue to a narrow life. Listen to others more informed than you are and don't be afraid to ask questions. Reading will increase your knowledge and open doors of learning and understanding. Remember that our "minds are like parachutes—they only function when they are open."

Progress and growth are impossible if you always do things the way you've always done things.

Wayne Dyer

In 1633, the English Colonists established a settlement on a peninsula between the James and York rivers in Virginia. They called it Middle Plantation because it lay in the middle of the peninsula. In 1699, they renamed their settlement Williamsburg in honor of King William of England and it became the capital of the Virginia colonies. At one time the most important city in the Virginia Colony, Williamsburg began to decline after the Revolutionary War. In 1926, John D. Rockefeller, Jr. became interested in restoring and preserving Williamsburg, and today it attracts more than a million visitors a year.

Visiting historic Williamsburg is a wonderful experience because we get to see how life was lived in the past. It is also a way to be thankful for the progress we've made up to the present time. But progress would not have come if the settlers and those who came after them had continued to do things the same way. If they had continued to bake food in an open fire, we would not have progressed to the microwave oven. If the military had continued to use muskets, our defense system would be totally inadequate.

Change is both good and necessary. Our evolution as a people and as a planet depends on change. We should always seek to find new and better ways of doing things in our individual lives as well. Just because we've always done things a certain way doesn't mean that way is the only way. We can experience change in our lives by beginning with little things. We can take a new route to work, or order a different item on the menu. As we consciously choose to see life in a different light, as we expand our minds to learn new things, growth will come. In order for us to see life with fresh eyes, we must keep our minds open to new and different experiences.

Each individual human being has the capacity to grow and become both useful and happy. In order for this growth to take place, we must allow the natural process of change to take place in our lives. There is a saying that "life is change, change is life." In other words, change is all about us. It is only when we resist change that progress and growth are stunted. But by forging ahead and looking for new and different ways of living, we can bring about progress and growth for ourselves and for others. Just as the Pilgrims experimented and learned new ways of living in order to survive, we, too, can experiment and not only survive but thrive in the process.

WEEK FORTY : LAW C

Holding onto grievances is a decision to suffer.
Gerald Jampolsky

Some of us choose to hold onto old and painful thoughts as though they were treasures. We seem to cherish memories of imagined or real mistreatment, or slights, and to forget the good and helpful things people have done for us, the good health we have been blessed with and the many successes we've enjoyed.

I know a man who still lives with negative thoughts of events that happened to him more than forty years ago; some of those things he remembers as being so terrible are really the result of his poor perception of what actually happened back then. He has allowed those negative thoughts to alienate him from his family and refuses every attempt they make at reconciliation. Instead, he chooses to be alone, cut off from all of those who could love and understand him.

We don't have to remain locked in negative thoughts nor do we have to react in a negative way to daily events. The way in which we choose to interpret what happens to us has a great deal to do with how important moments in our lives will be stored in our memory through the years. We alone have control of our thoughts, though many of us have forgotten how to exercise that control.

Try to hold this simple truth in mind: yesterday is gone. No matter what happened then, it's over. We can't go back. Tomorrow may never come, so the present may be all we have. We should strive to make the best, most positive use of it. The ill feelings and negative thoughts we had in the past were of no value to us then and have not increased in worth since. The choice is ours; we can keep them or let them go.

A mind that is occupied by positive thoughts is a beautiful garden, free of the weeds of negativity. Whether your mind is a beautiful garden or a weed patch is up to you. You can choose to overlook and forgive the shortcomings of others, or you can keep a mental ledger listing all the unkind things people may have said or done to you.

A mind full of love, laughter, forgiveness and thanksgiving refuses to dwell on past hurts. One man recites Abbott and Costello's "Who's On First" comedy routine whenever negative thoughts trouble him at bedtime. He laughs, his heart is light and the old grievances begin to fade. Prayer or the words to a song or poem may work equally well for you.

After all, you are the one who suffers most by holding on to grievances. For if you can't overlook and forgive the faults of others, how can you forgive your own?

WEEK FORTY : LAW D

It is more rewarding to give.

"If you want to get more out of life, you have to give more to life." Sounds like a contradiction, doesn't it? The chances are good that you may have reached the opposite conclusion. You may believe that if you want more out of life, you have to go get it—and quickly—before the other fellow beats you to it. Getting ahead in the world has become an obsession for many people, who believe that a satisfying life comes from acquiring and holding on to great wealth. Yet many of the world's most successful and influential people have proven otherwise. They seek and experience a greater reward in giving of their wealth than in getting it. Giving leads to more giving, and greater personal rewards. As Robert Dedman, a lawyer who has contributed $40 million to charity and who vows to give away at least one-third of his estimated $500 million before he dies, remarked in a 1986 interview in *Town & Country* magazine, "The more you give, the more you live."

There is certainly nothing wrong with getting ahead, or being in a position where you can be a positive influence on those around you. But it is through giving, not getting, that you can exert a truly positive force for good.

"It is more rewarding to give than to receive." If you only receive, that's all you end up having. If you give, you will have the pleasure of knowing that you've helped others, plus the rewards your giving brings back to you. If you want to be happy, strive to make someone else happy. Give happiness. If you want to have more love in your life, strive to be a more loving person. Give love. If you want to be successful, help others to succeed. It's not difficult to see how much better and richer your life will become if you yourself become a source of encouragement, inspiration and friendship to others. Giving makes you a magnet for success.

In nature, each species has to exist in a natural state of giving and receiving; otherwise, it creates unbalance in its environment, even to the point of its own extinction. A South American species of parasitic vine illustrates this point. This vine sustains itself by attaching to a certain kind of fig tree. The fig tree's nourishing elements are gradually diverted to the vine. The result is that the vine literally strangles the life out of its host, because it takes but gives nothing in return. And, once the fig tree dies, the parasitic vine must die.

Almost everyone prefers the company of givers over takers. Takers leave you feeling depleted; you are reluctant to be their friend. Givers, on the other hand, are a pleasure to be with because they help to establish an environment that blesses and enriches relationships. A taker becomes someone to avoid while a giver is always welcomed.

Instead of habitually asking what you can get from the various people and situations in your life, ask what you can give to them. The more you give to life, the more you will get back. This is a universal law that will go a long way toward creating in you an inner life that is well-balanced, prosperous, happy and fulfilled.

WEEK FORTY : LAW E

Love the unlovable.
Jesus

From *The Gospel According to Luke,* chapter 6, verses 27 through 38, in the King James version of the Bible: "But I say unto you which hear, Love your enemies, do good to them which hate you,

Bless them that curse you, and pray for them which despitefully use you.

And unto him that smiteth thee on the *one* cheek offer also the other; and him that taketh away thy cloke forbid not *to take thy* coat also.

Give to every man that asketh of thee; and of him that taketh away thy goods ask *them* not again.

And as ye would that men should do to you, do ye also to them likewise.

For if ye love them which love you, what thank have ye? for sinners also love those that love them.

And if ye do good to them which do good to you, what thank have ye? for sinners also do even the same.

And if ye lend to *them* of whom ye hope to receive, what thank have ye? for sinners also lend to sinners, to receive as much again.

But love ye your enemies, and do good, and lend, hoping for nothing again; and your reward shall be great, and ye shall be the children of the Highest: for he is kind unto the unthankful and *to* the evil.

Be ye therefore merciful, as your Father also is merciful.

Judge not, and ye shall not be judged: condemn not, and ye shall not be condemned: forgive, and ye shall be forgiven:

Give and it shall be given unto you; good measure, pressed down, and shaken together, and running over, shall me give into your bosom. For with the same measure that ye mete withal it shall be measured to you again."

LAWS OF LIFE INDEX

KINDNESS

LOVE

OPTIMISM

PERSEVERANCE